The Bataan Death March to MacArthur's Return

The Bataan Death March to MacArthur's Return

Revisiting the Battlefields of the Pacific War in the Philippines

Chris Hulme

Frontline Books

First published in Great Britain in 2026 by
Frontline Books
An imprint of Pen & Sword Books Limited
Yorkshire – Philadelphia

ISBN 978 1 03619 893 0

A CIP catalogue record for this book is available from the British Library.

Typeset by Mac Style
Printed in the UK by CPI Group (UK) Ltd, Croydon, CR0 4YY.

MIX
Paper | Supporting responsible forestry
FSC® C013604

The Publisher's authorised representative in the EU for product safety is Authorised Rep Compliance Ltd., Ground Floor, 71 Lower Baggot Street, Dublin D02 P593, Ireland.
www.arccompliance.com

For a complete list of Pen & Sword titles please contact:

PEN & SWORD BOOKS LIMITED
47 Church Street, Barnsley, South Yorkshire, S70 2AS, England
E-mail: enquiries@pen-and-sword.co.uk
Website: www.pen-and-sword.co.uk
or
PEN AND SWORD BOOKS
1950 Lawrence Road, Havertown, PA 19083, USA
E-mail: uspen-and-sword@casematepublishers.com
Website: www.penandswordbooks.com

Contents

Author's Note

I'd like to acknowledge John Grehan at Pen and Sword Books who helped me find a way to turn my Pacific journeys into books. Jon Brown, John McCullough, and Neil Murray all provided valuable feedback on the manuscript. Viv Griffiths and Connor Beighton at Influential lent creative support.

There were many historians, artists and poets who inspired me to visit the places described in the following pages, not least the American author James M. Scott, whose book *Rampage* seemed to be the standard text for every historical tour guide I met in Manila.

Their work is testament to a simple truth: artists and writers who chronicle war preserve not just what happened, but what it meant – and continues to mean. They guard against the most dangerous amnesia of all, embodying what may be the most important words in any language: lest we forget.

Chris Hulme,
February 2026

Foreword

This is a boots-on-the-ground exploration of a period of history that has always engrossed me and which was partly inspired by staring too long at maps of the Pacific Ocean.

I started out by looking at its islands through the lens of the Second World War but soon realised that this era was merely one chapter in a centuries-old contest for dry land – no matter its size – amid the immensity of water that covers almost one third of the Earth's surface.

Pacific Island nations that have been bargained over, conquered, fortified, abandoned, and reconquered in cycles that have repeated themselves across generations – shaped and reshaped by contests between empires, religions and ideologies. Yet in all my travels, the Philippine archipelago stood out as a place where these historical forces collided most vividly – and where their echoes remain most visceral today.

The Philippines is where Spanish galleons first imposed colonial rule in the 1560s, transforming an archipelago of diverse sultanates and barangays into a linchpin of emerging Pacific trade – Christianised and held for over three centuries. It is where that colonial order was shattered when the United States wrested control in 1898, only to face fierce resistance from Filipinos who had fought for independence from Spain. The Philippine-American War that followed (1899–1902) cost thousands of Filipino lives through combat, famine, and disease, as US forces suppressed the independence movement. Yet within a few decades of a truce and reconciliation, both would fight together as the forces of Imperial Japan rampaged across the Philippines. The siege of Bataan and fall of Corregidor in 1942 inflicted one of America's most agonising military defeats but did set the stage for a dramatic return – US forces eventually fighting their way back across the ocean for one last bloody reckoning in the islands.

The Philippines bookend America's experience of the Pacific War. It started with the astonished, reeling reaction to Japan's December 1941 onslaught on US territories – simultaneous attacks on Pearl Harbor, the Philippines, Guam, and Wake Island, along with British and Dutch colonies in Southeast Asia. Philippine society, colonised but never passive, endured the brutal occupation that followed, navigating it with defiance, compromise, and resilience. The beginning of the end came off the eastern shores of the Philippines at Leyte Gulf in October 1944, with history's largest naval battle. In Manila the following February, people would face the city's darkest hours with Japanese forces systematically massacring civilians as the street fighting raged, while American artillery added to the devastation.

With the Imperial Japanese Navy shattered at Leyte Gulf, American forces seized one remote ocean outpost after another, driving relentlessly toward the Japanese home islands. By 1945, the United States had become the most efficient and best-equipped military power the world had ever seen, capable of sustaining operations across thousands of miles of ocean in campaigns that consumed staggering quantities of men, materiel, and will.

General Douglas MacArthur looms large in this transformation – the highest-profile American combatant of the Pacific campaign, who held the Philippine islands and its people close to his heart. His career traced the emergence of the United States as a global power, from frontier republic to the nuclear age. Born just after Little Bighorn, he died in 1964 as US troops were preparing to deploy to Vietnam. The three biographies I absorbed included William Manchester's *American Caesar*, a title meant to reflect a powerful and complex leader capable of genius who nevertheless enjoyed neither universal acclaim nor routinely followed orders.

MacArthur came from a family of high achievers. His paternal grandfather served as a Wisconsin Supreme Court justice, a prominent figure in Milwaukee legal and political circles. His father, Arthur MacArthur, won the Medal of Honor in 1863 as an 18-year-old Union officer fighting at Missionary Ridge, one of several engagements that broke the Confederate siege of Chattanooga, Tennessee. A key moment in the battle saw the young Union officer lead a spontaneous charge uphill into Confederate fire, capturing a seemingly impregnable position and planting their colours at the summit.

The moment oddly foreshadowed the famous flag-raising at Iwo Jima in 1945, which produced one of the most iconic photographs of the Pacific War.

For all his father's heroics, I ended up with a sense that no matter how carefully historians detail Douglas MacArthur's achievements and personal bravery, few can forgive his career-long pomposity and his love of a press release. He was worshiped by some of the men who served under him and remains a hero of the Philippine South Korean nations, yet MacArthur was a giant ego who diligently stage-managed his own public persona as the swashbuckling commander outfitted with Aviator sunglasses, a rakish soft cap, and either a riding crop (First World War) or corn pipe (Second World War). The record shows a litany of vainglorious announcements at key moments, exaggerating his own contributions and diminishing those of senior officers around him. To his detractors, MacArthur's occasional brilliance as a military leader does not excuse these character traits, nor what some would characterise as a career marked by headstrong and imperious behaviour.

If only for balance, any commentary should reflect not just on his military triumphs, of which there were many, but also a somewhat forgotten irony: America's most famous Pacific War general invested his prestige and career in the Philippines, a theatre that many had already written off as doomed and indefensible. The strategic importance of the islands was acknowledged in Washington, but from War Department planners to President Franklin D. Roosevelt himself, rhetoric didn't translate into the resources MacArthur demanded in the pre-war years for defending a territory over 8,000 kilometres (5,000 miles) from the nearest US bases on Hawaii. Yet with sheer force of will, MacArthur eventually made his country stand up for a fledgling commonwealth nation facing daunting odds.

One of the more unexpected details I came to dwell on was MacArthur's insistence on keeping his wife and son with him overseas throughout much of the Pacific conflict. He used his seniority to bend the rules when other service families had long since been dispatched back to the United States. His one-time subordinate, Dwight Eisenhower, by contrast, saw his own family just once in three years of European command. MacArthur's wife Jean, and their only child Arthur IV, born in Manila in 1938, would stay at MacArthur's side during a reign of Japanese bombs and artillery shells, and were with him in a wooden PT boat during a desperate nighttime escape from Corregidor and the clutches of the Japanese.

MacArthur's choice to keep his family close may have been intended as an act of solidarity with the troops and civilians enduring severe hardships and risks. Yet I liked the idea that the MacArthurs shared an all-or-nothing family bond. In a war defined in part by absence, their togetherness is a reminder that history is not only made in battlefields and war rooms, but also in kitchens, in bomb shelters, and in the glances shared between people trying to stay connected as the world spins into chaos. Where possible, I visited the places where they lived during those war-torn years.

The only affinity I would ever claim to have with MacArthur is an enthusiasm for maps, which in my case I put down to the small satisfaction I take from planning things and curiosity about how geography affects us. As Supreme Allied Commander, South West Pacific Area, MacArthur pored over charts of all the places I would go; I felt his gaze had studied every palm-fringed beach, each rocky cove, and fertile valley that I explored.

My journeys, recounted here, blend the history of the outset of the war in the Philippines and its aftermath with a travelogue and reflections on what these battlefields are like to visit now. Mine are the experiences of an ordinary traveller. I had no special access to anything and operated on a modest budget. My ambition was to weave the threads of past and present into a tapestry that could satisfy my own search for meaning amid tumultuous events.

I got a taste for this early on – and much closer to home. As a child visiting London, I was made aware of the marks left behind by Second World War bombers, still evident in plain sight. I was shown brickwork and stone cladding peppered with shrapnel damage from exploding German munitions on older buildings such as the Victoria and Albert Museum on Exhibition Road, and Tate Britain, near the Atterbury Street entrance. The damage seemed miraculous. To gaze at the pockmarked stone was to step back in time to a blacked-out London of 1940, where the drone of Heinkel He 111s overhead was met by a cacophony of anti-aircraft guns. Bombs tumbled through a night sky criss-crossed with searchlights. Flashes of explosions illuminated the cityscape, revealing brief, jagged glimpses of the burning capital. The bombs whistled as they fell, followed by deafening blasts that echoed through the streets, sending chunks of debris through air thick with pulverised brick and mortar.

Why is a wall chipped by a bullet or a bomb fragment in London, Manila or anywhere else more interesting than a wall that is only marked by the passage of time in peacetime? Post-war German artists came up with the term '*Ruinenlust*' to explain our interest in the aesthetics of damaged things. Tate Britain itself once took the concept as the theme of an exhibition that featured over 100 works by artists all inspired by ruined buildings, from the seventeenth century onwards. A key moment seems to have been the excavation of the Ancient Roman city of Pompeii – buried by falling ash from Mount Vesuvius in 79 AD – which became a muse for painters and poets once it was uncovered in 1748. 'It's a theme in the arts and literature of that period, that the destruction of the past is a warning from history about what might happen,'[1] as one curator put it. 'It's to do with an unease about being modern. That no matter how modern we are, no matter how much progress we make – it will all come to an end, it will all fall away just like the civilisations of Greece and Rome.'

Manila is 10,748 kilometres (6,679 miles) from where I live, in Manchester, in the north-west of England. The further I got from home, the more I found myself reflecting on the act of travel itself – not just the movement between different points of physical geography, but across temporal space. Some of the connections that I made between past and present were unexpected and personal, reaching back to a father I never knew – a man who died when I was an infant, but who had once made his own journeys to the far side of the world as an observer with the Royal Navy's Fleet Air Arm, visiting the Philippines while serving aboard the aircraft carrier HMS *Eagle* in the 1960s.

Major historical events are told in the language of strategy, leaders, and decisive moments. Beneath all that, history is of course lived – and lost – in ordinary lives. It sits at the dinner table. It lingers in the old uniforms you find hanging at the back of the wardrobe when you are a child, and in the odd selection of personal belongings left behind. It's also there in the photographs that become stand-ins for memory. My father died during the Cold War, and not in the Pacific, but it did not take a huge leap of the imagination to understand that what happened within our family had played out countless times, in countless places, before and after my mother opened the door to the worst possible news. Once it happens, you are never quite free of wondering about the price we pay for our flags – or the unspoken reverie of those left behind to wonder at what might have been.

I think this kind of bereavement creates a certain disquiet about the future – an instinctive knowledge of how easily things can turn. Perhaps it was the same for Rudyard Kipling, one of the great chroniclers of empire and loss, who poured his anguish into *My Boy Jack*, the poem about his son missing in the First World War:

> 'Have you news of my boy Jack?'
> Not this tide.
> 'When d'you think that he'll come back?'
> Not with this wind blowing, and this tide.

So many wartime stories are about interruption – the son who never comes home, the father who dies young, the family that carries on without. Sometimes our travels are about trying to reconnect. Yes, with people, but also with the spaces they once moved through, the coordinates of their absence.

Travel, in that sense, becomes a form of watching and listening – to landscapes, and the artefacts fighting men once needed, used or looked upon. The feeling of standing in a place once defined by chaos and extreme violence, now hushed and overgrown, also carries with it a kind of intimacy. Sometimes it's the weight of your own footsteps on a path once taken by soldiers who moved warily through a world where every step involved risk. Or the way rust blooms across a piece of twisted metal half-buried in the undergrowth. It reminds you: history does not vanish – it settles, echoes, and waits to be heard.

Many Philippine islands are dotted with these markers – the airstrips now reclaimed by grass, the death markers left at the side of the road to remember the cruelty shown towards prisoners of war, and in old buildings and memorials weathered by the decades. The act of being physically present felt valuable and honourable. It was a way of acknowledging the weight of what had passed, and of bearing witness in a world that always wants to move on.

Maps

The Asia-Pacific. (*US National Archive*)

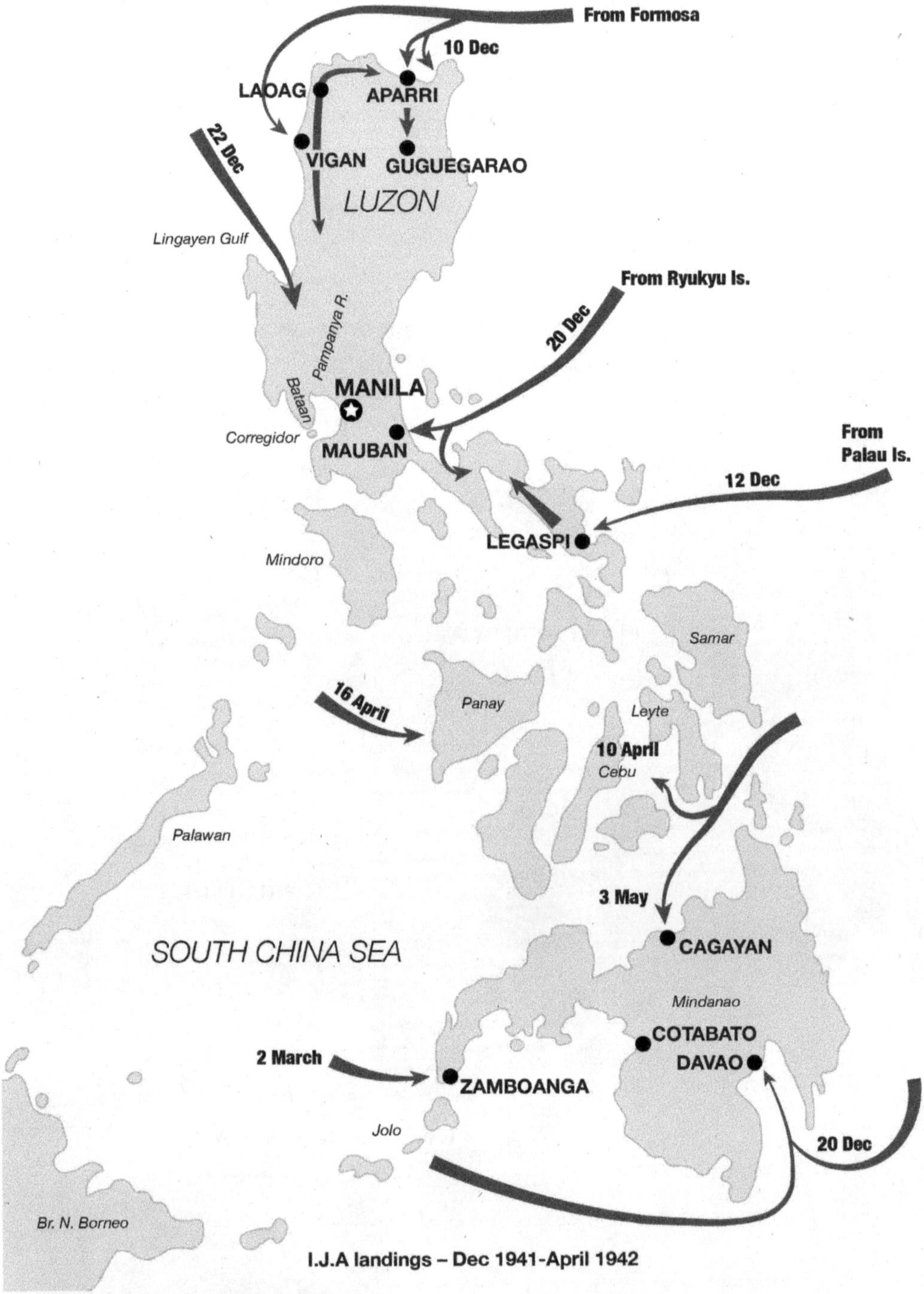

Japanese Invasion of Luzon. (*Connor Beighton*)

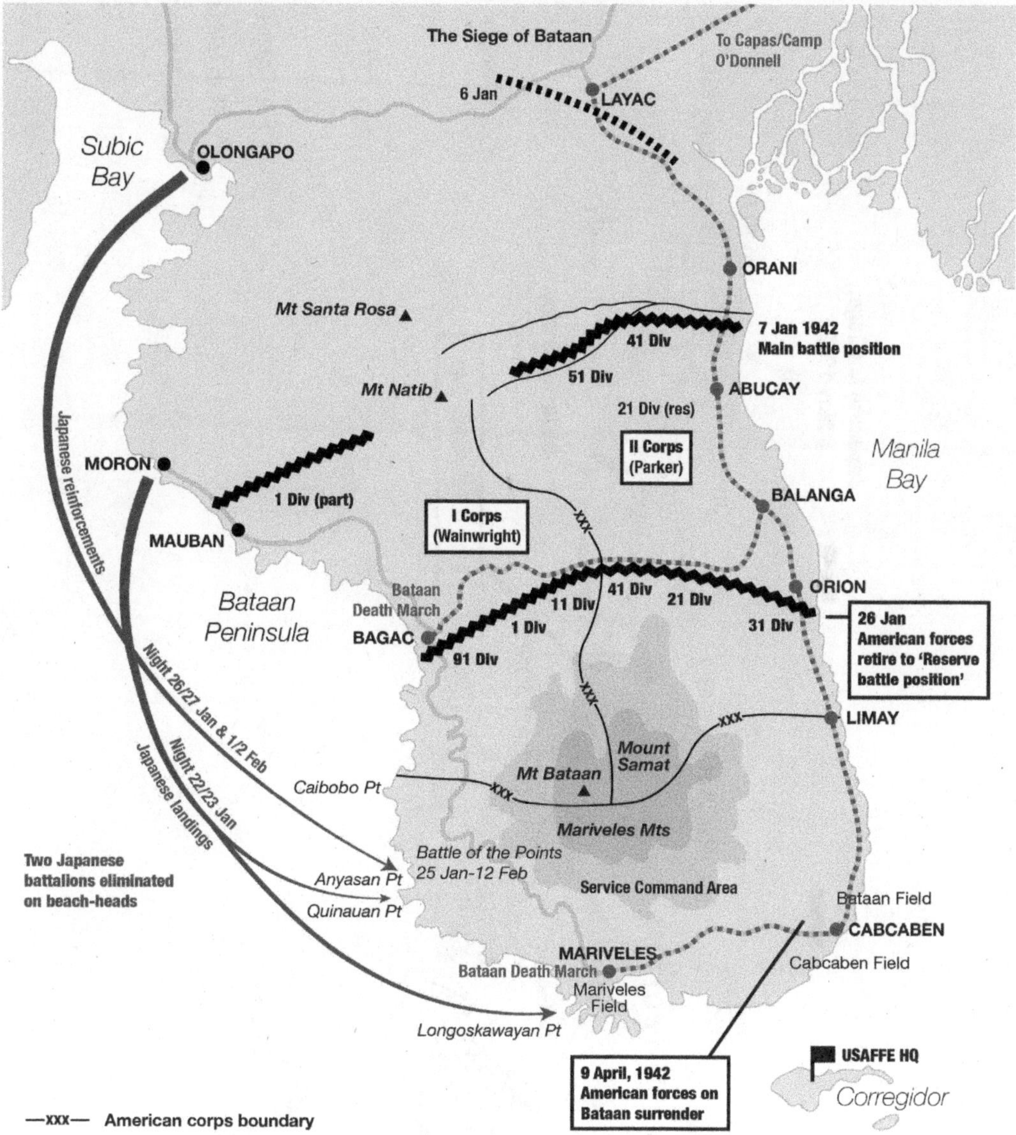

The Siege of Bataan. (*Connor Beighton*)

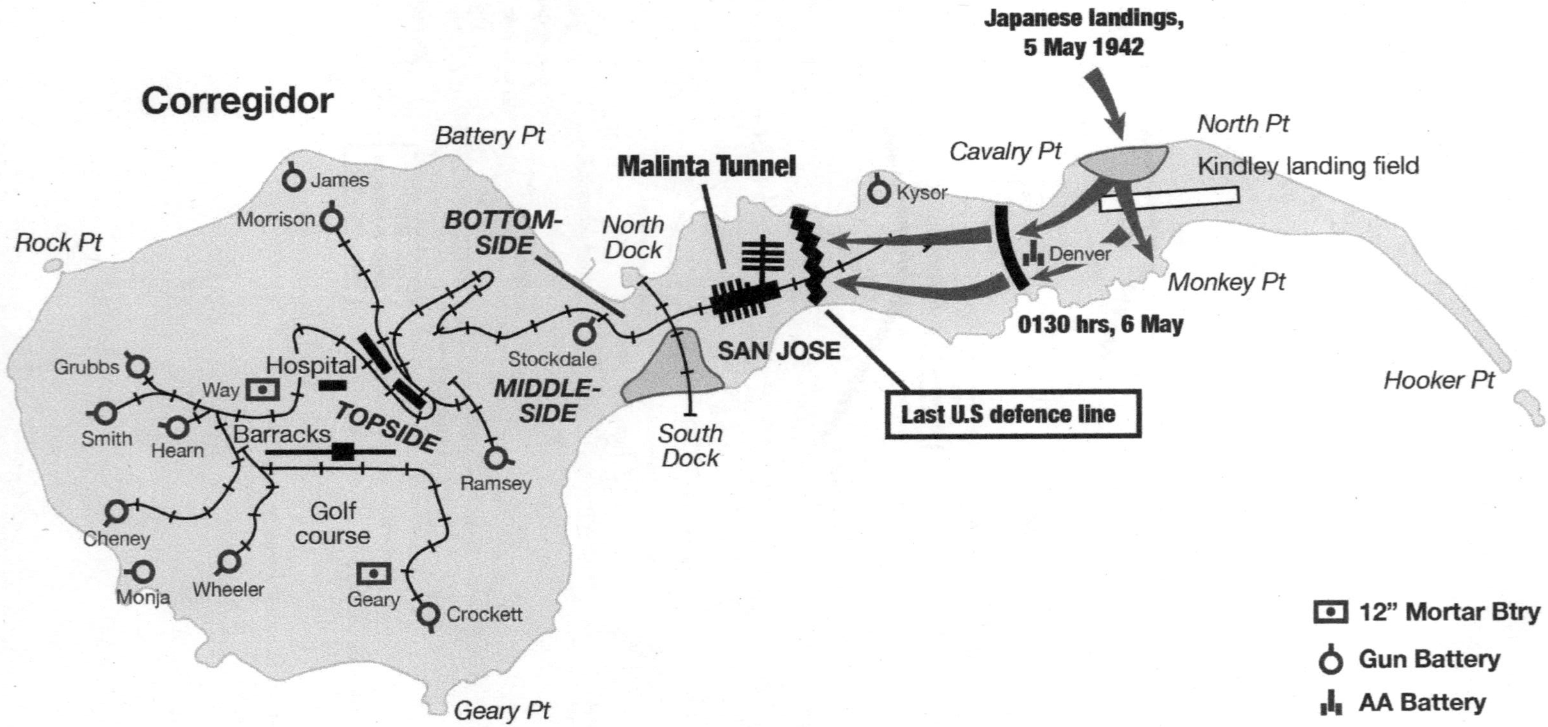

Corregidor. (*Connor Beighton*)

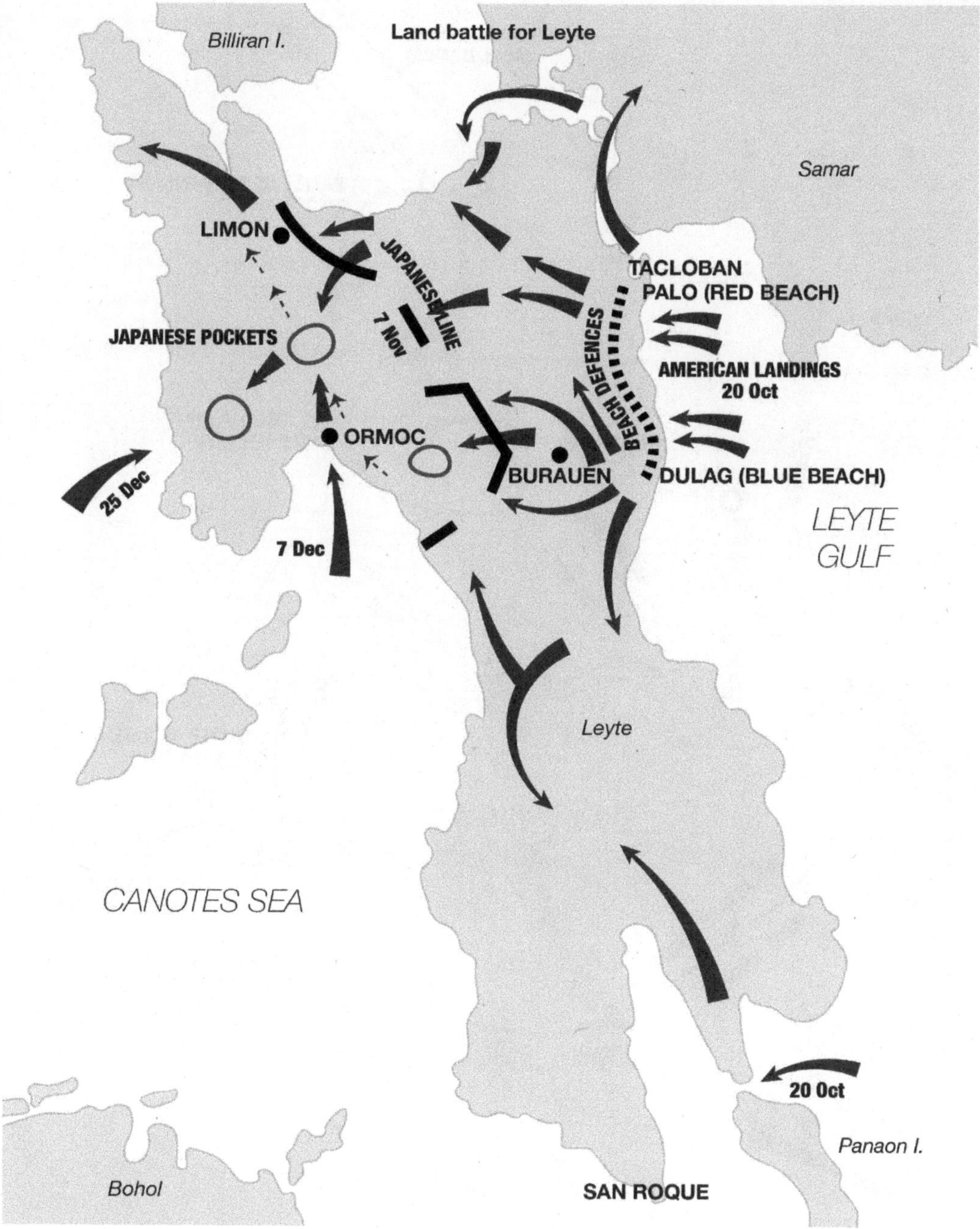

US Army Landing on Leyte. (*Connor Beighton*)

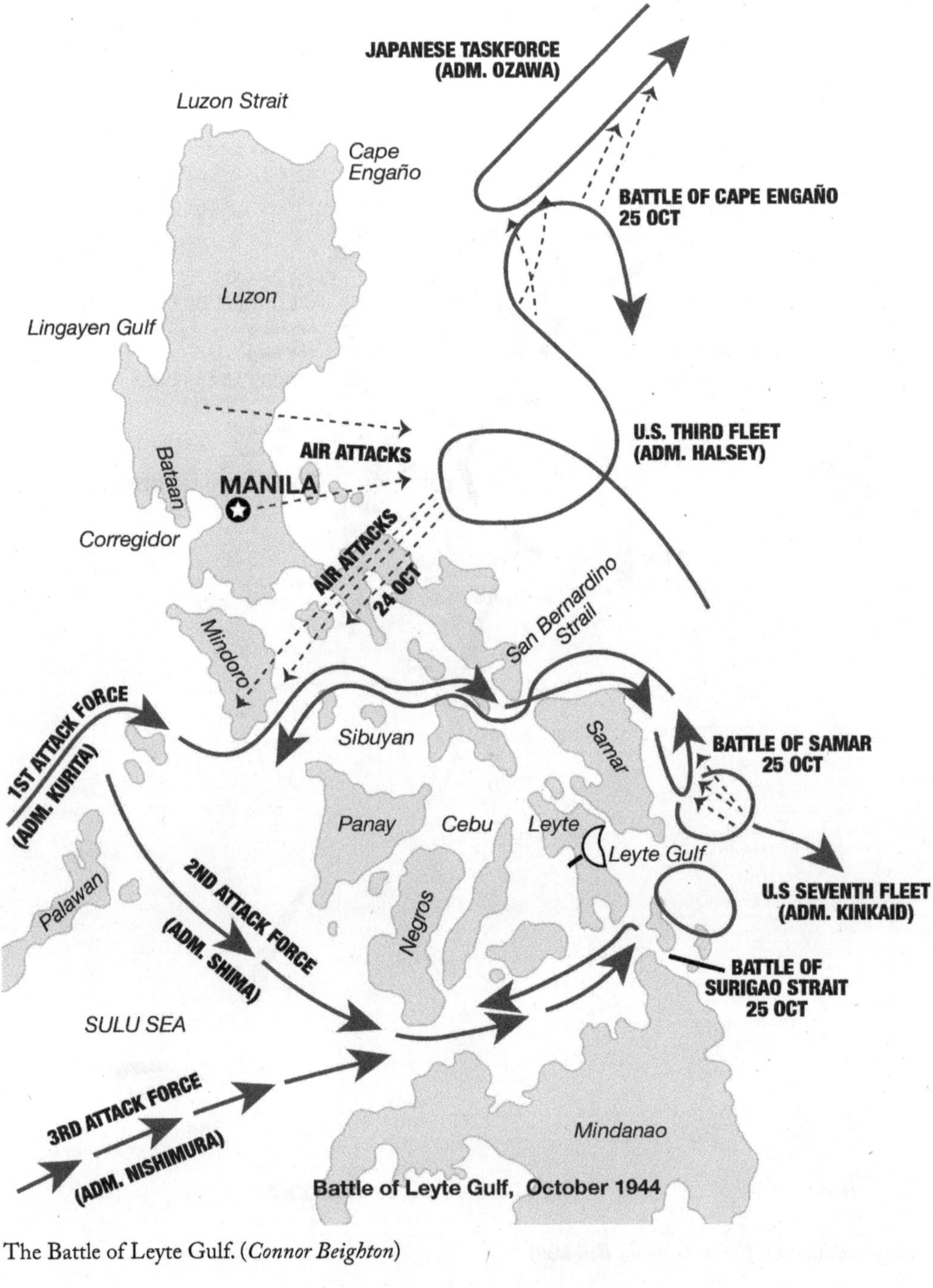

The Battle of Leyte Gulf. (*Connor Beighton*)

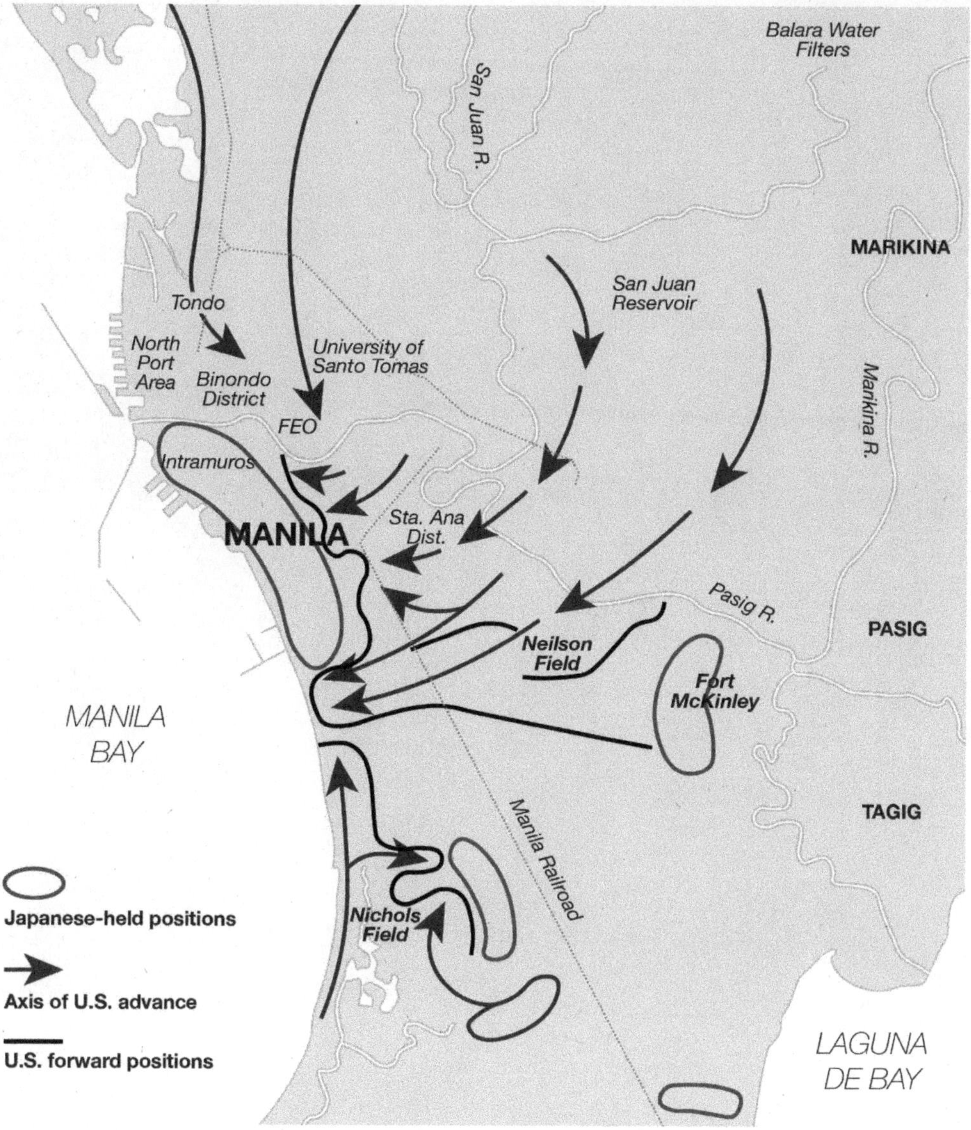

US Advance on Manila, 1945. (*Connor Beighton*)

Chapter 1

The Flags of Bataan

The rain was louder than the din coming from the air conditioning unit. On sliding back the curtains and folding away the old wooden blinds, there were no glass windows, only steel bars. I could not get a view of the heavens but watched torrents of water streaming from the scaffolding attached to the old building opposite. A walk around the narrow streets of Intramuros would have to wait.

As faux Spanish colonial places to stay go, mine was decaying and unloved, with long dead cockroaches in the dusty wardrobe and no cold running water. I wanted to spend as little time as possible in the White Knight Hotel but the reality of some of the worst traffic in Asia meant staying in the area I was exploring, the site of Japan's last stand in Manila during the final months of the Second World War.

To escape the room, I set myself up beside a portable air conditioning fan in the lobby downstairs and spent an hour trying to figure out getting to the Bataan peninsula and the island of Corregidor later in the week.

The ferry company that once made the latter a straightforward 50-kilometre (31-mile) boat trip to the mouth of Manila Bay had gone out of business during the Covid tourism restrictions. The only way to Corregidor now was a road journey all the way around the inside of the bay and down to the southern tip of Bataan, maybe six or seven hours out into the sticks, and then finding someone with a *banca* for the hop across the water to Corregidor.

Following a travel tip, I started by calling Imelda, manager of Villa Carmen, a small hotel on Bataan's southern coast. I rattled off my plans and requirements in the way of an organised Westerner with an itinerary. The voice that came back was modest and polite, the manner of hospitable Filipinos. English was not Imelda's first language. Her slight pause before replying only seemed to exaggerate my directness and her calm.

She told me to call Fidel. I got straight through but Fidel recommended I contact Albert, the boatman. 'Okay', said Albert, 'come at 06.00 Friday'. Understanding the fee for the passage was simple enough. The language gap only reared its head when I asked for a later crossing. Could he do 08.00 hours – and what time would they pick me up for the return from the island? Confused, he passed the phone to his wife and we muddled our way to an understanding.

As with all everyday travellers, I was looking at a lot of history in a short space of time. I knew that Manila escaped comparatively lightly at the outbreak of the Pacific War. The city was instead tested by degrees over four years until the conflict reached a pitiless climax, with street fighting of a kind more typical of the European war, and massacres of the innocent. The final shots were fired in Intramuros, a walled city within a city, which had served as capital of the Spanish empire in Asia and Oceania from the sixteenth century until garrisoned by the United States at the end of the nineteenth century.

Manila's tumultuous history all too rarely connects with international visitors today. The sprawling capital of nearly 14 million people has become a stepping stone as much as a destination. If you are coming to the Philippines from outside of Asia, sooner or later the question comes up: why hang around in a dysfunctional metropolis when you can fly in and out to one of the 7,083 tropical islands that make up the Philippine archipelago? The city has a chronic image problem, one that starts with Manila's traffic and the reality that getting anywhere is invariably a bumper-to-bumper chore.

It follows that unless you grew up in Manila, actually driving in the city is madness. Traffic congestion has evolved into a kind of crowd-sourced performance art, with an unrelenting cacophony of engines and horns from vehicles that don't run on batteries. Trucks, beaten-up taxis, colourful jeepneys, vans, scooters and motorcycle tricycles all jockey for position and change lanes without much warning. Standing at the junction of any intersection as this automotive monster is tamed by mere traffic lights is one of Manila's unheralded pleasures. By day, the tentacles of transport delays reach here, there and everywhere. In the humid, petrochemical dark, roads glitter and pulse. Routes are also confusing. Manila's traffic schemes include curfews and rule variations depending on the day of the week, a number-coding system, and frequent re-routings.

A pre-morning rush hour bus ride seemed the best means of escape. The plan was to travel far enough out of Manila to a town where I could still rent a car for exploring Bataan and drive the final leg down to the southern tip of the peninsula, from where it's about a twenty-five-minute boat trip to Corregidor. Two rival bus companies served Bataan province, each with its own depots. Once I figured out the one I wanted from the online timetables, I did a trial run the evening before to be confident of the location and distance from the hotel where I was staying.

Genesis Transport Inc. turned out to be a space between derelict-looking buildings. It was just off Avenida, a noisily congested arterial route directly underneath a huge flyover. At dusk the imposing columns of this inner-city Skyway loomed oppressively above one side of the bus depot, cutting across a time-worn backdrop of tower blocks. Everything felt dirty. Every painted sign and surface was chipped and worn. There was not enough money for graffiti. In the shadow of the concrete flyover, a small shantytown stood before the waiting customers and buses, as forlorn as all the other pocket slums dotted around the city. These deprived areas have nothing on the vast ghetto that is Tondo, one of the city's northern districts, which was never rebuilt after being flattened by artillery during the US Army's liberation of Manila in 1945. Today over half a million people live on Tondo's streets, but the Genesis depot showed that destitute Filipinos get by as best they can, wherever they can, crammed into any unclaimed space. I closed my eyes and listened to the rush hour apocalypse: an irregular symphony of roaring trucks, zipping scooters and horns. By one of the pillars a woman lay sleeping on a pavement blanket; stoned, exhausted or perhaps both. A little girl sat beside her, 3 or 4 years old, looking equally malnourished. She was playing on a tablet computer, which I guessed originated from one of Manila's fake goods markets. The city lights glowed indifferently.

Balanga, my destination amid the rice fields of Bataan, described itself as a city but would turn out to be a market town where swarms of motorcycles with sidecars – known locally simply as tricycles – are the main form of transport. The most promising car rental firm was a few miles out from the centre at Abucay. Via social media, for free-to-use Facebook was preferred by its owner over websites and emails for customer communication, I was provided with instructions on which of the two Genesis buses to board to get to the rental garage. One would take me to Abucay Plaza, near his place of business. The other meant being dropped off on the Balanga Highway and figuring it out from there. I am not someone of enormous faith but trusted his instructions for no other reason than the Facebook profile said God was the owner of his business and 'the unseen manager of every department, the silent partner.'

I woke earlier than planned and took a cab from my hotel to the Genesis station, arriving just before 07.00 hours. My driver deposited the bags on the oil-stained uneven ground. A bus grumbled, ready to depart. The conductor stood before it, wiry and stern like a drill sergeant impatient to round-up the last hapless recruits. Another bus behind it showed no signs of life. I pointed at the first vehicle. 'Balanga Highway?' The conductor regarded me sternly but said nothing. I pointed at the second bus. 'Abucay Plaza?'

'No,' he barked.

'What bus is this?'

'We go now. Get on. Balanga Highway then take a tricycle.'

Seizing the largest of my bags, heavy with scuba gear, he moved with a conviction that suggested an extinction-level event was about to strike Manila and the bus was my last and only chance to escape. I did what I was told and pushed my other holdall into the baggage store, the sound of the door slamming shut securing my evacuation. I would have to change at Balanga Highway and find a way to complete the journey, big bags and all.

I climbed aboard and passed a handful of other passengers before stationing myself near the back as the driver edged out of the bus depot. A TV screen at the front was already playing a Hollywood action film, *Crawl*, in which a giant alligator chases a woman around the flooded basement of a storm-collapsed house. I ignored the tinny clamour from the speakers spaced out down the centre aisle and got settled near the back, realising I was quietly enjoying the departure, the small glee of a plan enacted.

The bus made steady progress north-west through the urban sprawl. There were no suburbs. After about an hour we were abruptly free of the huge metropolis. The movie finished, leaving just the low and steady growl of the diesel motoring down the highway. Flat green fields slipped past the window, interrupted only sporadically by garish advertising billboards. This was tank country; I knew American M4 Shermans once roamed here. The conductor reappeared, less severe than before. Busily, he punched a pattern into the ticket, clicking away to register the date, the fact mine was a one-way journey and who knows what else.

* * *

The Philippines became a sovereign state in 1946 after over 300 years of colonial rule. The national flag is based around two horizontal bands. The upper stripe is blue, representing peace, truth, and justice. The lower band is red, symbolising patriotism and valour. On the hoist side, a white equilateral triangle denotes equality and fraternity. Within the centre of this triangle a golden sun of eight rays signifies the independence of the Philippines and its struggle for freedom. Each ray represents one of the eight provinces that led the revolution against Spanish rule.

At the corners of the triangle, a star symbolises the three main geographical regions – the Luzon group in the north-west, where I started my journey; the Visayas in the centre, where I would head to Leyte, scene of the largest naval battle in the Second World War; and Mindanao in the south, which I avoided because that's what Western governments tell you to do. The flag is unique in the sense that it can be flown upside down and with the red stripe on top to indicate a state of war.

Philippine independence did not get off to the start its architects had long imagined. Decades of political turmoil followed its recognition as a nation state. From the 1960s onwards the history was dominated by the Marcos family. Ferdinand Marcos, a lawyer turned tenth president of the Philippines, ruled from 1965 to 1986, which included imposing martial law from 1972 to 1981. He fraudulently claimed to have been a Second World War hero, attributing thirty-three military honours to himself. Marcos told stories of leading 100 Filipino troops against 2,000 Japanese during the fighting on Bataan – one of many yarns debunked by investigative journalists from *The New York Times*[2] and historians in the Philippines.

The penultimate controversy came decades later. Marcos was implicated in the 1983 assassination of his political rival, Benigno 'Ninoy' Aquino Junior, who was shot in the back of the head within minutes of returning from exile. A memorial plaque on one of the aprons at Manila's international airport marks the spot where Ninoy's life ended. Marcos was far from the only suspect in what turned out to be a pivotal moment in Philippine history but whoever wished death upon the exile it whipped up the typhoon winds of change.

Marcos won a rigged election in 1986 but was then swept from power by a people's revolution. It saw Ninoy's widow, Corazon Aquino, become president. A new constitution in 1987 created a proper separation of powers between legislative, executive and the judiciary, setting the country on the path it follows to this day. The hope was that while the old dynastic networks of power and wealth were unlikely to disappear overnight, modernisation would bring more transparency and accountability, especially regarding the police and judiciary.

In fact, six presidents-on from what became known as the People Power Revolution, the former dictator's son and namesake, Ferdinand Marcos Junior, won the 2022 election by a country mile. He asked the electorate to 'judge me not by my ancestors, but by my actions.' Bongbong – as he preferred to be known – campaigned on a broad pledge of bringing unity, as well as creating jobs, building infrastructure and cutting the cost of food. His critics described the appeal for unity as an invitation to forget the atrocities of his father's regime. They put Bongbong's victory down to decades-long historical revisionism and nostalgia perpetrated by the Marcos family, including massive disinformation campaigns on social media platforms.

International visitors arrive in Manila at Ninoy Aquino International Airport (NAIA), named in honour of the slain opposition leader. Part of the site was a wartime airfield, known as Nichols Field by the Americans, which in 1941 had the only paved runway in the Philippines. NAIA does not fare well in the age of online travel reviews. A new international airport is being built on reclaimed land to the north of the city but for now, on a good day, NAIA is a congested hub, with excessive queues. By other measures, it's the most stressful airport in Asia and Oceania, with numerous security checks and lost or delayed baggage all too common. I spent hours in the various terminals and did OK, passing through six times outside of peak season. I always made generous allowances for the bureaucracy, which just left the problem of getting to and from the airport on Manila's crazy roads.

Tourism makes up about 5 per cent of the national economy. For history buffs, Luzon, which is about the same size as Portugal, is the focus of everything that happened in the nineteenth and twentieth centuries, with Manila, Bataan and Corregidor its biggest draws. Other favoured destinations include Boracay, in the centre of the Philippine archipelago and part of the closely packed Visayas island group. It is said to have beaches that compete with the best that Southeast Asia has to offer. Palawan, an outlier way over to the east in the China Sea, can make similar claims and is a magnet for both Chinese tourists and its uncompromising fishing fleets.

The Filipino economy is in transition from an agricultural past to a future that's all about services and manufacturing. Considered one of Asia's so-called tiger economies, industrialisation sits behind the prediction that the Philippines will become the fourth largest in the region by 2050. The main exports include semiconductors, electronic products, garments, and petroleum-based goods.

The major internal hurdles before achieving the nation's development goals start with bridging the vast income divides between the different Philippine regions and social classes. There's also the challenge of securing investment for infrastructure and improving the nation's ability to withstand the typhoons that periodically sweep in from the Pacific, sometimes with devastating consequences.

Agriculture still represents about 30 per cent of employment and is focused on crops such as rice, sugarcane, bananas and pineapples. The land that works so well for cultivation is also suited to a certain era war movie.

Outside of its towns and cities, the Philippines stood in for Vietnam during the peak era of Hollywood's interest in that conflict, which ran from the mid-1970s until well into the 1990s. Most famously, *Apocalypse Now* was shot at various locations in Luzon. The Wagnerian helicopter attack on a little coastal village was filmed at Baler on the northeastern coast of Luzon in 1976. The helicopters that featured in the movie were provided by President Marcos and were being used around the same time to machine gun Filipino insurgents. The surfing beach so coveted by Colonel Kilgore is Baler Bay, today without the smell of napalm in the morning. Other productions followed – *The Boys in Company C* (1978); *Platoon* (1986); *Born on the Fourth of July* (1989) were all filmed in the Philippines.

The nation did in fact have a role during the Vietnam conflict. Subic Bay on the west coast of Luzon was once the US Navy's largest naval base in Asia and a major hub supporting the war. Disagreements over leasing costs in the post-Cold War era sent the US Navy home in 1992. The site has now been redeveloped as a commercial freeport and shopping centre.

Beyond its own borders, the Filipino travel brand has more than its share of issues. There's still a sense that the Philippines is a sequin in the rough when compared to the neighbours across the China Sea – deficient in glamour, adventure and cultural treasures, while somehow being rooted in both hard work and poverty.

The national brand is also beset by its association with middle aged European, Australian, Japanese and South Korean men, acquiring Filipino 'mail order' brides, who are typically much younger and looking for a way out of destitution. When I joined the check-in for my flight from the UK to Manila two fifty-something British men stood ahead of me in the queue. By simply removing my earphones it became apparent that one was already married to a Filipina and living inexpensively somewhere in Luzon. Their conversation made it clear that his companion was making his first journey to the Philippines, as did his wide-eyed, taking-it-all-in expression. How culturally sensitive is all this in a relatively young nation looking to assert pride in itself? Stuck in a Manila traffic jam one afternoon, I listened to what seemed to be a radio commercial for a soapy melodrama where a Filipina rejected the advances of a foreigner. 'Marry you? Go back to your country? We've only just met!' she said, her voice rising with daytime TV incredulity.

Mindanao is the second biggest landmass, a little larger than Ireland, and has a place in the history of the Second World War. I wanted to explore the big southern city of Davao, a Japanese stronghold in 1942. I was also intrigued by the Del Monte pineapple plantation near the island's north-west coast. It served as an American air base and features at key moments in the historical narrative, but the landing strip is today rice paddies and corn fields, with only a small monument erected by the local Chamber of Commerce to mark the heritage of the site.

The threat of terrorism in Mindanao and the other southern islands is the main barrier to travel. A semi-autonomous Muslim region, Mindanao has a long history of separatist movements and extremist factions who have fought with the national government. A long, drawn-out peace process has granted degrees of autonomy, but all progress is rejected by Jihadists who want to create an Islamic caliphate in this part of the Philippines. The British and American governments advise against visiting the western, central and southern areas of Mindanao, which means regular travel insurance is not available. The faraway Sulu archipelago to the south-west, where a string of islands almost form stepping stones to Borneo, is riskier still, with a view that any embassy would ultimately be powerless to help if you were foolish enough to travel there and got into trouble.

Sulu, the most intriguing in the sense that it is completely off limits, is regarded as a hotbed of extremism, private armies and maritime piracy. Tourists, journalists and priests have been seized during outbreaks of kidnapping and ended up held in the province. In most cases, they were released for a ransom paid.

Islam came to the southern Philippine islands some 200 years before Ferdinand Magellan, Catholicism and the European colonial period. Muslim guerrillas also fought alongside the Americans and Filipinos during the Japanese occupation in 1942. Yet the Moros, the name given to Filipino Muslims, have a hard baked and entirely plausible history of being disadvantaged and displaced by Filipino Christians.

The spirit behind Moro independence has endured across the centuries. Martial law and periods of fighting between separatists and the Philippine Army are all part of recent history while factions with various degrees of Islamic orthodoxy have evolved, some hostile to each other. The movement has succeeded in establishing Mindanao as a devolved region, Bangsamoro (Moro nation). It is run by the former rebels of the Moro Islamic Liberation Front. They have powers over taxation and a justice system based on Sharia law. Yet Jihadists outside of the peace deal remain a threat.

As I was planning my journey, I set up a Google News Alert for Abu Sayyaf, the highest profile extremist group, and watched the stories come in. It started with three Abu Sayyaf gunmen captured on Jolo, the biggest island in the Sulu province. The arrests made international news as the men stood accused of murdering two Canadians seven years previously. The tourists were kidnapped from a marina on Samal, an island just off southern

Mindanao. They were taken to a jungle camp on Sulu. When a ransom was not paid, the Canadians were beheaded.

Abu Sayyaf – Arabic for 'Father of the Sword' – was affiliated to Al-Qaeda before shifting its allegiance to Islamic State (IS). They fight under the IS flag. There are variations, but it usually consists of a black background with the Shahada, an expression of Muslim faith, emblazoned in white text across the centre.

* * *

At the turn of the nineteenth century, the old order was cracking. The Spanish lost the Philippines and other colonies to the power of independence movements and the fallout from the ten-week Spanish-American War of 1898.

Sparked over Cuba's struggle to free itself from Spain, the conflict broke out after the USS *Maine*, which had been sent to Havana to protect American interests, blew up in mysterious circumstances in the harbour. No one knew for sure who was to blame, but the crisis escalated and in Washington the headlines roared: 'Remember the Maine!' Blame fell upon the Españoles.

The brief but devastating conflict led to the destruction of two Spanish fleets and the loss of Manila, Spain's administrative centre in the Pacific since the sixteenth century. With its dominion in the Pacific shattered, Cuba emerged independent, while the United States claimed Puerto Rico, Guam, and the Philippines – the latter formally ceded through the Treaty of Paris in December 1898, its price set at $20 million.

Yet for Filipinos, the treaties signed in Europe meant nothing and their uprising was far from over. In the hills and jungles of Luzon, Emilio Aguinaldo – a slender young general who had once fought the Spaniards – now rallied his people to resist their new rulers. Aguinaldo was at the forefront of a long-running struggle for independence – and had designed the Philippine flag. Beside him stood thousands of *insurrectos*, men and women prepared to defy yet another empire to come across the Pacific.

The Filipinos were opposed by US colonial forces led by military Governor General Arthur MacArthur, a former Union officer and a hero of the American Civil War. Over the next three years, the Philippine islands bled as war, famine, and disease claimed some 200,000 civilians, while the combat dead numbered 20,000 Filipinos and over 4,000 Americans. Atrocities and reprisals happened on both sides – the brutal lexicon of war.

Turn-of-the-century American apologists for the bloody struggle stressed the strategic importance of the islands in terms of sea lanes, natural resources and trade – and expressed doubts about Filipino self-rule, fearing they might fall under German or Japanese influence. Yet annexation clashed with the values of many Americans cherished republican ideals. Opposition gathered in the form of the American Anti-Imperialist League, whose members included industrialist Andrew Carnegie and author Mark Twain.

In July 1902, the US Congress shifted course, promising eventual independence. With the casual authority of empire, President Theodore Roosevelt declared the Philippine conflict over and issued a general amnesty, though sporadic resistance continued.

By November 1935, however, the Filipino people had largely reconciled with American authorities and taken a significant step toward self-governance with the inauguration of the Commonwealth of the Philippines. Manuel Quezón, a lawyer by training, was elected the nation's first president. Under a ten-year transition plan, full independence was scheduled for 1946.

Yet even as the Philippines moved toward self-rule under American oversight, new anxieties were emerging in both Washington and Manila. Japan – once an ally during the First World War – was transforming into a formidable military power with imperial ambition for the Asia-Pacific region. For US strategists, the islands were no longer merely a colonial possession; they were becoming a strategic bulwark in an increasingly unstable Pacific.

In Japan, the drive for rapid industrialisation in the 1920s brought not only economic growth but also profound social upheaval: rural poverty, urban dislocation, and political unrest. Against this volatile backdrop – and amid the rise of fascist and communist movements across Europe and Asia – Japanese nationalist factions surged in influence. They rallied around the belief that Asia was Japan's rightful sphere of dominance – and that Western powers were colonial intruders.

In 1931, the staged Manchurian Incident gave the Imperial Japanese Army (IJA) a pretext to seize Manchuria – a resource-rich region that was part of

Chinese sovereign territory – triggering outrage in China and diplomatic condemnation abroad.

By 1937, border disputes and simmering tensions erupted into full-scale war. Within months, Japanese forces carried out one of the twentieth century's most notorious atrocities: the Rape of Nanjing. Over seven weeks, Japanese troops unleashed a campaign of mass murder and sexual violence. The International Military Tribunal for the Far East later estimated that between 200,000 and 300,000 people – the overwhelming majority civilians – were killed.

The massacre shocked the world and provoked international outrage. While some blamed a collapse of military discipline, others saw it as part of a calculated campaign of terror, a grim warning of the darker currents shaping Asia as the Second World War loomed.

The risk of large-scale conflict in the Asia-Pacific only escalated after the outbreak of war in Europe. With European powers weakened, their colonial territories were left exposed. Three months after the fall of France in June 1940, Japan signed the Tripartite Pact with Nazi Germany and Fascist Italy, formally joining the Axis alliance – regimes united not only by territorial ambition, but by the subjugation of perceived enemies at home and abroad.

In response to Japan's aggression in China, the United States imposed escalating economic sanctions. Japanese leaders viewed these measures as acts of war, convinced that Western powers sought to cripple their economy and deny them a rightful place among imperial nations.

By July 1941, tensions in the Pacific were reaching a boiling point. Japan had seized nearly every Chinese port except British-controlled Hong Kong. They also secured permission from Vichy France to establish military bases in southern Indochina. The Japanese fleet arrived in Cam Ranh Bay, one of Asia's finest natural harbours, while thousands of troops landed in Saigon.

Roosevelt demanded that the Japanese withdraw from mainland China. Until they did, Japanese and Chinese assets in the United States were frozen. The Panama Canal was closed to Japanese shipping. American businesses were also prohibited from exporting oil, iron and rubber to Japan. At Roosevelt's request, the British and Dutch also introduced similarly robust sanctions.

As the conflict with China had already stretched Japan to the limit, the nation's military and political elite were aware of the considerable risks of getting into a war with the United States. They understood that it could very well result in the destruction of Japan once the industrial might of the world's largest economy was focused on any opponent.

Voices for peace and serious diplomatic missions worked frantically in the hope of protecting Japan from a war that was unlikely to produce an outright victory. Yet the outlook of ultra-nationalists held sway. They were led by Hideki Tōjō, who by 1942 would consolidate enormous power as both prime minister and war minister, making him the dominant voice in Japan's military strategy. Tōjō enjoyed his nickname, the 'Razor', apparently given to him by army colleagues for his sharp decision-making.

Desperately short of raw materials and unable to acquire them because of trade embargoes, the crisis prompted Tōjō and his supporting cohort of military leaders to lash out in one of history's biggest rolls of the dice; a surprise attack on the United States, the day of infamy, 7 December 1941.

The raid on America's Pacific Fleet at Pearl Harbor in Honolulu was the focal point of an unprecedented firestorm that raged across Southeast Asia and the Pacific. At Pearl Harbor, eighteen warships were sunk or run aground. Some 2,403 Americans were killed – all technically non-combatants as war had not been declared. Within twenty-four hours, Japanese forces had swept across other Allied territories, starting with the Philippines, and beginning the process of toppling the United States as the dominant power in the Western Pacific. In a matter of weeks, the Dutch East Indies (today's Indonesia) and British-controlled Hong Kong, Burma (Myanmar), and Malaya (the peninsula that forms half of today's Malaysia), would also fall under the samurai sword. As the author William Manchester put it, 'The blitzkrieg, invented in Berlin, had been perfected in Tokyo.'[3]

From the American perspective, Japan's accelerating militarisation had demanded strategic consideration as far back as 1919. It took the form of War Plan Orange, a strategy that was revised repeatedly during the interwar years. The plan acknowledged a harsh strategic reality: in any conflict with Japan, US bases in the Western Pacific would be very difficult to defend.

The Philippines, the westernmost of all US Pacific interests, lay nearly 11,000 kilometres (7,000 miles) from San Francisco. Other vital outposts were not much closer to home – Guam, some 9,300 kilometres (5,800 miles) away, and Wake Island, a remote mid-ocean staging post approximately 7,000 kilometres (4,385 miles) distant. In Washington, the Great Depression and the relative poverty of US military resources in the interwar years, inspired a growing chorus of voices arguing that only Hawaii could realistically be considered the Pacific front line in any conflict – everything to the west, they warned, was simply too far away to supply and defend.

One of the loudest and most assertive voices taking the opposite view – that the Philippines could and should be defended – came from Douglas MacArthur, the son of the former governor general, a man who started his own military career in the archipelago and who had raced through the ranks to become Chief of Staff of the US Army. For him, the Philippines was not only a military bulwark, but a second home. There was no little irony here. His father, Arthur MacArthur, had been the colonial enforcer during the brutal turn-of-the-century pacification campaign. Now the son would speak up decades later as a defender of Filipino sovereignty and independence.

By the time Arthur MacArthur had completed his tour of duty in the islands he was one of America's most famous soldiers. He sailed home from Luzon to Milwaukee in 1907 with his wife, Mary Pinkney Hardy (Pinky), and their two sons. The former governor general would in time change his views and endorse the idea of Philippine independence, while also becoming a firm believer that American interests were best served by closer ties and cooperation in Asia as opposed to Europe.

Arthur MacArthur was to die of a heart attack in 1912 at the age of 67 while addressing a veteran's rally. In 1923, his eldest son, Arthur MacArthur III, a serving US naval officer, also passed away, having suffered a severe appendicitis. (A third son, Malcolm, had died in 1883, aged 4, from measles.) With the burial of Arthur MacArthur III, the legacy of one of America's most distinguished military families fell squarely on Douglas. His early army career would progress not just in the shadow of his father but was also subject to the ambition of his formidable mother. An intelligent, confident Southerner from Norfolk, Virginia, biographers chart Pinky's fierce devotion to her son Douglas's rise, instilling in him, from childhood onwards, the conviction that he was destined for greatness. Pinky was not content with the sidelines of military life. She lived with him during his early postings, often lobbying for his advancement and reinforcing the narrative of a divinely appointed destiny.

Douglas MacArthur had entered the service in 1903 with the Army Corps of Engineers in the Philippines. The posting sparked a lifelong fascination with the islands. There, he immersed himself in the practicalities of American colonial rule, overseeing the construction of wharves, landing strips, and roads at strategic points across the archipelago. He also nurtured the same conviction held by his father that American strategic interests were best served by prioritising economic and cultural ties with Asia.

As a soldier, MacArthur quickly rose in reputation and rank. He cut a dashing figure in the First World War, earning distinction for his boldness and tactical skill during the fighting in France. After the armistice, he returned to the United States to command the venerable but ossified West Point Military Academy, where, between 1919 and 1922, he launched sweeping reforms. Soon after, he was dispatched back to the Philippines for a second tour of duty. By then, MacArthur knew the terrain of Luzon and Mindanao as intimately as he knew the contours of US war strategy.

In 1930, aged 50, MacArthur was promoted to the top job in the US Army. Over the next five years MacArthur watched the deteriorating international situation with growing unease. Japan's withdrawal from the League of Nations in March 1933 – seven months before Adolf Hitler's Nazi regime pulled out – marked the unravelling of the post-First World War order. The League, founded to prevent another global conflict, was exposed as powerless in the face of rising authoritarian regimes. For military strategists like MacArthur, these exits were deeply ominous. The mechanisms of collective security were failing, and the world was drifting toward militarism, expansionism, and ideological confrontation.

MacArthur strongly maintained that the prestige of the United States military would be on the line in any conflict with Japan – and that the nation had both a strategic and moral responsibility to protect the Philippines' 17 million people. Pending full independence, they remained quasi-American: US non-citizen nationals who, in his view, could not simply be left undefended in the event of a crisis.

When his tenure as Chief of Staff ended in 1935, MacArthur reverted to his permanent rank of major general. Aged 55, he returned once again to the Philippines, this time in a dual role: remaining on the US Army's payroll while also serving as a paid military adviser to President Manuel Quezón and the Commonwealth government.

This unusual arrangement required the tacit approval of President Franklin D. Roosevelt, as accepting a position and payment from a foreign government while serving as a US military officer was prohibited. Yet Roosevelt allowed it, recognising that MacArthur's presence advanced Washington's broader goal: preparing the Philippines for eventual independence.

MacArthur had known Manuel Quezón for years. Their bond ran deep: Quezón would eventually become the godfather to MacArthur's only son, Arthur IV. As the historian Richard Frank recounts in *Tower of Skulls*, Quezón had long recognised MacArthur's sincere affection for the Filipino people – an affection 'manifested by his marked preference for the social company of prominent Filipinos rather than American expatriates.'[4] In an era marked by the easy condescension of colonial racism, Filipinos saw in MacArthur a rare figure: an American who respected them, who listened, and around whom they could rally.

The veteran US Army general was to supervise the creation of a Philippine Commonwealth Army, and lobby for support in Washington. Given the mounting sense of global disquiet in the late 1930s, MacArthur had a tough job. Resources were short everywhere, and the drumbeat of war was growing ever louder in Europe. MacArthur's cause was not helped by the vacillation of Filipino leaders who increasingly doubted whether America would ever come to their aid if there was a conflict with Imperial Japan. Quezón talked of speeding up the independence process with a view to declaring the Philippines a neutral state, making foreign aid even more unlikely.

In Washington, sceptical planners and politicians watched MacArthur's lobbying with dismay. To them, it was a refusal to confront a brutal truth: that the Philippines, isolated and poorly resourced, might easily be blockaded by the Imperial Japanese Navy (IJN) – which had the world's third-largest fleet, boasting ten aircraft carriers, ten battleships, and an air wing already blooded in combat. Holding out against a land invasion by the IJA was no less daunting a prospect, a force composed of disciplined veterans imbued with what Frank called a 'warrior ethos'.

The working assumption of War Plan Orange had always been that US and Filipino forces would fight delaying actions against Japanese landings on Luzon and other islands. The goal wasn't to stop the invasion but to buy time for an organised withdrawal. The plan called for forces to fall back on the Bataan peninsula and the fortress island of Corregidor, at the mouth of Manila Bay. These locations had been chosen because they were more easily defended (narrow approaches, rugged terrain). Stockpiles of food, ammunition, and supplies were supposed to be pre-positioned there. Manila Bay could shelter the US fleet if reinforcements arrived. The defence was designed to last about six months – the time planners estimated the US Navy would need to fight its way across the Pacific, defeating the IJN before relieving the garrison.

At his own request, MacArthur retired from the US Army at the end of 1937, but he was formally recalled to active service in July 1941, aged 61. As trade US embargoes pushed relations with Japan toward breaking point, MacArthur became commander of United States Army Forces in the Far East (USAFFE). At that stage, with peace hanging by a thread, and President Franklin D. Roosevelt stringing out negotiations with the Japanese to buy time for mobilisation, money, men, and equipment had finally begun to cross the Pacific – a modest influx of resources in preparation for the defence of the Philippines.

By October 1941, MacArthur's air force included 227 aircraft, including 35 of the new B-17 Flying Fortresses. Air superiority was to be a cornerstone of the defence, and the B-17s were viewed as a major strategic asset. War plans envisioned them striking Japanese air bases on Formosa (Taiwan), just 320 kilometres (200 miles) to the north of Luzon. They could also be dispatched against troop convoys at sea or deployed to disrupt landings on the beaches. Alongside them were ninety-one Curtiss P-40 Warhawks, proven and capable fighters. The remainder of the fleet, however, consisted largely of aging, obsolete aircraft – remnants of an earlier era, ill-suited for the modern air war that loomed.

By December 1941, MacArthur's ground forces had swollen to 107,000 men, most of them raw Filipino recruits under American officers. Their uniform – a telling symbol of the hurried mobilisation – was blue denim fatigues originally designed as workwear, complete with broad-brimmed denim hats. Material challenges were compounded by inadequate training, outdated weaponry, a scarcity of modern vehicles and radios, and a fractured linguistic landscape. While the Filipino elite typically spoke English or Spanish, the rank and file communicated in a mosaic of regional dialects – only Tagalog, widely spoken on Luzon, provided any common ground.

The best hope for effective resistance lay in the better-trained and more experienced units under MacArthur's command. Chief among them were 22,400 US Army regulars and 12,000 Philippine Scouts – professional soldiers renowned for their discipline and combat readiness, in stark contrast to the fledgling Commonwealth Army. There was also the 3,000-strong Philippine Constabulary, a paramilitary force with policing experience. Augmenting this were 1,500 men of the US 4th Marine Regiment, recently evacuated from Shanghai.

MacArthur made nothing of the reality that he was in command of a patchwork force, and his ground forces might well be outmatched by an adversary battle-hardened from four years of fighting in China. Most of his forces were deployed for the defence of the two main islands, Luzon and Mindanao. Many historians also feel MacArthur put too much faith in what a relatively small number of B-17 bombers could achieve, given the size of the force they would face.

Crucially, MacArthur rejected War Plan Orange's retreat-to-Bataan strategy. He secured permission for a more active defence, which called for confronting the Japanese at the beaches. This change would have profound consequences and prove to be one of the most controversial aspects of the forthcoming conflict. It affected where the American and Filipino forces stockpiled and hoarded the food, medicine and ammunition essential to sustaining a long-term defence of the island – and how easily or otherwise these supplies could be accessed once the fighting was underway.

Hindsight would show that MacArthur's decision to discard War Plan Orange was a fatal miscalculation – one shaped perhaps as much by pride and principle as by strategic reasoning. Once the Japanese launched a land invasion his idealism collided with the brutal chaos and unforgiving arithmetic of war, leaving his forces vulnerable, over-matched and in full retreat. Then again, critics maintain that MacArthur often made decisions based on how he wished the world to be, rather than how it was – a tendency that contributed to the military disaster that began unfolding on Luzon at the end of 1941.

* * *

The war came not in a sudden lightning bolt, but in the long shadow of an attack already unfolding half an ocean away.

By the evening of 6 December 1941, Japanese air power had massed on Formosa: land-based Mitsubishi G4M bombers (Allied code name Betty) and Mitsubishi A6M (Zero) fighters, engines fuelled, crews briefed. Their mission was bold and clear – destroy the American air threat to the landings planned for Luzon.

Army and naval aircraft would fly from separate bases, striking targets across the island. The main blow would fall on Clark Field in central Luzon, home to the new B-17 Flying Fortresses – the core of MacArthur's defensive plan. No carriers would join the raid; every Japanese flattop was committed to Pearl Harbor. Surprise was reserved for that historic mission alone.

The International Date Line divided the assaults across two calendar days. In Hawaii, the first bombs were set to fall at 08.00 hours on 7 December – a bright, sunlit morning – but in Manila it would already be 02.00 hours on 8 December. Darkness over Luzon ruled out a simultaneous attack. The Formosa squadrons were ordered to launch in the early hours, cross the 250 kilometres (155 miles) of the Luzon Strait, and arrive at daybreak – expecting to find American fighters already aloft and spoiling for a fight, and B-17s clawing north toward Formosa in retaliation for Pearl Harbor.

One part of the plan began well enough. In the pre-dawn hours, two small bomber groups droned south over the water toward northern Luzon, ready to strike at American fighter airfields near the coast.

At the main Formosan base, however – where the Clark Field strike was coiled to strike – the weather betrayed them. A heavy fog clung to the runways, thick and unmoving. Pilots and crews sat waiting, fearing the spectre of American bombers appearing out of the dawn murk. They did not take flight until 10.15 hours – a delay that should have been a gift to the defenders of Luzon, but which was squandered.

About an hour later, radar screens lit with the trace of a big formation of aircraft over Lingayen Gulf, on the north-west coast of Luzon: 105 bombers, flanked by 85 Zero escorts. American fighters finally scrambled, but their radios filled with contradiction and confusion. Was Manila the target? Or were the Japanese turning back to Formosa after the earlier strikes in the north? By one account, one group of fighters actually passed beneath the armada without ever seeing it.

At Clark Field, the B-17s sat parked and refuelling. It was more than ten hours after Pearl Harbor, yet nothing circled above in the powder blue sky to protect them when, at 12.40 hours, Japanese aircraft arrived in V-shaped formations. The first bombs fell in long, deliberate walks through the lines of Flying Fortresses. Each warhead carried enough TNT to bring down a building, shred an aircraft, or blast a crater in the runway. Incredulous, ground staff and crews ran for cover as one sharp crack after another was swallowed by the enormous rip of explosions, tearing open the air and sending deep shudders through the ground.

Petty Officer First Class Saburo Sakai, flying fighter cover for the Japanese bombers, watched as the bombs struck. 'The entire air base seemed to [rise] into the air with the explosions,' he recalled. 'Pieces of airplanes, hangars, and other ground installations scattered wildly. Great fires erupted and smoke boiled upward.'[5]

Then came Sakai's turn. The Zeros circled down to 13,000 feet, still without enemy opposition. With his two wingmen in tow, Sakai nosed over, dove steeply, and picked out two B-17s untouched by the blasts. He 'poured a fusillade of bullets into the big bombers.'

Unopposed, Japanese pilots simply ran amok. The one working radio at Clark Field that might have summoned help was smashed in the opening salvo. Half the B-17s were destroyed on the ground, including three being readied for reconnaissance over Formosa. Ten P-40 fighters were blown up as they prepared for take-off; others were shot to pieces or crash-landed during the forty-five-minute melee. A second wave from Formosa smashed hangars, machine shops, bomb stores, and fuel dumps. Other Japanese formations swept the remaining fighter bases on Luzon. By nightfall, MacArthur's Far East Air Force had been decimated.

Over the following week, mopping-up raids erased what was left. A few P-40s and B-17s remained airworthy, but not for long. The surviving B-17s at Del Monte Field in Mindanao were flown to the safety of Australia. The last twelve P-40s went to Bataan, where they flew reconnaissance and the occasional harassing strike. The skies over the Philippines belonged to Japan.

The cascade of disaster had in fact only just begun. With the skies lost, the US Asiatic Fleet's surface ships withdrew south to Australia. Only a few submarines remained – their torpedoes unreliable, their threat minimal. The Philippines lay wide open.

In 1941, with the crisis in full flood and the world reeling from the scale of the Japanese blitzkrieg in the Asia-Pacific, there was no time to pick apart the events on Luzon. Today historians reflect that the strategy of relying on the B-17s at Clark Field to spearhead the defence of the Philippines was flawed. Richard Frank points out that the base had not been developed properly to serve its purpose. It was poorly defended and lacked the solid, prepared ground to allow for the adequate dispersal of aircraft.

Another factor in the opening day disaster was that orders to locate the entire bomber force at the more secure airfield, Del Monte, had not been carried out in full. Historians note the 'incredibly inept' performance of the officers directing American fighters to intercept the incoming Japanese strike aircraft as also contributing to the disaster.

Attempts to understand why the response was so poor can read like an account of a criminal negligence trial. They centre on the time it took MacArthur to react to the incredible news that Pearl Harbor had been hit and hit hard. Unofficial reports of the attack reached Manila around 03.00 hours local time. MacArthur was woken up and informed before 04.00 hours. In the hours that followed he repeatedly refused to see Major General Lewis H. Brereton, commander of the Far East Air Force (FEAF) in the Philippines, who was best placed to intercept and counter the first strike.

Brereton had been given the news by MacArthur's Chief of Staff, the priggish Brigadier General Richard Sutherland at 04.00 hours. He wanted permission to attack Formosa, as was set out in the war plans. Sutherland continued to deny Brereton access to MacArthur and maintained that an American strike could only take place with the express permission of the general. Remarkably, further requests to see MacArthur were denied, even as intelligence reports came in advising of the escalating gravity of the situation. These included notification before 09.00 hours of an American destroyer, *William B. Preston*, coming under fire from Japanese aircraft in Philippine waters. At 08.50 hours Sutherland even called Brereton to reaffirm MacArthur's order to defer bombing Formosa.

In fact, between 05.00 and 05.30 hours MacArthur had received a cable from Washington DC directing him to activate the war plan. This sanctioned striking at any Japanese forces and installations within range. A series of disputed discussions and decisions cover these desperate hours, but it's accepted that MacArthur did not authorise an attack until 10.15 hours at the earliest, when he personally called Brereton. Even then, the initial permission was only granted for a strike at sunset. The order was to count for nothing: the Japanese had long since taken off from Formosa and were about to wreak havoc.

In the chaos of that morning, and aware that his aircraft could be destroyed on the ground, Brereton had ordered his B-17s aloft between 08.00 and 08.30 hours to circle the airfield, but they had not been loaded with bombs and had all landed to refuel when the Japanese swarmed over Clark Field four hours later.

MacArthur's biographers have explored the failure to bring American forces to a proper state of readiness. In one of the more supportive accounts, *American Caesar*, William Manchester described MacArthur's mental condition at the outbreak of hostilities as verging on 'catatonic' and suffering from a paralysis of indecision due to conflicting pressures.

The latter likely came from the restraining influence of his friend and benefactor, Manuel Quezón. The Philippine president harboured a belief that by remaining neutral and not provoking the Japanese his nation could somehow avoid the worst effects of occupation or full-scale war. Any news of the damage inflicted at Pearl Harbor may have oddly made Quezón double-down on this conviction, with the prospect of American reinforcement of the Philippines receding with every update on the astonishing events on the other side of the Pacific.

Quezón was to be disabused of his fantasy over the coming weeks and months, with legions of Filipinos killed for their allegiance to the United States. What's more, the stark reality of being isolated on the edge of Asia only increased as the hours passed, with reports of Japanese aircraft bombing Guam and Wake Island, the two American outposts between Hawaii and the Philippines.

Unlike at Pearl Harbor, there were no high-level commissions to hold the commanders to account for ill-preparedness. After the events in Hawaii, Army General Walter Short and Admiral Husband Kimmel were both demoted and retired from the military soon afterwards. No formal inquiries took place into what went wrong in the Philippines. For years afterwards, MacArthur blamed Brereton and stood behind statements about being under orders not to provoke the Japanese by taking the first aggressive act. The key officers involved were all subsequently plunged into the defence of the Philippines, some becoming prisoners of war, which, along with the loss of papers, the distances involved, and the passage of time pushed the issues ever further from scrutiny.

Two days after the fiasco at Clark Field, some two thousand Japanese troops had landed at two towns in the north of Luzon, Vigan and Aparri. This was a preliminary to a full-scale land invasion, their collective mission to seize airfields in the northern part of the island that would bring their shorter-range aircraft into the battle. They marched under the Rising Sun flag. It featured sixteen rays radiating from a red sun – centred in the army version but positioned slightly off-centre, closer to the hoist, in the navy equivalent. Many soldiers also carried something more intimate: personalised Yosegaki Hinomaru or good luck flags. These were Japan's simple national flag – a red circle on a white background – transformed into personal talismans. Before departing for war, soldiers would have family members, friends, and neighbours sign these flags with messages wishing them victory, safe return, and good fortune. The practice embodied Japan's identity as the 'Land of the Rising Sun' while connecting each soldier to his home community.

The Japanese brushed aside the troops defending the northern area and moved south to prepare for the linkup with the main invasion group that would land at Lingayen Gulf in a matter of days, some 177 kilometres (110 miles) north-west of Manila. During this time, other small landings occurred elsewhere in Luzon and in the southern Philippines on Mindanao and the Sulu archipelago.

Another large-scale air attack also devastated the US Asiatic Fleet's main base at Cavite in Manila Bay, destroying torpedo reserves.

Finally, in the early hours of 22 December, the ground began to tremble as some 43,000 IJA troops from two divisions of Lieutenant General Masaharu Homma's 14th Army came ashore on the grey to black sand of Lingayen Gulf, a U-shaped bay.

They landed at three points along the northern shoreline and faced two poorly equipped and inexperienced Philippine Army divisions, only one of which had artillery. The defenders were unable to hold their ground against some of the best trained soldiers in the world and the Japanese duly pushed inland and south towards the capital, with the American and Filipino forces conducting a fighting retreat. On Christmas Eve, a second landing of some 7,000 troops on the coast Lamon Bay, 64 kilometres (40 miles) south-east of the capital, threatened to catch MacArthur's troops in a giant pincer.

MacArthur's revised version of the defensive plan to defend the beaches was in ruins. It became apparent there was no choice but to mount a defence on Bataan, as set out on the original War Plan Orange. Most of his men made it through, but food, weapons, ammunition and other critical supplies that had been dispersed around four massive supply depots on Luzon were abandoned amid the chaos of truck shortages, congested roads, and harassing air attacks.

Before escaping to the fortress island of Corregidor at the opening of the bay, along with Quezón and his staff, MacArthur declared Manila an open city on 26 December in the hope of saving it from destruction. The Japanese bombed it anyway as the Americans still used the anchorage for logistical purposes and were busy burning stocks of fuel to prevent them falling into the hands of the enemy.

Chapter 2

The Deluge and the Flood

I was only corrected once on my puzzling pronunciation, but Filipinos say *Bata-ann* as opposed to the American English *Bat-tan*. Before reaching *Bata-ann* proper, my bus made one stop at an historical crossroads of sorts. The terminal was attached to a shopping mall on the outskirts of San Fernando, the regional capital set amid the agricultural plains of central Luzon. The town was a key waypoint in the battle, with American and Filipino forces passing through here once MacArthur ordered a fighting retreat towards Bataan. The roads were held open long enough to allow troops to funnel onto the peninsula. The idea was that the relatively narrow width of the land on Bataan would allow for a defence in depth.

The escaping Allied units had to get through the first of two bottlenecks where the roads into Bataan from the north and south converged at the only crossings over the Pampanga River – the road and rail Calumpit Bridges, just south-east of San Fernando. By blowing both spans, they placed a deep and wide obstacle in the path of the advancing Japanese. A ferocious delaying action was also fought on the plains just to the west of San Fernando. Known as the Porac-Guagua line, it is once again peaceful farmland today.

I sat on the bus staring at the signs for other historically interesting places. The depot has connections to Clark Field, where the US Air Force maintained a base until 1991. At that time, it suffered extensive damage as a result of the eruption of Mount Pinatubo, a giant volcano that sits on the plain between San Fernando and the west coast of Bataan, hastened a closure that was already pending because of disagreements over leasing costs. It's a regional airport and business park today.

Without much of a delay, the bus trundled out of the shade of the San Fernando depot and headed south-west towards Bataan down Route Three.

We passed through Layac Junction, the second and final bottleneck that had to be navigated in 1942. A bridge over a river here represented the last crossing before Bataan proper. I saw a sign that marked the 'First Line Of Defence of Bataan' and a monument that acknowledges the barrios' short-lived role as a focal point in the conflict. Heroic statues of larger-than-life Filipinos in combat positions and carrying a Philippine flag stood proud in the middle of an unceremonious traffic island.

On 4 and 5 January 1942, Layac Junction overflowed with an army of around 50,000 men in full retreat, the township choked with Americans and Filipinos, to say nothing of trucks, buses, artillery, tanks, oxcarts, horses, and large numbers of staff and command cars. A strafing air attack would have produced absolute carnage but the Japanese, focused on taking Manila, missed the moment. By the early hours of 6 January, the fleeing troops had all crossed over and the withdrawal from north and south Luzon was complete. When the order was given to blow up the span, the siege of Bataan began.

A little while after passing through Layac I was finally deposited at the side of the north-south highway that runs parallel to the east coast and Bataan's farming plains. As the bus pulled away, I was relieved to find that I was not completely stranded in rural isolation – a couple of tricycles were waiting for customers. I approached the one rider with a luggage rack of sorts. For 300 pesos he was prepared to tackle me and my big bags. I'd worked out the route from Google Maps – turn off the highway at Laon proper, a feeder road that went directly to Abucay Plaza, then across a bridge over the Abucay River and take the first right. I showed him the route and he nodded. A certain amount of confusion and gesticulation followed as, once we got off the highway, motorcycle and sidecar veered here and there around the Bataan countryside, me trying to make myself heard (he was wearing a crash helmet) and pointing in exasperation at the map on my phone.

It turned out that the man who owned the car rental business with God had recently sought election as the mayor of Abucay. A campaign poster still decorated the garage wall where I stood waiting to collect my vehicle.

In person, Armando Estrella Madrid was tall, and somewhat solemn, with a shaved head and the imposing physique of a recently retired basketball player. In the election poster he had an enigmatic half-smile. I was not entirely clear whether the cash I put on the table meant I was insured or not. He looked at me gravely and spoke about taking responsibility for the car with the tone of someone handing over a child for adoption.

I pointed at the poster and asked, 'did you win?'

'I was not elected', he replied, less priestly than before. I must have said something like 'unlucky' which brought forward his own conclusion.

'After the pandemic, everything is about money. Everybody wants money. I don't have.'

With the discipline of the devout, I backed the car slowly out into a narrow street flanked by a rainwater gully. Closely packed single-storey houses lined the road – all tin and tile roofs, modest yards, and laundry hanging in the afternoon sun.

Already hating the tricycles that ruled every thoroughfare in Abucay, I managed to drive out of sight of the defeated mayor before taking a wrong turn and getting pulled over by the police for going down a one-way street. I talked my way out of missing the 'Do Not Enter' sign – written in plain English – with some 'I've just got off the bus from Manila' shrugs and apologies. Surprised that I was an international visitor, the officer asked where I was from, laughed as though I had said something ridiculous, and waved me on my way.

I'd rented a studio apartment in a low rise and uncharacteristically modern block in the centre of Balanga, ten minutes south of Abucay. A security man, who was probably somewhere in his sixties, sat on a stool by the entrance gate. My unit turned out to be Asian and funky inside: a futon instead of a bed, a projector rather than a TV, and chopsticks in place of knives and forks. I imagined a young couple had either lived there or designed it. The air conditioner produced a blissful blast of refrigeration.

Taking a break to get my body heat down, I researched the Abucay election results online. Car rental man finished third, with 2.51 per cent of the votes. He stood as an independent. The two other mayoral candidates slugged it out securing 43.65 per cent and 53.84 per cent respectively, with Robin Tagle of the National Unity Party getting elected. Changed into fresh clothes, I decided to explore the town and try buying some cutlery I could use. I was supposed to deposit my keys with security but the guard and I could only communicate with shrugs and other gestures. He gave me one of those genial, half weary smiles of the semi-retired and I kept the keys.

Balanga is a city on account of its population of around 100,000 people and the Spanish-era cathedral located in front of the central plaza. It had the feel of an untidy market town, one where everyone has some form of employment. The first thing that caught the eye was the long and ugly lines of overhead wires suspended above and along the length of almost every street, gathering in bundles at junctions. The black spaghetti is apparently a consequence of a telecommunications boom in the 1980s when new providers were allowed to hang cables on existing poles to quickly and cheaply catch up with the established providers.

A series of streets branched off from the main road threading through the functional centre of agricultural supply sheds. The general stores were augmented with a small and brightly lit shopping mall, along with commercial spaces for wholesalers and enterprises in manufacturing, insurance, financing and the like.

During the Spanish era Bataan began to see paved roads and stone bridges. The colonists also introduced stone and masonry construction for homes, at least for the upper echelons of society. Well into the twentieth century, Balanga and other rural areas were still dotted with traditional Filipino huts built with readily available and affordable local materials. Woven *sawali* panels of flat bamboo strips formed the walls beneath roofs made from bamboo joints and thatched palms. The American colonial era encouraged more Western ideas such as higher ceilings, bigger living rooms, inside bathrooms and private garages to secure vehicles. During this period the bungalow became the most common type of house outside of the Filipino big cities. Abucay, where I had rented the car, seemed to be almost exclusively bungalows. Balanga looked a little more varied, but inexpensive single-story homes made from concrete walls and galvanised metal roofs, each with a yard, garden, and garage, were a big part of the townscape.

Balanga and Abucay may seem workaday and residential, but they once stood on the front line of the battle for Luzon. They were shelled by the Japanese in 1942 as they fought their way down the Manila Bay side of the peninsula. Their story was told in the Bataan War Museum. It was only a short walk from where I was staying but no signage marked the way. After some wandering around, I discovered it was located within the grounds of Balanga Elementary School. Lola, a retired teacher, welcomed me, quite possibly the first and only visitor that day. The building itself was a rather elegant old army barracks. I spent time reading the exhibition boards retelling the story of the battle for Bataan. A variety of artefacts in glass cases were set around the museum's unusual centrepiece, a large diorama made up of 120 dolls depicting scenes from the struggles and strife of 1942. I bought a souvenir from the gift shop – a fridge magnet featuring MacArthur, still a bona fide hero in these parts.

Outside, the wartime stories gave way to the steady pulse of present-day Bataan. The peninsula is little troubled by foreign travellers. From its edge of Manila Bay, the shoreline is not a sweep of golden beaches or a chain of attractive rocky coves, but a stretch of mudflats. Yet as I was to discover the next day, by climbing one of the high points at the peninsula's southern reaches, the glass towers of Manila could be seen in miniature across the bay, gleaming like a mirage of the tiger economy.

Highway 301 threads through farmland before meeting the southern highlands. The most compelling is Mount Mariveles, a sleeping colossus draped in forest and cloud, its volcanic slopes spilling down to the sea. At 1,388 metres (4,554 feet), Mount Mariveles is not so much a solitary summit as a vast landmass, its base sprawling across much of southern Bataan and claiming the horizon. Between its broad shoulders, a caldera yawns 4 kilometres (2.5 miles) across – a brooding reminder of the cataclysm that tore it open in an age when fire ruled the Earth.

Just 9 kilometres (5.5 miles) away, on the lower slopes, Mount Samat lifts its smaller crown to the sky – 545 metres (1,787 feet) of green-clad elevation. The younger brother – less mighty, yet no less proud – stands in the foreground of the peninsula's topographical icon. On clear days they are both prominent and distinct, green-robed guardians steadily emerging as you head south. Yet the skyline conceals other hulking monoliths away in the central plains, especially Mount Natib, whose steep, untamed flanks would play a decisive role in the opening weeks of the siege.

Once the retreating troops reached Bataan, MacArthur reorganised his remaining forces into two corps, forming a shore-to-shore line of resistance across the peninsula's northern neck. The only break in this front was Natib – its volcanic mass rising to over 1,280 metres (about 4,200 feet). In 1942, the tangle of dense jungle covering its slopes and the complete absence of roads made it all but impassable to vehicles or artillery. To the soldiers, Mount Natib was less a point on a map than a fortress raised by nature itself. On its western flank, Major General Jonathan M. Wainwright's First Corps – some 22,500 men – held a defensive line stretching to the village of Mauban on the South China Sea.

On the eastern flank, Second Corps led by Major General George Parker covered the area from Natib to Abucay out by Manila Bay. He had about 25,000 troops. MacArthur had one stroke of luck: on 2 January 1942, the day the Japanese marched into Manila, Lieutenant General Masaharu Homma's most experienced division, the 48th Division was reassigned to support the invasion of the Dutch East Indies and Dutch Borneo. Inexperienced reservists from the 65th Brigade took their place for the push down into Bataan province. The brief halt in hostilities, as Homma reorganised part of his force, allowed MacArthur's officers more time to prepare defensive positions.

In the opening stage of the battle the defenders of Bataan used artillery to great effect to disrupt Japanese attempts to advance. In scenes reminiscent of the First World War, the frontline edged slowly forward and back as the two sides slugged it out through a series of piecemeal exchanges. Nevertheless, as the fighting wore on, the IJA began to find gaps, partly by showing that the mountainous terrain around Mount Natib was not as impenetrable as had been presumed.

On 10 January, MacArthur left his emergency HQ on Corregidor for his only visit to Bataan during the battle. He crossed by boat to the southern tip, Mariveles, and was then driven around the dusty roads on the peninsula in a battered Ford sedan, with stops where he tried to bolster morale. He got as far north as Abucay, where I had picked up my car. Thereafter, he sent his besieged troops messages designed to bolster their fighting spirit. 'Help is on the way from the United States. Thousands of troops and hundreds of planes are being dispatched. The exact time of arrival is unknown as they will have to fight their way through.'

A convoy had in fact been dispatched from San Francisco in late November 1941 led by the heavy cruiser *Pensacola.* It featured transports packed with troops and supplies to reinforce Luzon, but this lifeline was diverted to Brisbane, Australia after the attack on Pearl Harbor.

MacArthur doubtless believed the briefings and assurances from Washington at the outset, but his blustery promises to his own troops faded away without explanation as the weeks began to pass. It seemed the US Navy had accepted that it could not break the Japanese maritime blockade.

As if to prove the dire state of the supply situation, the first month did produce the last cavalry charge in American military history. On 16 January 1942, First Lieutenant Edwin Ramsey of the 26th Cavalry Regiment led a horseback counterattack against Japanese troops trying to break the defensive line at Morong, a village near the China Sea coast. Ramsey and the rest of his twenty-seven-man platoon, consisting mostly of elite Philippine Scouts, galloped headlong into a far larger force of enemy infantrymen. The surprise charge scattered the Japanese, even though they were backed by light tanks, and helped buy time to reorganise the defensive line.

'Bent nearly prone across the horses' necks, we flung ourselves at the Japanese advance, pistols firing full into their startled faces,' Ramsey wrote in his memoirs. 'A few returned our fire but most fled in confusion. To them we must have seemed a vision from another century, wild-eyed horses pounding headlong; cheering, whooping men firing from the saddles.'[6]

American planners had reckoned that the Bataan defence forces required enough supplies for 43,000 soldiers to last at 180 days without any form of resupply. However, the actual number of troops that had withdrawn to the peninsula was around 80,000, along with 26,000 civilians who had followed in their panic-stricken wake. Supply problems were acute and made worse by the vast quantity of food, fuel, ammunition and medicine that had been destroyed or left behind. From his headquarters on Corregidor, MacArthur had no choice but to order that his Bataan troops be placed on half rations in January.

The Japanese punched decisively through the defensive line as the month ended. Forced to withdraw further south, the two corps either side of Mount Natib retreated under the cover of artillery fire and a tank group. They formed the second and final line of resistance from 22 January. It ran from the village of Bagac on the South China Sea coast without interruption to Orion on the shores of Manila Bay.

Over on Corregidor, President Quezón, bitter at being abandoned and written off, asked Roosevelt to grant the Philippines full independence so that he could announce neutrality. His request on 8 February read:

> After nine weeks of fighting not even a small amount of aid has reached us from the United States. Help and assistance have been sent to other belligerent nations … but seemingly no attempt has been made to transport anything here … [The] United States has practically doomed the Philippines to almost total extinction to secure a breathing space.

Roosevelt turned down the request, partly in the belief that the Japanese would not acknowledge such a late statement of neutrality. MacArthur was ordered to keep the Stars and Stripes flying as long as possible.

Having been given only fifty days to conquer the entire Philippine archipelago, Lieutenant General Homma was himself under enormous pressure. The failure to quickly eradicate the stubborn American-Filipino resistance on Bataan was a source of personal embarrassment and fierce criticism from Tokyo.

What Homma did next also drew scorn: rather than waste his men in all out frontal assaults, Homma tried to outmanoeuvre his enemy by conducting a series of flanking amphibious landings. The idea was to get behind the American-Filipino line and establish beachheads at points along the rugged west coast and fight inland from there.

Homma, who was 55 years old, had spent eight years as a military attaché in London in the 1920s and 1930s. During the First World War he was an observer with the British Army in France. All of which was held against him in some quarters – Homma was too 'Western'. Any approach that focused on conserving his men was considered timid by hardliners, but the flanking missions went ahead anyway. Between 23 January and the start of February the amphibious raids came to be called the Battle of the Points.

Homma's force did not face elite troops. American and Filipino personnel held in the rear consisted of a ramshackle collection of grounded pilots, members of the Philippine Constabulary, and headquarters staff, none of whom had infantry training. Louis Morton, the official historian of the US Army, reports that the defenders 'wore different uniforms and came from different services' and formed a group that even under peacetime conditions 'would have given any commander nightmares.'[7]

The improvised outfit made so much noise and moved around in the bush with so little regard for infantry discipline that one surviving Japanese diarist recorded that his unit thought they had encountered a special suicide squad that did not care if it was spotted.

Yet the rear echelon defenders managed to hang on until more experienced units arrived to take control. Homma made further attempts at reinforcing his troops on 26 January and 2 February at different points along the shore, but these beachheads were slowly whittled down. By 13 February, the IJA raiding forces had been eliminated.

The Battle of the Points went forward about the same time as Japanese units managed to infiltrate the second defensive line in the centre of the peninsula. A force of around 1,000 IJA broke through in what became known as the Battle of the Pockets. They crossed in three different places in the centre of Bataan (the Little, Big, and Upper pockets) only for each pocket to be isolated and closed. Over half of the raiders were wiped out, with about 400 soldiers escaping back to Japanese lines.

The bastards of Bataan, as the American-Filipino hybrid of mostly raw troops saw themselves, had inflicted a significant setback on the previously marauding IJA. Since moving onto Bataan, almost 3,000 of Homma's men had been killed, at least 4,000 more were wounded, and as many as 12,000 were sick or dying from malaria, beriberi, and dysentery. As March 1942 approached, Homma had slipped well behind the Tokyo schedule.

Yet for all the undoubted pressure caused by failing to meet the timetable, the fundamentals of the situation remain unchanged. Homma's forces could still be replenished. In the war of attrition, the Japanese enjoyed decisive advantages over the now completely bottled-up American and Filipino forces. Homma duly asked for experienced reinforcements and paused offensive operations until they arrived from Shanghai. By the middle of March, Homma had received enough replacements in battle-hardened men and artillery to launch a fresh assault.

* * *

I drove south through the sun-baked plains before turning onto a winding road at the foot of Mount Samat. The route climbed toward the Shrine of Valor, a national memorial marked by a stark white cross rising 92 metres (302 feet) into the sky.

At the base camp car park, I bought a ticket and filed into a reception hall where a short orientation film played. It spoke in careful tones of reverence. Social media posters were asked to show respect. Couples should avoid excessive displays of affection. Drones, the narrator warned, risked being shot down by the army.

The humidity pasted my shirt to my back as I walked up the last steep rise. At a curve in the path, I stopped, taking in the view to the north. The tangle of thick jungle that once challenged the footsteps of weary soldiers in the 1940s had long since yielded to agricultural order. Fields of sweet potato, turnip, and watermelon now quilted the plains of Bataan. Balanga and Abucay appeared as grey smudges along the shoulder of Manila Bay. The coastline stretched away into the haze, gradually fading from view as it curved right toward San Fernando and central Luzon, some 80 kilometres (50 miles) away. There was a hush to the land, a sense of rural ways. Yet I knew that for the American and Filipino gunners once dug into the slopes of Mount Samat, waiting for the coming barrage, this view would have offered no such peace.

Higher up, the terrain levelled into a broad clearing the size of several football fields, ringed by forest. At its centre stood a rectangular shrine complex, its sides defined by a colonnade of marble, with architecture that blended the stillness of the sacred with the stature of the civic. Each panel was lined with high-relief sculptures by Filipino artist Napoleon Abueva. His parents, Teodoro and Purificacion, had fought in the resistance before being killed by the Japanese. Abueva, a teenager at the time, was captured and tortured, but survived. I climbed a flight of wide steps that tapered toward a flagpole, where the Philippine flag barely moved in the light breeze above two immense bronze urns flanking the entrance. Behind the main building, the Shrine of Valor cross rose, steadfast and solemn.

Inside, tablets along the walls recounted the story of the Bataan campaign. At the centre, an altar stood before three stained-glass murals depicting religious scenes. Above, dark brass chandeliers – their forms inspired by the sampaguita, the Asian jasmine and national flower of the Philippines – evoked the garlands still offered in honour and respect.

Back outside, I wandered across the surrounding esplanade, its floor patterned with geometric designs. An entrance led to a museum beneath the colonnade, and before the stairwell one wall displayed a gallery of head-and-shoulders portraits of Filipino war heroes. In each painting, the men faced the viewer with direct, open gazes, formally dressed in civilian clothes. Their expressions varied – calm, alert, contemplative – but all shared a common air of dignity. Some looked like partners in a prosperous law firm; one robust man had the commanding presence of a restaurant owner, the kind who greets patrons with easy charm and runs his kitchen with uncompromising authority. Here were shopkeepers, teachers, and businessmen – ordinary men who had defied an empire and lived to tell the tale.

One stood apart. Colonel Ruperto Kangleón, chiselled and unsmiling, possessed the spare frame and inward steel of a soldier. He had led the resistance in Leyte and was awarded the Distinguished Service Cross by MacArthur himself for heroism.

Each portrait carried a terse inscription of valour. Beneath the image of Lieutenant Simeon C. Medalla, of the Reserve Officers' Training Corps, it read:

> Member 47th Infantry Hunters ROTC Guerrilla – who, completely disregarding his personal safety, led a special force assaulting an enemy stronghold. The battle lasted six hours and cost the invaders 40 dead and allowed for the seizure of a considerable quantity of firearms and ammunition, with only four men wounded on his side.

Afterwards, I followed a zig-zagging footpath paved with round stones mottled red, their colour – local lore insists – the blood of Japanese soldiers, though in truth it comes from mineral-rich quarries on Corregidor. The path wound upward toward the memorial's crowning structure: a bold, modernist white steel cross rising from a sculpted base carved with scenes from Filipino history. At its foot stood a massive bronze door, forged from melted artillery shells, sealing the entrance to the interior. The elevator that once lifted visitors to a gallery in the arms of the cross stood silent, currently out of service.

* * *

For the besieged soldiers and civilians trapped on the peninsula, there was little reprieve from dwindling rations, festering wounds, and the slow, wasting grip of tropical disease. In a decision born of sheer desperation, Major General Jonathan Wainwright ordered the 250 horses of the 26th Cavalry to be shot and butchered to feed the starving men. It was a heart-breaking command for any cavalryman, but Wainwright made no exception for himself. He personally shot his own mount – Joseph Conrad, his trusted charger for years. With daily rations reduced to little more than a cup of rice per man, the troops turned to whatever protein they could find: mule, dog, cat, monkey and iguana. Worse still, by the middle of February, the defenders of Bataan were short of mosquito nets and had run out of quinine, the first line drug used at the time for the prevention and treatment of malaria. Dysentery proved no less widespread and debilitating. Surrounded by their own stench, American infantrymen increasingly felt abandoned by their government, forced to fight a war on their own, without basic resupply, much less air or naval support.

MacArthur stayed on Corregidor – earning the sobriquet 'Dugout Doug' from men still waiting for the much-promised relief. Weary of scanning the skies for B-17s and P-40s that never came and perplexed that the promised convoy of supplies and reinforcements had not appeared on the horizon, they came up with their own stanza to mark their stand.

> We're the battling bastards of Bataan
> No mama, No papa, no Uncle Sam

The wartime diaries of some of the officers who served on Bataan detail the fraught conditions. The entries written by Major Achille C. Tisdelle are particularly evocative as are photographs of him in the field. Lanky and thin faced, with a painter's brush moustache, Tisdelle had a spare, hardy bearing. A native of Chicago, Tisdelle was in his early thirties but looked a decade older. At first glance I thought he looked like the novelist George Orwell, but he was in fact a career soldier. On 2 February, he reflected: 'Everything has been against us since war started. We could coordinate fire from mortar batteries and Corregidor to much better advantage if the batteries had shrapnel rounds. The armour-piercing 12-inch shells are not very effective on light material and personnel.'[8]

He was more expansive on 16 February:

> Routine bombing front and rear areas. Nip radio today claims cruiser *Houston* has been sunk Feb 4th with Admiral Hart aboard. The damned Nips have got a new propaganda program that does not help our morale any. The men joke happily but underneath they are disquieted. KZRH in Manila plays American songs to American soldiers on Bataan and Corregidor at 21.45 hours every night. Theme song 'Ships that never come in' followed by popular records. Nips continue holding front lines loosely and with impunity knowing that unless we receive support we will not dare to extend our flanks by advancing.

As the end of February approached, Wainwright reported to MacArthur that only 25 per cent of his malaria-stricken and starving First Corps soldiers on the west side of the line were fit for duty. Parker's Second Corps on the eastern flank had fared little better. Most of the men had lost about a third of their body weight.

Recognising how precarious the situation had become, President Roosevelt made the fateful decision to order General MacArthur to abandon his command on Corregidor and transfer to Australia. It was a departure steeped in guilt and the sting of perceived failure – a moment that would haunt MacArthur for the rest of his life. That sense of unfinished duty would come to shape not only his personal conduct but also the arc of American strategy throughout the remainder of the Pacific War.

Though derided by some as 'Dugout Doug', MacArthur had repeatedly demonstrated personal bravery during his career, and no one doubted he believed he should remain and fight to the end, whatever fate awaited him. Roosevelt was told plainly that MacArthur was ready to sacrifice his own life, his men, and even that of his wife, Jean, and young son, Arthur IV, who – against all army regulations – had stayed by his side on Corregidor. It took a direct and uncompromising order from the president to force him to leave. For Roosevelt, the risk of one of America's most famous military leaders falling into Japanese hands was too great to bear; such a blow would feed the growing fear that, after crushing the British Army in Singapore, Japan would steamroller American forces wherever they met them.

Given no choice, on 10 March MacArthur briefed his highest-ranking officer in the Philippines, Major General Wainwright, that he was leaving. Wainwright, then 59 years old, was tall, naturally gaunt, and nicknamed 'Skinny' by his friends. The meeting handed him the unenviable role of Allied commander in the Philippines. Soon after, he moved his headquarters from Bataan to Corregidor. Before departing, MacArthur presented him with a box of cigars, two jars of shaving cream, and a final instruction: make it known to all ranks that he was leaving only over his repeated protests. For the men left behind, and especially the veterans of the First World War, the departure of MacArthur was a grim milestone indeed, a sure sign that relief was never coming. They were to be sacrificed.

The first feature film based on the events, *Bataan*, produced within twelve months of the battle, did not conceal that sense of bewildered abandonment from American audiences. It tells the story of a fictional mishmash unit trying to prevent Japanese forces crossing a bridge.

Bataan could almost have been a stage play where soldiers do their duty and are picked off one-by-one as they follow their orders in the face of insurmountable odds. After one of the men is killed by a Japanese sniper, the arch sceptic in the group, Corporal Barney Todd, joins a debate about whether they will ever be relieved. 'Sarge,' he says, 'You better bury the rest of us face down so we don't keep lookin' up for planes that ain't coming.'[9]

The transfer of command from MacArthur to Wainwright left the Luzon force in urgent need of leadership on the ground. That responsibility fell to Major General Edward King, a seasoned officer who had been overseeing the artillery on Bataan.

Louis Morton, the official US Army historian, later described King as 'an extremely able soldier of high intellectual calibre.'[10] Born in Georgia, he had earned a law degree from the University of Georgia, only to disappoint his family by abandoning a legal career for the army. Known to friends as Ned, he was driven less by convention than by a hunger for purpose and challenge. A veteran of the First World War, King was remembered by those who served with him as modest, thoughtful, and instinctively respectful of all ranks.

Before his departure, Wainwright gave King a direct and unambiguous order: under no circumstances was he to surrender. It was a command that would weigh heavily in the weeks to come – a moral and military burden no American general had yet borne in the campaign. When the moment of reckoning arrived, King would be left alone to navigate the fine line between duty and sacrifice.

As March 1942 ended, Japanese artillery barrages and air attacks grew in intensity. They launched a full-scale assault at Mount Samat on 3 April. A large array of artillery guns, howitzers, and mortars began to register on their targets from 10.00 hours and kept firing until 15.00 hours, pulverising the area where the Shrine of Valor stands today. The thunder of artillery was accompanied by 60 tons of bombs dropped along the defensive line during 150 sorties flown by unopposed Japanese aircraft. Fighters swooped low, strafing the exposed positions.

In his diary Achille Tisdelle recorded 'a sky black with planes.' The barrage shook and churned the earth, setting ablaze the mountain, destroying painstakingly constructed barbed wire defences while covering everything in smoke and dust. Amid the chaos, artillery observers on Mount Samat found it difficult to direct return fire. Once the big Japanese guns stopped, thousands of IJA troops worked up the slopes. By 5 April, the remaining American and Filipino troops holding the position were defeated.

The same shell-shocked day that the Mount Samat offensive began the Japanese launched a major thrust against Second Corps on the South China Sea side of the line, with a similarly sustained aerial and artillery bombardment. Over the following seventy-two hours, IJA infantry were able to achieve another decisive breakthrough. Lieutenant General Homma had reckoned that forcing a second breach would require a week. When it took just three days, he pushed his forces even further south on 6 April to meet the expected counterattacks head-on.

King's forces duly engaged the advance, even summoning malaria-stricken men from their sickbeds but it was to no avail. Three months of malnutrition, malaria, and intestinal infections had left the bastards of Bataan weak. The Japanese drove a decisive wedge between the two corps. Defensive lines were formed and abandoned before they could be fully occupied and marauding Japanese aircraft raked the starving, retreating army.

The western side of the line crumbled into a complete rout. Bataan's roads jammed with emaciated soldiers who had abandoned their arms and equipment, fleeing the torrents of Japanese infantry and armoured columns flowing south. They passed overturned trucks, bombed-out tanks, and shattered guns. 'Thousands poured out of the jungle,' wrote one observer of the collapse, 'like small spring freshets pouring into creeks which in turn poured into a river.'[11]

On 7 April, Major General Wainwright instructed King to launch another counterattack but there was a sense of chaos and collapsing lines everywhere, with communications breaking down. It was clear to King that the end was near. The troops he did have were weak and diminished. To be considered combat effective and able to fight was defined as a soldier being able to carry his weapon 100 yards and still shoot it. By King's reckoning, only about 15 per cent of the troops, some 27,000 men, were available in cohesive units that could meet the standard.

King also became concerned that within hours the Japanese would have free passage to Limay on the east coast of the peninsular. It was the location of two open air jungle hospitals where there were some 12,000 men, wounded or too ill to move. They would be stranded behind enemy lines on the Manila Bay side of Bataan and face an uncertain fate.

Approaching midnight on 8 April, King held a conference with his Chief of Staff and his operations officer. In *The Fall of the Philippines*, Louis Morton recounts that in going over the tactical situation King and his officers could see no way to stop the Japanese reaching the high ground above the little port town of Mariveles within twenty-four hours, from where the enemy could dominate the southern tip of Bataan. Trapped at the water's edge, King considered that fighting on would lead to the pointless waste of the lives of his exhausted soldiers, achieve no military objective, and result in the heavy loss of life among the civilian population under his control.

He concluded they had to open negotiations with the Japanese for a surrender. Once he gathered his senior staff to his tent at midnight to tell them of his intentions, King made it clear that he had not called the meeting to ask for the advice or opinion of his assistants. From eyewitness accounts, Morton describes the moment King explained his decision to his officers. King made it clear that the choice was entirely his and he did not wish anyone else to be 'saddled with any part of the responsibility.' The message was – 'Remember this, you did not surrender … you had no alternative but to obey my order.' King told his men he had not communicated with Wainwright 'because I do not want him to be compelled to assume any part of the responsibility.'

They all knew MacArthur had forbidden surrender. There would be consequences if King survived captivity. 'Though the decision to surrender could not have surprised the staff, it hit with an awful bang and a terrible wallop,' wrote Morton. 'Everyone had hoped for a happier ending to the grim tragedy of Bataan, and when General King walked out of the meeting there was not a dry eye present.'

In those last desperate hours Wainwright did not learn of King's decision until it was irreversible, but he was in many ways simply a conduit for MacArthur, and implacably instructed to fight to the bitter end, whatever the view of anyone on Bataan or Corregidor. Long before the defence crumbled, Wainwright had on his desk a direct order from MacArthur prohibiting surrender under any conditions. When Wainwright had queried it, pointing out that if supplies did not reach him soon the troops on Bataan would be starved into submission, MacArthur again denied his authority to surrender and ordered that, if they ran out of food they should counterattack, whatever the cost in lives.

In messages to MacArthur that day Wainwright dutifully acknowledged the impending defeat. He reported 'with deep regret' that the troops on Bataan were 'fast folding up' and that the men were so weak from malnutrition 'they have no power of resistance.' Wainwright still followed his orders and sent King a fresh command to launch a counteroffensive at dawn on 9 April. King chose to ignore it – which he knew, if he lived, would probably lead to disgrace and court martial hearing.

King had more pressing concerns. All units had to be notified of the decision to surrender and given specific instructions; the remaining supplies of anything of military value had to be destroyed, and there was still time for selected individuals and units to be extracted and sent over to Corregidor, including the nurses at the open air Limay hospitals.

Given thirty minutes to make ready for the journey, the nurses were cautioned to take with them only what they could carry. In the darkness they boarded trucks that crept south along the congested road running down the Manila Bay side of the peninsula, where there was still a semblance of order.

The group from General Hospital No. 2 at Limay were delayed by the massive explosions from an ammunition dump which went up just as their convoy passed; there was no time to move the remaining stocks to a safer area.

The delay was costly: shortly before daylight, the barge departed to Corregidor without the Limay nurses. It was only through the 'vim, vigour, and swearing' of one of King's senior officers that a motorboat was sent from the island to carry the nurses to relative safety across the channel.

Small groups of Americans and Filipinos had already fled into the mountains to continue the war as guerrilla fighters. The last organised remnants of the force defending Bataan fell back to the docks at Mariveles on 9 April. No doubt some still carried hopes of getting across the channel to Corregidor, but they were out of time. Later that day, when the Japanese forces pushed into the little port town, they were met with white flags.

* * *

Just outside the Bataan War Museum, in a fenced-off garden shaded by a mango tree on the school grounds, the Surrender Site Marker commemorates the moment 75,000 American and Filipino troops became captives. Four bronze statues of American officers sit across a table from two Japanese counterparts.

Colonel Everett Williams, one of the defeated officers, rests a hand to his face – the unthinkable has come to pass. Beside him, General King is haggard but composed, leaning forward as if politely listening to the interpreter. Major Wade Cothran sits back, arms folded, his chair slightly askew, reluctantly present. The diarist Achille Tisdelle, hollow-cheeked, stares ahead with the abject dismay of a man just given a life sentence. Across from them sit Colonel Nakayama, acting on behalf of Lieutenant General Homma, and his interpreter.

The Americans had been taken to the Balanga school to be interrogated; their intention to surrender had been signalled a few hours earlier in Limay, a small town to the south.

In the prelude to the main event, two American officers – bachelors with no children – volunteered to carry the white flag and arrange the initial meeting. After saying their prayers, they crossed into Japanese lines and were confronted by screaming troops jabbing bayonets. Waving a flag made from a bed sheet, they were spared when a Japanese officer appeared and agreed to escort them to the local commander. One of the emissaries then returned to summon King and his aides.

The formal surrender party travelled north in two jeeps. For the sake of dignity, King wore his last clean uniform, though it was soon sullied; Japanese aircraft strafed the convoy several times, forcing the Americans into roadside ditches. They met a Japanese officer at an agreed point and were led to a farm, now an anonymous street in Limay. A simple plaque marks where the Americans asked for a cessation of hostilities – a site nearly absent from the Bataan visitor narrative, partly redeemed by the memorial at the Balanga school.

In the school's fenced garden, four bronze American officers face two Japanese counterparts. The statues are based on a Japanese photograph displayed on a nearby sign. In the still image, the Americans' uniforms hang loose from months of malnourishment; fatigue and scepticism are written in their postures. King, moustachioed and broader faced than the sculptor's version, sits with a quiet humility. He was 58 years old, but the burden of command had aged him far beyond that.

I kept returning to the photograph, struck by the moral courage of a man defying orders that no longer served any purpose and would only lead to the destruction of those under his command. Going against a lifetime of training and a deeply ingrained military ethos must have caused King private agonies, yet he bore them alone.

Tisdelle's diary recorded the moment: 'As they approached us, General King rose from his chair. The Jap colonel ignored him and [sat down] stiffly at the end of the table. General King resumed his seat across the table, sitting erect with his hands folded in front of him. I never saw him look more like a soldier than in this hour of defeat.'

The negotiations were curt and unsatisfactory. The Japanese demanded the surrender of Corregidor, which King insisted was outside his authority. When he asked for assurances about the welfare of his starving, disease-ridden men, Colonel Nakayama replied sharply: 'We are not barbarians.'

* * *

I had been warned about the rainy season. Once I was on the road again, driving south from Balanga to Mariveles Bay, here it was abruptly: bounteous rain, pouring down, splashing and cascading across the road surface. The wipers flailed but could not keep pace. I had never seen a downpour so intense. My eyes strained to pick out the surface, scanning for standing water, worried about aquaplaning on the streams flowing across the tarmac. I searched for a safe place to pull over. Nothing appeared.

On the map, this stretch of Bataan – provincial Mariveles – looked mostly rural, but the coastal highway ran through an industrial corridor pressed against the shores of Manila Bay. Big trucks roared past, ploughing through rippling sheets of water, each one drenching my God-given rental car with even more blinding spray. Beyond the road, somewhere in the rain-haze, loomed an oil refinery, a power station, a grain terminal, and a scattering of large-scale plants.

Eventually the highway tilted west, climbing through wet, dark trees before narrowing to a two-way road that twisted down toward Mariveles Bay. Every corner demanded precision; my shoulders stayed hunched, my jaw locked, eyes moving between slick tarmac and blind bends. The volcano loomed over each turn, its steep flanks crowding in, too close, its shadow pressing on the road like the gaze of something disapproving and unblinking.

By the time I made it into eastern edge of Mariveles, the clouds had given their all. The wipers rested at last, the windscreen clear, the road calm. Slower streets replaced the hard rush of the highway.

Warehouses lined the port, their corrugated flanks glistening from the retreating storm. Soon the metal sheds of manufacturing and logistics gave way to older low-rise buildings and the narrow, bustling streets of the town centre.

Nothing seemed more important than stopping for having a coffee and resetting myself. I pulled into a Western-style roadside fast-food joint, but disappointment awaited. The regulars at this particular Jollibee weren't coffee drinkers. The server told me they had a machine somewhere out back, but it would take thirty minutes to rouse it into service. I gave up, crossed the road, and stood at the edge of the grey, crumpled South China Sea.

Mariveles was a supply port in 1942; MacArthur himself, as a junior officer, had spent some time here. Both the US Navy and Army had basic facilities in the town. In the twenty-four hours before Homma's troops arrived personnel began dumping equipment in the sea and destroying installations around the harbour, with explosions and fires illuminating the night sky. They also scuttled the *Dewey*, a sizable floating dry dock, and an assortment of other vessels, including submarine tenders.

Renewing the search for coffee, I climbed back into the car and took a chance on a right turn, which delivered me into a tangle of narrow, bustling streets. The road became a labyrinth – lined with small shops, fruit stalls, and repair kiosks, all spilling over with life. Within minutes, I was cursing my decision, caught in an intense, byzantine one-way system where tricycles, pedestrians, and bikes swirled, all seemingly defying traffic logic. After a slow, painstaking reverse from a dead end I finally guessed correctly and found a road that led up and out of the chaos. And there, as if conjured by the gods of caffeine, stood a roadside coffee shack.

Having taken a break here, the road climbed around the opposite flank of Mount Mariveles and towards the China Sea side of the peninsula. It was all wind-scoured, rugged coastal wilderness. In places where the grassy slopes had been gashed open, for drainage works or some other kind of construction, the soil revealed itself as a vivid orange red.

With elevation came more spectacular views. The windswept mountainside panned down towards the ocean where a series of five finger-like promontories jutted out into the water, each with hidden bays. I had noticed that tour companies offer trips to the aptly named Five Fingers. The finger closest to Mariveles, Longos Kawayan, was pummelled by the American big guns on Corregidor during the Battle of the Points when IJA units landed on the beach here.

The road came down from the outback into Bagac, a small town sat on the plain between the two dormant volcanoes. Mount Natib sat majestically in the drizzle to the north, with Mount Mariveles behind me.

To this day the slopes of Natib remain difficult to navigate and are covered with thick, undisturbed forest, home to giant fruit bats, wild monkeys, boars, and eagles. Getting to the top requires a tough trek and a local guide but there are rewards. When Mount Natib last erupted around 18,000 years ago, its summit collapsed to form a vast acorn-shaped caldera – a primeval amphitheatre nearly 7 kilometres (4.3 miles) across. Its a hidden world that few get to see.

During the Battle of Bataan, MacArthur's final defensive line had stretched from Bagac across to Orion on the Manila Bay coast. Bagac today is for the most part a peaceful coastal town, without industry. Its centrepiece is Las Casas Filipinas de Acuzar, an upmarket hotel and conference centre set before the South China Sea. I'd seen the resort on the itineraries of organised military history tours but, even if my budget had allowed a stay, it was fully booked months in advance.

* * *

Once the surrender took effect, starving and disease-ridden troops were rounded up in both Bagac and Mariveles. Some 10,000 Americans and 65,000 Filipinos became captives. They were stripped of their canteens, rations, and personal items. Any prisoners found in possession of Japanese money or mementos were summarily executed, as their guards assumed it had been stolen from dead Japanese soldiers.

The first large-scale atrocity took place just outside of Bagac. Between 350–400 troops from the Philippine Army's 1st, 11th, 71st, and 91st Divisions were separated from the American officers and taken to a site inland by the Pantingan River. With their hands tied behind their backs, the soldiers were systematically massacred, typically beheaded or bayoneted by Japanese who mistakenly believed the Filipinos had fought on after the surrender. The testimony of five survivors was later used in war crimes trials.

The remaining captives in the two towns were organised in groups of about 100, guarded by four men. They were to be force-marched 105 kilometres (65 miles) north from starting points in Bagac and Mariveles that merged into one route just below Balanga. The grim procession would march further north towards a railhead at San Fernando.

The Office of the Provost Marshal General, which has the role of ensuring the safety and discipline of US Army personnel, produced a report in 1945 that drew together the work of various agencies in trying to detail what happened during what became known as the Bataan Death March. It found that since Major General Wainwright, in overall charge, had refused to comply with the demands of the IJA that Corregidor be surrendered at the time Bataan capitulated, the men were told they would be treated as hostages, not as prisoners of war.

Whatever the context, from the outset Japanese soldiers began dishing out executions and savage beatings, denying food and water and making every attempt possible to humiliate the Americans in the eyes of the Filipinos. April is early summer in the Philippines, and the prisoners were forced to march through temperatures that averaged 27°C (81°F) to 33°C (91°F).

The captives began collapsing in the middle of the second day. James Bollich, a 20-year-old corporal in the US Army Air Corps explained to one historian: 'We hadn't had water in a day and a half and in the tropics it's almost beyond what you can take. And of course once anybody collapsed, the Japanese immediately killed them, it looked like they were really trying to kill us all.' At night they were taken into fields to sleep. 'You would lie down and pass out right there,' recalled Bollich.[12]

The route passed artesian wells, but prisoners risked death if they tried to get water. Raymond Vasquez, an infantryman, recounted: 'We didn't dare ask for water. You'd get a bayonet in your back. You just had to keep going. No matter what, we had to keep going. If we got food, it was a small bowl of rice, and if that rice was cooked, we were really lucky. Some of us had canteens. The Japanese took them and gave our water to their horses.' Vasquez remembered several Filipino women who gave the passing prisoners water, only to be attacked by the guards. 'They were raped,' he said. 'We could hear their screams.'[13]

Over five days, the heat, unchecked disease and executions brutally culled the group, with hundreds of marchers dying as the grim procession edged north. Men too weak to continue were finished off by bayonet squads following behind and, in some cases, trucks drove over those who had succumbed to fatigue.

Severe thirst produced sheer desperation. One American captive, a tank commander called Lester Tenney, recounted:[14]

> You would see water on the side of the road in carabao wallows. The carabao would sit in there and bathe. We would see that and spread the scum along the side and just drink the water. The result was dysentery, real bad dysentery.

> It was called the Death March, because of the way they killed you. If you stopped walking, you died. If you had to defecate, you died. If you had a malaria attack, you died. It made no different what it was; either they cut your head off, they shot you, or they bayoneted you. But you died, if you fell down.

Once the exhausted marchers finally reached San Fernando, they were packed into sweltering rail box cars for a journey to Capas. From here the prisoners walked the final 14 kilometres (9 miles) to Camp O'Donnell, a former US Army base, further north at Tarlac.

The horrors only continued within its barbed wire fences. Camp O'Donnell was designed to accommodate about 10,000 men. The figures are debated to this day, but the Japanese crammed around 54,000 captives inside its grounds, where there was little running water, sparse food, no medical care and only slit trenches along the sides of the site for sanitation. Over the following months, the heat, vast clouds of flies rose out of the latrines and malaria, dysentery, beriberi and a host of other diseases swept through the crowds of men, claiming an appalling death toll. The emancipated prisoners began to perish at the rate of 400 per day.

By July 1942, Camp O'Donnell was considered unacceptable even by IJA standards. They began moving the American prisoners to another series of camps near Cabanatuan, in central Luzon. They also started to parole Filipino prisoners who signed an oath not to become guerrillas, making the mayors of their hometowns responsible for their conduct.

When Camp O'Donnell finally closed in January 1943, it had become a mass grave. More than 20,000 Filipino soldiers and 1,547 Americans had perished within its boundaries. Today, the site is the Capas National Shrine, a 54-hectare (130-acre) memorial planted with thousands of trees, each one representing a life lost in those pitiless days.

By the most conservative estimates, between 5,000 and 10,000 Filipinos and about 650 Americans died on the Bataan Death March. The entire route, from southern Bataan to Tarlac, is now marked by white-painted concrete obelisks placed 1 kilometre (0.6 miles) apart. In all, there are 138 markers: 97 in Bataan, 33 in Pampanga, and 8 in Tarlac, ending at the gates of the former Camp O'Donnell.

The markers were installed in stages, with key markers like the Zero Kilometre markers in Mariveles and Bagac, where the atrocity began, unveiled in 1968. In Mariveles, the Zero Kilometre Death March monument marks the place where, on 10 April 1942, thousands of Filipino and American soldiers started their 160-kilometre (99-mile) ordeal. A second stands in Bagac, where another column set out the following day. Both monuments are modest in scale but formal in presence, raised on concrete plinths and cast in relief. They depict a figured slumped forward, embodying the march's brutal toll; beside him, another stands upright, a quiet symbol of endurance in the face of suffering.

The markers along the route have a simpler design – white concrete posts set directly into the ground, mostly without plinths or figurative scenes, and set by busy roads. Most display only the kilometre number and the Death March insignia. They serve more as milestones, recording the distance covered rather than the grim ceremonial outset of the journey.

Yet even in their simplicity, the roadside markers are powerful – confronting passersby with a bleak reminder of the cruelty inflicted along the route. When I stopped beside one, its paint was thin, the edges worn by decades of tropical heat and pounding rain, and the tile plaque faded. Later, on the bus to Manila, I watched them slip past in the window, one after another, each a mute witness to lives cut short. Their unbroken repetition over 105 kilometres (65 miles) conveyed the relentlessness of the suffering they commemorate. Repeated across the Bataan landscape, they also seem to remind us that remembrance itself can be a form of protest and warning.

In the end, the succession of markers made me think not just about the cruelty of Bataan, but about how atrocity has taken shape elsewhere. Sometimes history shows violence to be deliberate, organised and bureaucratic, hidden behind forms, orders, and procedures. The perpetrators never touch the victims; the violence happens far beyond their presence. It was not like that on Bataan.

The philosopher Hannah Arendt famously grappled with the question of how ordinary people can commit extraordinary crimes. Covering the 1961 trial of Adolf Eichmann, the Nazi bureaucrat who oversaw the mass deportation of Jews to extermination camps, she expected a flamboyant and sadistic monster. Instead, she found in the dock a small, self-important man speaking in clichés, seemingly unable – or unwilling – to think about the human consequences of his actions. From this came her idea of 'the banality of evil': that atrocity can be committed not only by the openly brutal, but also by the thoughtless and dutiful.

On Bataan, the cruelty was face-to-face, vicious, unrelenting and without distant bureaucracy. The deaths were a product of long manufactured hatred and abject indifference to the survival of thousands of prisoners. The starvation, beatings, bayonetings, and denial of water were carried out in full view of locals, sometimes with apparent relish but often simply as part of a day's work by Japanese troops. Therein may lie the harshest truth of the Bataan war crimes: atrocity doesn't require legions of sadistic monsters. It can emerge from ordinary people operating within systems that normalise cruelty, whether through bureaucratic distance or cultivated hatred. Both reveal how moral thinking can be systematically disabled.

On the journey back, I thought of some lines written by Lieutenant Henry Lee, a 27-year-old soldier from Pasadena, California, who served in the 31st Infantry Regiment. Lee survived the Bataan Death March, but not captivity. While a prisoner of war, he secretly composed poems in two elementary school notebooks, hiding them beneath a hut floor. When the camp was liberated in 1945, a combat photographer discovered them and later sent copies to *The Saturday Evening Post*, which went on to publish nine of Lee's works.

In *The Death March*, the author captured the horrors in a few of the bleakest lines:

> So you are dead. The easy words contain
> No sense of loss, no sorrow, no despair.
> Thus hunger, thirst, fatigue, combine to drain
> All feeling from our hearts, anesthetize the mind.
> I cannot mourn you now. I lift my load,
> The suffering column moves. I leave behind
> Only another corpse, beside the road.

Chapter 3
Corregidor

The boat slipped away from an old wooden jetty that reached out into the water from rough ground at the back of Villa Carmen. Two twenty-something Filipino couples visiting from somewhere outside of Luzon were aboard; my solo trip had been folded into a guided tour.

It was a decent-sized *banca*, with a slender wooden hull, open sides and outriggers for stability. An orange tarp sagged between timber uprights, providing a patch of cover above the benches. Once we donned the lifejackets, Albert the boatman cranked the outboard to a growl and we left the southern tip of Bataan for open water. The boat ploughed across a 3-kilometre-(1.8-mile) wide channel, with only the sea spray for company. The Rock, as the Americans called Corregidor, rose from the mouth of Manila Bay, a grey, irregular mass against the pale sky. The particulars of its form – the way the island looks like a tadpole, with the head to the South China Sea and tail twisting into the huge bay – belong to maps, or the gaze of circling birds.

Corregidor measures about 6 kilometres (3.7 miles) in length and up to 2.5 kilometres (1.5 miles) at its widest point. Three hill masses step down gradually from the head to the low, flat, and narrow tail. Most of the terrain is blanketed in tropical trees and vegetation. A single road circuit links the main points of interest.

The island is managed by a non-profit organisation based in Manila, the Corregidor Foundation. As we docked there were a couple of its people waiting under a temporary-looking gazebo. The point of arrival was called the Sabang East North Boat Terminal on the Bataan-facing north coast. Back in the day, it was simply Engineer Dock. They signed us in, checked our temperatures and Covid vaccination passes, and took the required Filipino pesos – just shy of 50 US dollars.

A guide would show us around the old fortress in a four-wheeled tram with stops at key points. Given the humidity, the insect noise and the unruly vegetation, it was a bit of a *Jurassic Park* start. And, in an odd way, the inhabitants were running wild too. The only hotel on the island, the two star-ish Corregidor Inn, was closed for business but travel forums were full of advice about closing windows. Otherwise, monkeys – specifically long-tailed macaques – would get inside.

Amid the peak of pandemic anxiety, a debate had opened about relocating Corregidor's primate population as it was said to have become unmanageable. At any one time at least 100 macaques have been counted on the island but many more inhabit its forests. Some visitors may delight in glimpses of the monkeys, darting through trees or mischievously approaching the road, but not everyone. Cynthia Carrion, chair and CEO of the Corregidor Foundation raised concerns about infection. 'Remember they are also possible carriers of a virus and can trigger a zoonotic disease and cause another pandemic,' she told Manila's *Business Mirror*.[15]

Claims by an official from within the Department of Agriculture that the monkeys are native were swiftly disputed. The non-believers say the macaques were captured on Mindanao for breeding and commercial sale – and later released on Corregidor when the venture faltered. Yet since the American soldiers once garrisoned on The Rock routinely complained of soap bars and flashlights being pilfered by monkeys, there clearly was a primate population of some description before bombs and shells stripped away most of the island's forest and vegetation in 1942. Aside from breeding in the wild, the Department of Agriculture official said that natural migration from Bataan may contribute to the numbers of primates on Corregidor today.

While trying to process the news that monkeys are excellent swimmers and might be doing the front crawl in the very same channel I had just crossed, I noted Cynthia Carrion's remarks that macaques are territorial and have become 'too aggressive to the point of lurking inside hotel rooms, stealing food and on several occasions, run[ning] after tourists.'

The colonial Americans formally designated Corregidor as Fort Mills when it became an active military base. Construction began in 1902, shortly after the Spanish had been sent packing and a new chapter began. Over the following years, the garrison expanded to house 5,000 men, and a formidable array of defences were carved into the island's hills, and facing the open mouth of Manila Bay. When Bataan fell in April 1942, The Rock became the final redoubt – its tunnels and barracks swollen far beyond their limits, sheltering some 11,000 American and Filipinos under relentless assault from air and sea attacks, and land-based artillery.

Prior to 1942, Corregidor was regarded as a plum positing. 'A legend in its own time,' said the historian Eric Niderost, and a place so bristling with guns it seemed impregnable. Niderost interviewed Marine Private Donald Versaw, part of the 4th Marine Regiment, which had transferred to Corregidor to bolster defences in December 1941. 'I heard that it was armed to the teeth with big guns and was protected by a big minefield,' recalled Versaw – 'It was known that one gun ashore is worth three or more afloat.'[16]

Corregidor was less an island than a fortress – a defiant mass of rock and steel, built from reinforced concrete casemates and armoured turrets, its presence announced by the relentless pounding of its guns. Along its ridges and headlands, some fifty-six coastal guns guarded the sea approaches. Behind them, the great mortars sat in clusters of four, their black maws tilted toward the clouds, ready to lob explosive shells toward enemy positions.

This was no peaceful citadel. Its strength lay in a web of defences spun decades earlier, when the United States still held the Philippines as a colonial possession. Corregidor was flanked by three smaller island forts: Fort Hughes to the south, Fort Frank to the west, and the armoured stronghold known as Fort Drum.

Fort Drum began as nothing more than a jagged splinter of rock in the channel south of Corregidor. Engineers pounded it flat, clad it in steel and concrete, and shaped it into a warship that would never sail. Within its rock and metal armoured hull, 200 men lived, fought, and endured. On its 'deck' stood two immense turrets, each with twin 14-inch barrels capable of reaching 21 kilometres (13 miles). Japanese guns pounded it day after day from the bay shore, but as long as the Stars and Stripes snapped in the wind, Fort Drum answered, its voice a thunderclap rolling across the water.

Today Fort Drum still squats in the channel – rusting, defunct, and abandoned. Its turrets are frozen in place, weathered by decades of exposure, with only the twin barrels at its concrete bow still pointing seaward. Falling within a Military Reservation Zone managed by the Philippine Navy, it can now be seen only from afar, binoculars required.

This network of armaments covered every conceivable angle of approach to Manila Bay from the South China Sea. Across Corregidor itself, gun barrels jutted from fortified positions, some mounted on disappearing carriages – counterweighted systems that lifted the weapon to fire above a reinforced parapet, then dropped it back into cover for reloading.

Among these, Battery Hearn reigned supreme – the island's longest-range weapon. Mounted on a 360° rotating platform, it could hurl a 1,000-pound (453-kilogram) shell up to 27 kilometres (16 miles), far enough to strike Japanese positions on southern Bataan. A crew of thirty-four operated it, two stationed in a chamber beneath the carriage during action. At full pace, Hearn fired one round every fifty-five seconds.

Battery Hearn is now one of Corregidor's most visited relics – especially by Japanese tourists, drawn by a wartime photograph etched into history. In it, a crowd of IJA soldiers pose around the base of the massive gun, their faces relieved and triumphant. They cluster like hunters around a slain beast, the enormous barrel before them something once feared, now silent.

In fact, for all this immense firepower, Corregidor's defences were built for what was already a bygone era. The system worked well so long as the main threat came from warships, but the rapid rise of air power in the mid-1930s changed the equation. The island's fixed guns were vulnerable to high-flying Japanese bombers, its anti-aircraft weapons too old to threaten them effectively.

The big coastal guns were also ill-suited for counter-battery fire against land-based artillery. Most, like Battery Hearn, lacked the elevation to hit Japanese guns positioned on high ground. Only the mortars, with their steep arcs, could reach – and even they were crippled by ammunition shortages. As Bataan diarist Achille Tisdelle noted, much of the available stock was the wrong type: armour-piercing, delayed-fuse shells meant to punch through a ship's decks before exploding. On land, they simply buried themselves deep underground and did little damage. 'What was needed,' historian Eric Niderost explained, 'was anti-personnel instantaneous fuse ammunition – something that would detonate in the midst of an enemy battery and wreak havoc.'[17]

Drinking water was another pressing concern. Corregidor had no natural source of freshwater. Supplies had to be brought in by barge or captured from rainfall, funnelled into wells that tapped the island's limited groundwater. During infrastructure upgrades in the early 1930s, engineers made efforts to conceal new water storage facilities – burying them beneath tennis courts in the hope of avoiding detection. Yet the attempts at secrecy were undone by watching eyes. Japanese intelligence operatives had already marked their locations. When the bombing began in 1942, those hidden reservoirs were among the first targets struck.

Corregidor's power plant was another critical weak point. Nestled in a low-lying area and lacking proper fortification, it was essential to operations – supplying electricity to pump water from the wells, ventilate the labyrinth of tunnel shelters, and operate the elevation systems of the heavy coastal guns. Yet despite its importance, the infrastructure remained exposed. Power and communication lines were strung across the surface or buried only shallowly, leaving them dangerously susceptible to bombardment. With each blast, the lifelines of the fortress – its firepower, water, and underground air ventilation – grew ever more precarious.

Upgrading Corregidor had long been a complicated affair. The Washington Naval Treaty of 1922 – an effort to prevent another arms race among the major Allied naval powers of the First World War – placed explicit restrictions on the construction of new fortifications. The United States, Great Britain, Japan, France, and Italy were all signatories, and the treaty effectively froze coastal defence development.

It wasn't until the mid-1930s, when Japan and Italy formally renounced the agreement, that the treaty began to unravel. Yet even then, momentum for reinforcing Corregidor remained sluggish. When the US Congress passed legislation setting a firm date for full Philippine independence the signal was clear: the islands would soon go their own way. And with that looming separation, there was little appetite in Washington to spend precious tax dollars fortifying territory the United States was preparing to relinquish.

Then as now, fortress Corregidor is divided into four distinct areas. I guessed their names came from a no-frills officer who liked to call things exactly as they were.

Topside is the island's crown – the highest ground and once a key hub of military operations. Big guns are positioned along its ridges, and a parade ground sits at its heart, a place for drills that later became a battlefield. These days, it's also home to the Pacific War Memorial Museum.

Middleside held a mix of accommodation and administrative buildings. Here you'll find landmarks such as the skeletal ruins of the Mile Long Barracks – a highlight for most visitors – and a colonial-era lighthouse that once guided ships into Manila Bay. Built in 1853, its beam shone for nearly nine decades before going dark in the hours after the Day of Infamy.

Bottomside marks the start of Corregidor's tail section. In wartime it was a place of warehouses, workshops, and other support functions. It also held the small civilian community of San Jose – a tiny seaside barrio with a church, facing the island's southern shore.

Where Middleside narrows into Bottomside, the island's broad body begins to taper, and here the ground hides something extraordinary. At the base of a steep hillside is Corregidor's most distinctive man-made feature: the Malinta Tunnel.

Bored into the hill by army engineers starting in 1922, the tunnel's original shape resembled a fish skeleton – a main east-west passage with twenty-four lateral tunnels branching from it. Built first as a bomb-proof storehouse and bunker, it was later expanded into a network of underground grids, including a 1,000-bed hospital. The main corridor became General MacArthur's headquarters after he escaped Manila in December 1941 and also housed the Philippine Commonwealth government in exile.

The Americans had sidestepped Washington Treaty restrictions by disguising the project under a maintenance budget. Filipino convicts did most of the blasting and digging, overseen by US Army engineers. It was gruelling, filthy work – the name 'Malinta' comes from the Tagalog for 'infested with leeches.'

Finally, Tailside extends back into Manila Bay as the island's easternmost point and curls slightly south at the tip. It featured an airstrip Kindley Field and a radio intercept station, along with some artillery positions. Corregidor does have several beaches, with similarly unfussy names – North Beach, which saw action during the amphibious assaults, South Beach, and Bottomside Beach.

With the fall of Bataan, a Japanese invasion was inevitable. The first lines of defence were hastily assembled and formed by a mixed force of around

1,500 men of the 4th Marine Regiment, topped up with leftovers from US Army units, flyers with nothing to fly, navy stragglers and Filipino militia.

The 4th Marines had arrived from Shanghai via Subic Bay in late December, occupying Middleside Barracks before moving to bivouac positions in the three most likely landing areas. Its 1st Battalion became responsible for everything east of the Malinta Tunnel towards the tail of the island – which, in the event, proved to be the epicentre of the battle when the Japanese eventually stormed ashore under the cover of darkness.

We climbed aboard the tram, and the guide kicked things off with a few quips. On a map, he said, Corregidor looks like a tadpole – but, according to fertility doctors, it bears a resemblance to something else entirely.

Soon after, we wound up a hill from Engineer Dock towards Topside, stopping at a plateau beside the ruined Middleside Barracks.

In my mind, soldierly accommodation is functional and spartan. Yet photographs from the 1920s and 1930s show the architects had a grander brief for Corregidor. Middleside Barracks resembled well-to-do university housing. It comprised a couple of three-story buildings set in a straight line on a flattened stretch of land. Their facades were a procession of large rectangular windows – broad enough to welcome light and breeze in the tropical heat. Inside, rooms had high ceilings and, in some cases, sliding panels of Capiz (mother of pearl) instead of glass, casting a soft, milky glow when the sun hit just right. Outside, well-kept tropical gardens framed the buildings. Palm trees and broad green fronds were trimmed precisely to the height of the first floor – as if the island outback had been tamed just enough to let order and refinement have their day.

Further up the hill stood Mile Long Barracks – a much larger version of the same. We got off the tram at each site and took in the mournful spectacle. In their pomp, both buildings spoke of symmetry and good order – designed with confidence, built to last. Today they are concrete skeletons, missing roofs, windows, and doors. The once smooth, putty-coloured facades are blackened by fire and stained with tropical mould. The structures still suggest a framework: the bones of something, with empty spaces opening to blue sky and bright grass. Amid the steady background chirp of crickets, it was possible to imagine the low murmur of soldiers, far from home, going about their daily routines.

In bomb-ravaged towns and cities, destroyed buildings are almost always cleared away – flattened, erased, replaced to recover the value of the land. On Corregidor, the architect's vision remains before you, roofless and scorched, just as it was when the explosions stopped and the flames guttered out. It is starkly engrossing, strangely beautiful, partly because there is a uniformity to the disorder. Both barracks are severely damaged and only warm, humid air moves through the repeating grid of rectangular frames that once held windows and doors. Every surface bears the marks of violence, which began with the first wave of Japanese bombing on the morning of 29 December 1941. Standing before Corregidor's wrecked barracks felt like witnessing two histories at once – the destructive hours where they blasted and burned, and the slow, patient claim of nature pressing in to fill the void.

The same interplay between destruction and natural renewal draws artists to ruins. The French photographers Yves Marchand and Romain Meffre, for instance, have documented abandoned spaces in their project *Ruins of Detroit*. 'Seeing nature growing back in those buildings, there's a certain sense of morality or irony within the ruins when they are reclaimed,' Marchand told one journalist.[18] In some ways, war – like industry – exploits nature. And there is, undeniably, a peculiar satisfaction in watching nature take it all back.

On the south side of the island, the wreckage of Battery Geary stands as an even more sombre reminder of the thunderous barrage that once shook Corregidor. A sunken, levelled concrete platform – roughly the size of eight tennis courts – lies recessed into the landscape, its silence now at odds with the fury it once unleashed and suffered.

In January 1942, Battery Geary played a crucial role in striking Japanese troops during the Battle of the Points, its guns targeting enemy positions along Bataan's western coast. Its fourteen-man gun crew operated four 12-inch M1890 mortars, which were designed to drop huge shells through the decks of battleships. Given the size and close proximity of the mortars, they could only be fired two at a time.

Homma's 14th Army would obtain restitution on a single day, 2 May 1942. They fired 2,600 artillery rounds at Battery Geary alone during an earth-shattering blitz. At 16.27 hours, one of the rounds penetrated the site's central magazine, igniting 40 tons of explosives. The detonation that followed obliterated Geary, killing everyone within the perimeter, while tossing 10-ton guns around like toys and hurling large chunks of concrete over a kilometre away. I walked past the displaced guns, the ruptured buildings and chuck of concrete debris in the grass. The site retains a sense of dreadful violence, as if the concussive blasts still echo around the perimeter today.

Our next stop, Battery Way, occupied roughly the same footprint as Geary and housed an identical set of four 12-inch mortars. Unlike its twin to the south, Battery Way remains mostly intact – an enduring symbol of the defiant spirit shown by American artillery units in the island's final days.

As with all the surviving big guns on Corregidor, time has worked its alchemy. The oxidation of copper in the steel has turned their surfaces a uniform jade – a matte green patina that lends them the look of relics unearthed from the sea.

During the morning of 6 May 1942, Major William Massello Junior lay seriously wounded on a stretcher here, having refused to be evacuated as the battle for Corregidor approached its climax. As over four months of air raids and artillery barrages reached their zenith, Battery Way was one of the last big guns operating, with Massello and his fourteen-man crew still in the fight. From his stretcher, Massello pulled the lanyard firing his one remaining serviceable mortar while his men remained under cover. All around the mortar pit lay debris from the heavy pounding their position had taken. Somewhere amidst the rubble was the telephone which Massello had ordered ripped from the wall so, he said later, he could not receive the order to surrender.

* * *

Lieutenant General Masaharu Homma was running out of time. His fifty-day timetable to conquer the Philippines had already slipped, and though Bataan had fallen on 9 April, the final prize – Corregidor – still held out in Manila Bay. Taking it would finally open the harbour, cut the Allies' last lifeline, and likely force the surrender of every remaining defender in the archipelago.

Major General Jonathan Wainwright, the gaunt, weathered cavalryman who had taken over from MacArthur, commanded some 20,000 US and Filipino troops formed of Corregidor garrison and forces scattered across Mindanao, and Cebu. Day after day, Japanese bombers and artillery gnawed at the island, smashing gun emplacements, collapsing tunnels, and crippling water and power systems.

For Homma's 14th Army, victory was anything but straightforward. Landing craft were scarce, and his troops bivouacked in the fever-ridden valleys of southern Bataan were succumbing to the same malaria that had wrecked Major General King's forces weeks earlier. Yet the clock was ticking too loudly to wait for starvation to do the work – and Homma could not have known that Corregidor's food stores would be gone within a month.

Quinine reached his troops only days before the landing craft finally did – nearly three weeks after being summoned from Lingayen Gulf and Subic Bay, where they had been kept out of range of Corregidor's big guns. Now they had to slip south under cover of night, hugging the coast in small groups while Japanese artillery pounded the island to mask their movement.

By nightfall on 5 May, the assault force was ready. The first wave consisted of 790 men from the 61st Infantry Regiment under Colonel Gempachi Satō. They set out in 19 assorted landing craft, the smallest carrying 30 men, the largest 170. In darkness, one hour before moonrise, they churned across the Bataan Channel toward the island's northern tail, three staggered lines riding the high tide.

Before they moved, Japanese guns had plastered the target beaches. Trenches, pillboxes, barbed wire, mines, and anti-boat obstacles were methodically laid to waste. At the chosen landing zone lay near Kindley Field, where the 1st Battalion, 4th Marines waited, dug in and braced for the worst. American searchlights found the incoming craft but were quickly silenced by precise counter-fire. Tracer rounds lanced through the dark; explosions lit the surf in red and white flashes. The first few Japanese boats were shredded, but wave after wave pressed forward into the chaos.

The IJA was an infantry-heavy force, often lacking heavy weapons, but Homma's men were equipped with a lightweight and effective killing machine that Japan's enemies came to know well – the Type 89 mortar. A kind of grenade launcher, it was described as the 'knee mortar' by Allied troops who erroneously believed it could be fired by bracing it against the thigh just above the knee (the recoil would in fact break your leg). The Type 89 proved well suited to assaulting Corregidor's beaches. Despite the carnage in the flashing surf, the landing forces began to get traction, killing Marines in their foxholes or forcing them back.

The second landing – 785 more soldiers – fared worse. Strong currents pushed some into their own artillery zone, and they struck the strongest Marine defences head-on. The beach became a slaughterhouse. Most Japanese officers were killed. A group of observers, watching through binoculars from Bataan, called it 'a spectacle that confounded the imagination, surpassing in grim horror anything we had ever seen before.'[19] Yet the Japanese kept coming, joining forces with the first wave and cutting across the island's tail, trapping the surviving Marines at its tip. Gingerly at first, Homma's troops began to move inland.

To reach the American command post in the Malinta Tunnel, the attackers would have to fight over three bare ridges to where the tail meets the island's body. Their first objective was Battery Denver, the largest anti-aircraft position in the area, whose guns had been depressed to fire directly on the beach. Taken at 01.30 hours, it became the focal point of three furious counterattacks. In the moonlight, grenades, rifle fire, and bayonet charges shredded what remained of the 1st Battalion's strength.

In one of those counterattacks, two veteran Marines – Sergeant Major Thomas Sweeney and Quartermaster Sergeant John Haskins – assaulted a stone water tower where Japanese machine guns had set up. They killed the crews, scaled the tower under fire, and hurled grenades from its summit into Japanese positions. They climbed up and down repeatedly to resupply until, finally, one was cut down at the base; the other's body was found weeks later atop the tower.

Throughout the nighttime battle, the officer in charge of the 4th Marines, Colonel Samuel Howard, and the army's Major General George Moore were beset by poor communications. Lines between the front lines and their headquarters in the Malinta Tunnel had been cut. In the chaotic engagements they had to rely on piecemeal information from field radios, runners, and patrols to direct the response.

At the same time, the ferocity of the defence led Homma to fret that the attack was falling apart. He was concerned that his men would run out of ammunition. Scores of Japanese troops had already paid for Tokyo's impatience to end the siege of Corregidor, drowned in the channel, or killed on the beaches. But at 05.30 hours another 880 Japanese troops did manage to land, followed by three tanks that came ashore at 09.30 hours. The reinforcements tipped the balance.

By the time the battered Marines pulled back to the ruins of a concrete trench a few yards from the west entrance to the Malinta Tunnel, the last bastion of American power in the Asia-Pacific was on the brink. American and Filipino troops protecting other potential landing sites had yet to get into the fight, but Homma already had a knife at the throat of the defenders. Mindful that the Japanese could now land tanks and troops under far less threatening conditions at the north shore, and had complete control of the skies, Major General Wainwright had to consider the slaughter if the tanks clanked towards the opening of the Malinta Tunnel. Over 1,000 men lay wounded in its overcrowded recesses, effectively trapped along with 150 nurses and scores of other non-combatants. The game was up.

* * *

The western entrance to the Malinta Tunnel was the grander of the two – a flat concrete arch set into a sheer wall of exposed rock. Retaining walls flanked the approach, lending it a symmetry almost at odds with the desperate fighting that once surged towards it. Tall steel gates barred the mouth, reinforced by heavy wooden blackout blinds that kept the tunnel's secrets hidden from prying eyes.

Inside, the main passageway was roughly the width of a two-lane road, with generous headroom. The broad, echoing space lay empty and silent, the air cooler and drier than outside. Tram rails still ran the 252 metres (831 feet) of the main shaft, once linking Corregidor's north and south docks to this command centre. Spartan reinforced-concrete walls rose to a domed ceiling. At its highest point, a line of electric lights cast a pale, even glow. During the war, fluorescent tubes had flooded the space with harsh, clinical brightness. A more atmospheric scheme was introduced during renovations in 1998, perhaps to help recreate the foreboding that once filled these walls when Malinta served as a command centre, hospital, shelter – and, in the end, tomb.

With the crickets gone, the only sound was our guide's low, measured voice, softly reverberating through the void. In busier seasons, a sound-and-light show tells the story of the Malinta Tunnel, but none of the equipment was running. With just the five of us on the island, it was hardly surprising – the whole experience felt as if tourism here was running on a skeleton crew and a touch of improvisation.

Torches were needed as soon as we branched off the fishbone spine into any of the twenty-four ribs. These laterals had much lower ceilings than the main shaft. Averaging 49 metres (160 feet) in length and 4.6 metres (15 feet) in width, they felt far more enclosed – giving them something of a haunted-house aspect. Here and there, the beam would catch an unlit mannequin of a soldier or staff member frozen in place, plastic face mid-motion, waiting for orders that would never come.

Drop-down lights had once illuminated the offices and sleeping areas created here, swaying and flickering under surface barrages. We picked our way past authentic artefacts – old wooden desks, rusting typewriters and radio equipment by torchlight. In places, army-green metal storage barrels and wooden boxes lined the damp walls.

In one shadowy passageway, the guide stopped at a spot where the floor, walls and ceiling were badly pockmarked, as if wax had been splattered with hot oil. Later in the island's torrid history, Japanese soldiers had apparently gathered here in a circle and pulled the pins on grenades, blowing themselves up rather than surrendering.

For lack of time, or because of restricted access, we did not visit the underground hospital – a separate but connected grid of tunnels added after the original structure was completed. Instead, one of the laterals off the main drag featured a makeshift display: a mannequin soldier, bloodied and bent, being helped toward a metal-framed bed, simulating a field ward. The tours are indicative, not exhaustive; we avoided the tunnels once devoted to ammunition and gasoline storage (where damp had rendered many shells ineffective in 1942). Other parts of the labyrinth will remain forever off-limits: in 1945, suicidal explosions collapsed some tunnels, entombing hundreds of Japanese occupants.

I was grateful for the absence of crowds. Yet I still wanted a moment away from our small group and its holiday chatter – a chance to better imagine the distant rumble of bombs, the echo of boots. The guide consented. I waited until the others turned a corner and were out of sight and sound.

Alone in the tunnel, I switched off my torch. The darkness closed in from all sides, swallowing the light, the very air around me. A rush of suffocating disquiet filled my every pore, as if the tunnel itself had been waiting for this moment. I switched the torch back on and was soon hurrying to catch up with the others – hoping I wouldn't be surprised by a long-tailed macaque lurking just beyond the beam of light.

* * *

The tunnels had begun to fill up after the Japanese landings on Luzon in December 1941. First came the survivors of the air attacks on the Cavite naval base, set ablaze in the early days of the conflict. The headquarters staff and service troops from Manila soon followed as the tunnels became MacArthur's centre of operations on 25 December. President Quezón, his deputy and their key staff also took refuge.

The general set himself up an office in Lateral No. 3, near the communications centre. MacArthur had a desk while, to the rear were metal bunk beds where some of his staff slept. In his memoirs, *Reminiscences*, MacArthur recalls a new headquarters 'carved deep in the rock' and as a place 'bare, glaringly lighted, and [containing] only the essential furniture and equipment for administrative procedures.'[20]

His wife Jean and 4-year-old Arthur IV had watched the destruction of the Cavite naval base from the family's suite at The Manila Hotel. Now they lived with the general in a cottage on the north of the island, near Infantry Point, on Topside and with a view of Bataan. The house was an obvious and inviting target for air attacks and had only had a modest air raid shelter nearby, with old iron doors that wouldn't close properly. During raids MacArthur was in the habit of standing outside, and watching Japanese bombers approach, perhaps even further tempting fate by smoking a Lucky Strike.

Quezón and others felt the general was taking ridiculous risks but MacArthur believed it was something his men needed to see. He told Quezón: 'I know I have no right to gamble with my life, but it is absolutely necessary that at the right time a commander take chances because of the effect down the line, for when they see the man at the top risking his life, the man at the bottom says, "I guess that if the old man can take it, I can too."'

Bloggers have tried to locate the MacArthur house among the overgrown ruins on Topside but none of the various memoirs are precise about which of the small row of ruined buildings was used by the family.

Soon enough, one of the bombing raids found and destroyed the cottages. The MacArthurs subsequently moved to a different bungalow in the Bottomside area. He continued to flaunt fate and run extreme risks, albeit with Arthur eventually made to sleep in a cot in one of the Malinta laterals. Before it got too crowded, Arthur was in the habit of running up and down in the tunnel singing 'The Battle Hymn of the Republic' or shouting 'Air raid, Air raid!' when the warning sirens went off.

As the days passed the tunnels overflowed with exhausted and hungry people. The 809th Military Police, two ordnance companies, an engineer unit, and other service detachments took up residence. Headquarters staff and nurses also stayed in the crowded complex, while enlisted men lived in the barracks before they were bombed out, or in bivouac camps in the field.

On 30 December 1941, an improvised ceremony at the west entrance saw Quezón, by now seriously ill with tuberculosis and confined to a wheelchair, inaugurated for his second term as president of the Philippine Commonwealth, along with his vice president Sergio Osmeña. This produced one of the most poignant moments in the long struggle for the Philippine self-determination. Six years earlier, their first inaugural had been a great show of pageantry in Manila to acknowledge the formal birth of a nation state. Now an improvised wooden platform was built near the mouth of the stinking tunnel, with two chairs on it. 'Hail to the Chief' was played on a chaplain's organ before Quezón took the oath, his voice interrupted by coughing spasms.

He told MacArthur: 'No words in any language can express to you the deep gratitude of the Filipino people and my own for your devotion to the cause, the defence of our country, and the safety of our population.' When it was MacArthur's turn to speak, his voice was quiet and low:[21]

> Never before in all history has there been a more solemn and significant inauguration. An act, symbolical of democratic processes, is placed against the

> background of a sudden, merciless war. The thunder and destruction dropped from the skies, can be heard in the distance. Our ears can almost catch the roar of exploding bombs. Such is the bed of birth of this new government.

MacArthur's face was streaked with tears.

Over 4,000 people eventually took shelter in the crowded subterranean complex, squeezing in besides the boxes, equipment and growing numbers of wounded. I was visiting during the September rainy season and found the air relatively cooler compared to the outside; untypical of the more humid weather between January and May, when the island was under fire. During its peak occupation, electrical blowers pushed fresh air around Malinta, but the ventilation was poor and the environment deteriorated as the siege stretched from weeks to months. Despite the humidity, the intermittent power failures, and the stench of confined humans, many of the occupants became reluctant to go outside. They were considered 'tunnel rats' by troops still out in the field, braving the bombing and artillery barrages.

After the fall of Bataan a grim reality had in fact settled over the fortress: there was almost no hope of relief or escape. The best they could do was delay the overwhelming Japanese firepower. The sense of what was to come must have increased with the arrival of around 2,000 soldiers, army nurses, and civilian workers who escaped from Mariveles in the final hours on Bataan. The starving, dirty and diseased veterans were of course the lucky ones, the survivors of a force once numbering tens of thousands of men, now mostly dead or POWs. Many of the Bataan troops hung around in the already crowded tunnels. They were in a desperate state, unfit for service. Filipino diplomat Leon Maria Guerrero, a controversial wartime figure and critic of the Americans during the Japanese occupation, wrote of the stubbornness of spent, disillusioned men that defied command or insult, was impossible to allow them to remain, not only because they made normal traffic in the tunnels difficult, but principally because their shame and despair was contagious – it was a sinister and insidious disease that daily infected the garrison of Corregidor.'[22]

Although food shortages had not been as desperate as on Bataan, everyone had lived on reduced rations for months. The islanders were also forced to eat cavalry horses as supplies dwindled towards critical levels. Going months without a proper diet created even more risk as men in a weakened state lacked reliable night vision. Drinking water was only distributed twice a day.

From about mid-February the Japanese blockade made it impossible for even small ships to slip through the defences and bring in a trickle of supplies and evacuate non-combatants. After this point, there was no guarantee of any more opportunities to escape and any that came along would be fraught with danger. Yet remaining on Corregidor was an even grimmer prospect, with death during the raids or capture as a Japanese POW both highly plausible outcomes.

For all the risk, Jean MacArthur refused to leave and or even discuss it with her husband. When Doña Aurora, the Philippine's First Lady, suggested it Jean said: 'We have drunk from the same cup … and we three shall stay together.' Later, in conversation with an aide, MacArthur explained that his wife had chosen to stay and endure 'the rigours of war with me.' When another aid asked about Arthur's fate, MacArthur said crisply, 'He's a soldier's son.'

For some historians, this was emblematic of MacArthur's leadership style: intensely personal, dramatic, and imbued with symbolic meaning. The presence of his own family symbolised resilience and confidence in the face of adversity. By keeping them with him, MacArthur may have sought to inspire his troops and civilian staff, projecting the image of steadfastness and courage under siege. It also underlined his commitment to the defence of the Philippines. His family's presence demonstrated that he was willing to share the risks faced by others on Corregidor.

Manuel Quezón and Doña Aurora had been evacuated with other government personnel via submarine in February. Soon after, President Roosevelt ordered MacArthur to leave the Philippines and make his way to Australia, from where he could continue the fight.

That order was carried out on the night of 11 March, when MacArthur and his family departed for Mindanao aboard a fleet of four blacked-out PT boats. These wooden vessels were fast and highly manoeuvrable, with shallow drafts suited to reef-strewn coastal waters – but they were far from comfortable on the open sea. MacArthur later likened the experience to being inside a washing machine.

For two days, they battled rough seas, island-hopped through hostile waters, and dodged Japanese warships. Upon reaching Mindanao, the

MacArthurs boarded a pair of B-17s at Del Monte airfield, eventually arriving in Melbourne by train on 21 March 1942. The journey had taken ten days.

Meeting the press upon arrival, MacArthur famously declared: 'I came through and I shall return' – a promise that made headlines around the world.

On 29 April, two navy PBY flying boats managed to land off Corregidor in the darkness with medicines and anti-aircraft fuses. They staggered away from the island with fifty nurses and officers from MacArthur's staff aboard, barely making it off the water. The last successful evacuation was made on the night of 3 May. The US submarine *Spearfish* took on another party of officers and nurses who had been ordered out, as well as important records and details of every person still alive on the fortified islands.

In the final hours, from somewhere inside the tunnels, a Brooklyn-born radio operator named Irving Strobing tapped out a series of telegraph messages back to America. One quipped about their plight, others were emotional. They made the 22-year-old briefly famous when later published.[23] 'We've got about 55 minutes and I feel sick at my stomach,' he signalled.

> I am really low down. They are around now smashing rifles. They bring in the wounded every minute. We will be waiting for you guys to help. This is the only thing I guess that can be done. General Wainwright is a right guy and we're willing to go on for him, but shells were dropping all night, faster then [*sic*] hell. Damage terrific. Too much for guys to take … The jig is up. Everyone is bawling like a baby … They are piling dead and wounded in our tunnel … I know now how a mouse feels. Caught in a trap waiting for guys to come along and finish it up…

By 10.15 hours on 6 May, Wainwright had reached the same conclusion as King before him when confronted by the bitter dilemma: fight on and take responsibility for a slaughter or surrender and deal with the consequences.

He sent his final message to President Roosevelt:[24]

> There is a limit of human endurance and that limit has long since been passed. Without the prospect of relief, I feel it is my duty to my Country, and to my gallant troops, to end this useless effusion of blood and human sacrifice. With profound regret and continued pride in my gallant troops, I go to meet the Japanese commander.

Wainwright had agonised over the decision but, unlike King, he at least knew that he would not face a court martial. The month before, on hearing news of the surrender of Bataan, President Roosevelt had taken it upon himself to send a direct message to Corregidor giving Wainwright freedom of action for any decision he felt he had to make. Roosevelt wanted to make clear there was no sense in taking the orders to an illogical extreme. The original orders were issued in a different time and context, when the purpose was making clear the robust defence expected at the outset of the fighting on Bataan and Corregidor.

Pointedly, MacArthur received Roosevelt's message before Wainwright with the instruction to pass it on if he agreed with the substance and timing. It stayed on MacArthur's desk. When Wainwright sought to clarify the situation directly with MacArthur, the reply simply stated that the president had made it clear that Wainwright had the authority to do as he saw fit. What's beyond doubt is that MacArthur was dismayed at Wainwright's surrender: within a few weeks he blocked a proposal to award Wainwright a Medal of Honor.

* * *

No complete figures exist for the casualties suffered by either side during the Battle of Corregidor but estimates of the Japanese losses start at around 1,000 men. Many drowned in the straits between Bataan and Corregidor as landing craft and other vessels were destroyed on the approach. Accurate figures for Allies are just as elusive. This is partly because the 4th Marines that bore the brunt of the assault was a mixed service regiment patched together on Corregidor, but around 1,000 men defending the island were likely killed and as many again wounded.

The surrender was even more logistically difficult and humiliating than it had been for King on Bataan. Prior to asking for a cessation in the fighting, Wainwright had released his southern Philippine commanders back to MacArthur's remote authority in Australia before he attempted to meet the enemy commander – a ruse to try limiting any surrender to the fortified islands of Manila Bay alone. Homma's emissary would have none of it.

The Japanese would not accept Wainwright's surrender unless it meant the capitulation of every man in his command, everywhere in the Philippines.

To underline the point, the Japanese carried on bombing and shelling Corregidor throughout 6 May even as white flags flew over the island and after its big guns had been put out of action. Wainwright eventually accepted the terms. He was taken to the KZRH in Manila, the Japanese-controlled radio station that had long served as a kind of perverse diversion for his besieged troops, with its mixture of propaganda intended to induce homesickness and war weariness.

At midnight Wainwright broadcast a surrender message to all his commanding officers in the Philippines. Even then, it took some weeks to convince senior officers on Mindanao and the Visayas to accept the order – they had somewhere around 20,000 men scattered around the islands, ample supplies and wanted to break into small units and fight on as guerrillas. But in the end, on 9 June 1942, the surrender was reluctantly accepted, and the hostages formally became POWs.

* * *

It was merely overcast when the boatman handed out disposable ponchos. Disliking single-use plastics, I decided to take my chances under the overhead tarp. It was still dry when we pulled away from Engineer Dock, although about halfway across the channel the heavens opened. The rain came down with a vengeance, soaking me as surely as if I had been swimming with the monkeys.

By the time we reached the Villa Carmen jetty, the downpour had become absurd – a dense, vertical river from sky to ground. We scattered wordlessly, abandoning goodbyes, each of us bent on escape.

My car was parked on uneven ground, and I hurried, imagining the mud loosening to liquid beneath the tyres. The rear windscreen lacked a wiper, so reversing in that torrent was like peering into a liquid curtain. I knew there were large rocks nearby to avoid.

Disorientated, I then made a wrong turn and found myself on a dirt track crossed by a torrent of water a few metres wide. Reversing did not seem an option, so I decided that driving through the water was an acceptable risk.

Gritting my teeth, I got across only to find myself in the gloom of a small, ramshackle settlement of huts and trees, with no onward track back to the main road. Forced to turn around, and dreading what the surging water might do to my vaguely insured car, I pushed through the water again amid ominous clunks of bodywork against rocks, all the while cursing my own stupidity.

The tumbling sheets of rain on the way back to Abucay did a reasonable job of cleaning the bodywork. I had just about regained my calm when, after dark, I was back standing before the man who owned the car rental business with God. Armando Estrella Madrid surveyed the vehicle silently before returning my deposit and licence without comment. To my surprise, he did not ask if I had been driving off-road and generously offered to give me a lift to Balanga, from where I would get the bus back to Manila.

Given the ordeal I'd put his car through – and a lingering guilt and anxiety about whether I'd damaged it in some way – I was grateful for any conversation that wasn't about my Bataan travel experiences.

Soon, talk of the Pacific War in these parts led him to mention a local legend: that Japanese officers buried looted Philippine treasure somewhere in the province – maybe in Limay, or directly beneath Balanga's cathedral.

Gold hunting apparently began in earnest in the late 1980s and has touched most parts of the country. For a time, the government even issued permits to foreign treasure hunters and authorised several digs.

We let the conversation trail off, choosing to ignore the lack of evidence. Perhaps the truth of it was like the tracks from my earlier off-road detour – there for a moment, then washed away by rain, leaving no trace that could survive the scrutiny of newspapers or the claims of insurance lawyers.

Armando didn't seem ready to call it nonsense, as if belief in the gold was some kind of treasure. And sitting there in the dark car, the rain still needling the roof, I was prepared to imagine it – a last, glittering secret, stashed somewhere beneath the soil of Bataan or sealed under Balanga's cathedral floor, waiting for someone lucky enough to find it.

Chapter 4

Typhoon Leyte

MacArthur had vowed to return to the Philippines. I stood at the water's edge where he fulfilled the pledge, two and a half years after his dramatic exit from Corregidor. The general strode theatrically from a landing craft and through the shin-high surf onto the island of Leyte, marginally ahead of six other men in khaki uniforms.

Gaetano Faillace, a New Yorker who served as his personal photographer, was in position to capture the moment. It proved to be one of the defining images from the Pacific War, showing MacArthur's determination to reclaim both the Philippines and his own reputation, along with his instinct for how to stage-manage events for the news media.

MacArthur wore his khaki uniform, Aviators and a peaked cap. I was sporting a disposable poncho to cope with a blustery Sunday morning where rain threatened to lash down at any moment. An artwork created by the Filipino sculptor Anastacio Caedo acknowledged the general's 'I have returned' moment. It served as the focal point of a promenade just above the landing zone the Americans called Red Beach.

Seven double life-sized bronze figures stood in a ceremonial pool of water. The lofty statues were framed by the backdrop of Leyte Gulf, ominously grey and at the eastern extreme of the nation. MacArthur, forever leading the way, loomed above me, flanked on his right by the Philippine president-in-exile Sergio Osmeña and his Chief of Staff, Richard Sutherland on the left. At the rear of a group of officers and aides, CBS Radio correspondent William Dunn followed the others inshore, typewriter under his arm.

The tide was in, making it impossible for me to walk where MacArthur had spoken with GIs on the landing beach years before. The general had remained oblivious to repeated warnings that snipers were still active in the area. I took some pictures and bid good morning to a security guard who, I imagined, had little to do as the bad weather meant hardly anyone else was around what is designated a national monument.

MacArthur had wandered around in the sun before settling on a log, his back to the surf. He stared at the Leyte shoreline as if in awe of finally having boots back on the ground. Spontaneously, he scrawled out a letter to Roosevelt, the president with whom he endured a complex relationship, one marked by mutual distrust, opposing political views, and grudging respect. The moment was bigger than all their differences. 'This note is written from the beach near Tacloban where we have just landed,' he wrote. 'It will be the first letter from the freed Philippines. I thought you might like it for your philatelic collection.' The page was marked 20 October 1944.

MacArthur's presence on Red Beach was a moment of relative calm in the Pacific tempest south of the equator. After evacuating from Corregidor, he had reached Australia, from where he commanded one of two major Allied offensives driving Japanese forces back toward their home islands.

While the US Navy spearheaded the campaign to reclaim the Solomon Islands, MacArthur concentrated on nearby New Guinea, a theatre where his leadership shone brightest. All of the Solomons and most of New Guinea had been seized during Japan's 1942 expansion, marking the empire's southernmost reach and posing a direct threat to Australia. Under his direction, American and Australian troops perfected a daring leap-frogging strategy on New Guinea – bypassing some heavily fortified Japanese positions to strike at more strategically valuable targets, thereby cutting enemy supply lines and weakening their overall hold in the region.

Yet the way to the Philippines was far from certain. In the war councils of 1944, Admiral Chester Nimitz, commander of the US Navy, and several of the Joint Chiefs urged a bolder leap – to bypass the islands altogether and strike at Formosa, a stepping stone they believed would lead more directly to Japan's own shores. MacArthur bristled at the notion. To him, the Philippines were not simply coordinates on a map. They were the keystone of the South West Pacific, the artery through which Japanese supply lines pulsed from the south. To abandon them, he argued, would be both a strategic misstep and a moral failure.

Beneath the language of strategy lay something obviously personal. He sought redemption for the fiasco on Luzon at the start of the conflict and had left the Philippines under orders in 1942 with a promise – 'I shall return.' To fulfil it was to redeem a pledge of honour to the Filipino people, whose resistance had endured under the harshest occupation. In the end, it was MacArthur's unyielding advocacy and the strength of the case he made that won the day. The Philippines would be the next great objective. And as the plans took shape, MacArthur drew on the resourcefulness of Filipino guerrillas behind enemy lines, and the weight of his own conviction to prepare the campaign that would carry him back across the sea.

Unlike other artworks commemorating the fighting, which tend to depict bristling defiance, the bronze statues show a calm, business-like purpose to get the job done. And once MacArthur got his bearings on the shoreline he went much further than mere quiet confidence.

In a messianic radio address to the Filipino people, he declared:[25]

> I have returned. By the grace of Almighty God our forces stand again on Philippine soil – soil consecrated in the blood of our two peoples. We have come, dedicated and committed, to the task of destroying every vestige of enemy control over your daily lives, and of restoring, upon a foundation of indestructible strength, the liberties of your people.

The skies had opened when MacArthur began speaking, and the crack of distant gunfire could still be heard as US Army troops headed inland. Yet he pressed on through the downpour, praising the Filipino guerillas who had many bloody victories on Leyte, and promised an end to the nation's suffering. 'The hour of your redemption is here. Your patriots have demonstrated an unswerving and resolute devotion to the principles of freedom that challenges the best that is written on the pages of human history.'

Then came the call to arms.

> Rally to me. Let the indomitable spirit of Bataan and Corregidor lead on. As the lines of battle roll forward to bring you within the zone of operations, rise and strike. Strike at every favourable opportunity. For your homes and hearths, strike! For future generations of your sons and daughters, strike! In the name of your sacred dead, strike! Let no heart be faint. Let every arm be steeled. The guidance of divine God points the way. Follow in His Name to the Holy Grail of righteous victory!

The landing speech also featured a reference to re-establishing a Philippine government. It was classic MacArthur in the sense of being both grandiose and premature: a tough fight lay ahead for Leyte, which was defended by about 20,000 IJA troops in units which could still be reinforced. Beyond Leyte, at least 260,000 combatants from Japan's 14th Army were prepared to fight to the last man on the larger Philippine islands, not least Luzon and Mindanao. And that was only the land battle: three Japanese naval groups, featuring the two largest battleships ever built and sixty-seven other warships, were also steaming towards Leyte to confront the US invasion fleet.

I had flown into Tacloban, a small coastal city on the north-east coast of Leyte, the night before. A commercial port since 1874, Tacloban is dominated by the fishing industry and has a deepwater wharf used for lumber and agricultural exports. It also operates as the gas station for the region, with a major petroleum depot located on its shores. The Daniel Z. Romuáldez Airport where my AirAsia flight touched down was built on the site of a wartime airfield, but it was dark and my arrival experience posed more immediate intrigues.

I could not find any evidence that buses or cabs ever served the airport – and my hotel was about a 25-minute drive away in a city of 250,000 people. After asking a security guard, I was directed to a man who was hanging around, presumably looking for work. Amid the bustle of departing passengers and where the bright lights outside the terminal faded to gloom, I tried to decide if he had an honest bearing. Carlos appeared out of the shadows and introduced himself with a gravelly, sonorous voice. Wishing to avoid a fleecing, I haggled with practised theatrically over the quoted 500 pesos, so much so that he might have wondered if he'd somehow insulted my late mother.

On the drive into Tacloban, I felt guilty about my performance. Carlos talked about the rising cost of gasoline, the scarcity of work and how tough things had been in Tacloban since Covid. He managed a bar at one point but now had time on his hands. He offered himself and his pick-up truck as a tour guide. We swapped numbers just in case, but I had to tell him I'd already arranged a car rental firm to collect me the following morning – and planned to drive myself around the island.

Leyte is about the size of Corsica and part of the Visayas islands group. American English is widely spoken but Leyteños tend to talk to each other in one of two dialects – Waray in the more populated north and Cebuano in the agricultural south. As with most of the pieces in the nation's watery jigsaw, Leyte is awkwardly shaped and much longer than it is broad. As the crow flies it is some 180 kilometres (110 miles) north-south and about 65 kilometres (40 miles) at its widest point. A relatively pinched waist forms the midpoint of the island. Outside of its ports, much of the land is farming plains or densely forested highland areas. Sugarcane is the predominant crop in the north, rice and coconuts in the south.

Any painter hoping to capture the essence of Leyte would require an ample supply of green on the palette. Evergreen palm trees are the island's defining feature and, in the less developed areas, crowd the landscape.

For American military planners, two areas were of special interest in the 1940s. The east coast beaches looked like the obvious place to bring in a large amphibious force. On the other side of the island, a rugged mountain range running down most of the coast offered the Japanese defensive positions. This rocky margin extends over two thirds of the west coast and looms above the port of Ormoc, a counterpart to Tacloban.

A 20 kilometre (12 mile) wide band of flat land stretches from the northern shores on a diagonal down to the invasion-friendly east coast, just south of Tacloban. These low-lying plains, Leyte Valley, are still all farmland and palm trees today, with only a basic network of roads.

I would come to regard the Leyte Valley vista as somewhat monotonous compared to the intrigue of the densely covered jungle hills in the west and south-west, where waterfalls are hidden away by languid mists drift over a dense covering of trees, and steel framed road bridges suddenly appear to allow you to traverse unexpected ravines.

Leyte tends to be much less celebrated as an international visitor destination than its Visayas neighbours Cebu and Bohol, both of which are considered world class scuba diving destinations and about eleven hours by ferry to the west.

Yet Leyte can at least claim to have a bigger economy than its much nearer neighbour off the east coast, Samar, which is so close that, at a quick

General Douglas MacArthur. (*US National Archives*)

Surrender on Bataan: American officers, left to right: Colonel Everett Williams, Major General Edward P. King Junior and Major Wade Cothran; Major Achille C. Tisdelle facing Colonel Nakayama and another Japanese officer. (*US National Archives*)

American newsstands announce the fall of Bataan. (*US National Archives*)

POWs on the Bataan Death March. (*US National Archives*)

A march without mercy: left to right Samuel Stenzler and Frank Spear. (*US National Archives*)

Corregidor, 1945. (*US National Archives*)

Inside the Malinta Tunnel – Lateral No. 12, Corregidor, 1945. (*US National Archives*)

Major General Jonathan M. Wainwright. (*US National Archives*)

The Malinta Tunnel today. (*iStock*)

Battery Hearn today. (*Chris Hulme*)

One of Corregidor's surviving mortar batteries. (*Chris Hulme*)

A view of south dock, Corregidor, 1945. (*US National Archives*)

Ruined barracks, Corregidor. (*Chris Hulme*)

MacArthur returns – tribute above Red Beach, Palo. (*Chris Hulme*)

I Have Returned. (*US National Archive*)

US landings, Leyte, the 382nd Infantry disembark. (*US National Archives*)

US infantry pinned down on Red Beach by Japanese mortar and machine gun fire. (*US National Archive*)

US Army inland landings, Leyte, October 1944. (*US National Archive*)

Landing ships unload on Leyte. (*US National Archives*)

US tanks push inland on Leyte. (*US National Archives*)

US Army soldier, Leyte landing, October 1944. (*US National Archive*)

Leyte – fatalities from the 34th Infantry and navy personnel from *LST 171* killed by mortar and small arms fire on Red Beach. (*US National Archives*)

US anti-aircraft artillery unit, Leyte. (*US National Archive*)

Tacloban, 1945. (*US National Archive*)

MacArthur HQ, the Price Mansion, Tacloban, 1945. (*US National Archive*)

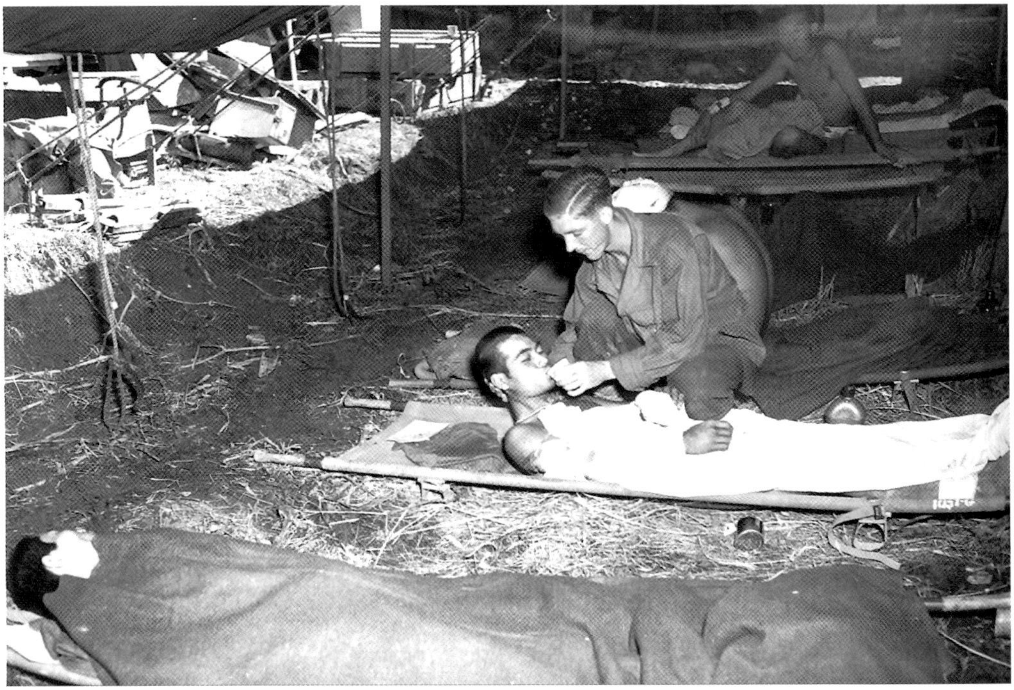

Seargeant Maurice Buckley assists a wounded Japanese officer at a Tacloban field hospital. (*US National Archives*)

The Manila Hotel wrecked in 1945. (*US National Archives*)

glance, the islands appear to be conjoined. Just above Tacloban, Leyte is in fact connected to Samar by the spectacular San Juanico Bridge.

Much larger and more rugged than Leyte, Samar suffers from a chronic lack of civic infrastructure beyond the impressive bridge. In a throwback to another era, Samar is also regarded as a holdout of communist opposition. The New People's Army rebellion is a Marxist-Leninist-Maoist group in conflict with the Philippine government. From somewhere in Samar's hills and barangays it operates what has been described as the world's longest ongoing communist insurgency.

For Filipinos, Leyte is closely associated with the rise of Imelda Marcos, the wife of the nation's former elected leader/dictator, Ferdinand Marcos. During her time as First Lady, Imelda Marcos painted a nostalgic portrait of the place where she was raised. Born in 1929, Imelda Romuáldez was eight years old when her mother died and her father, managing a struggling legal practice, relocated to the family Manila. She returned to Leyte to study for a degree in education at Tacloban's Saint Paul's College in 1952. Two years later, back in Manila, she met an ambitious 36-year-old congressman. After a whirlwind courtship they got married and soon established themselves amongst the nation's social elite.

Imelda gave birth to three children before Ferdinand was elected president in 1965. Her interest in high fashion and hard politics meant she was dubbed 'the Steel Butterfly'. Famously, her extravagant tastes would one day see a collection of 1,060 pairs of shoes found by the revolutionaries who entered Manila's Malacañang Palace in 1986 (the shoes are now in the National Museum). It was easy to imagine the Marcos couple amid the bustling post-war reconstruction of the capital as opposed to Leyte, a rural backwater where farmers and fishermen care not for political intrigues and haute couture.

Then as now, Leyte revolves around its workaday port cities, Tacloban and Ormoc, that serve as the main inter-island transport hubs. The airport is named after Imelda Marcos's uncle, Daniel Romuáldez. The rest of the island features some nondescript lesser hubs and market towns. The average international visitor stays for just two days.

Tacloban's most celebrated attraction is the Santo Niño Shrine and Heritage Museum. It is one of the twenty presidential palaces built by Ferdinand Marcos for his wife. It boasts an Olympic-size swimming pool, state dining rooms, conference rooms, a replica ballroom of the one in Malacañang Palace, and several bedrooms, each room having a diorama of the former First Lady, as well as a signed photograph of the couple. For all its grandeur, Imelda is believed to have only stayed in the house once. The shrine element celebrates a Catholic priest – who was said to have healed and saved people from a cholera epidemic that plagued Tacloban in 1889. Southern Leyte, meanwhile, does have some international renown with scuba divers, a favourite location for encounters with whale sharks.

Leyte's significance in reconquest of the nation is dominated by the naval Battle of Leyte Gulf, which began three days after MacArthur walked up Red Beach. Leyte Gulf is a large body of open water beyond the invasion beaches and off the east coast. It is framed by an overhanging stretch of Samar to the north and the jagged edges of Mindanao to the south.

A complex engagement, routinely described as the largest naval engagement of the Second World War, the Battle of Leyte Gulf reads more like four or five ferocious exchanges in one. They took place off Leyte, Samar, Luzon and faraway Palawan. In essence, the Japanese launched a three-pronged naval attack to try to defeat an American land invasion. Two of the IJN thrusts headed east from Singapore. The third was a decoy IJN taskforce sailing south from the Japanese home islands.

Scores of books and documentaries retell the story of the epic chess match of air and sea power. The main action took place over three days, but there is next to nothing to see today unless you have connections with the operators of the world's most sophisticated underwater exploration equipment. The vessels that were destroyed sank in some of the ocean's deepest water. The one place devoted to the battle, the Surigao Strait Museum, was either permanently closed or shut for a long-term redevelopment – I could never tell which from the information publicly available. For me, getting there would have involved a four-hour ferry crossing from the southern end of Leyte to Surigao at the northern tip of Mindanao, but the channel crossing was not to be.

Severe weather has made its mark throughout the history of the Philippines, but especially in the Eastern Visayas, where gigantic weather systems occasionally roll in from the Pacific. The destructive power of typhoons became a factor in the battle to reclaim the Philippines from late 1944 onwards and, if anything, the risk seems worse today. Population growth has made more people and places vulnerable.

Leyte and Samar were the focus of global attention for a few days in November 2013 when Super Typhoon Haiyan – known locally as Yolanda – slammed into the islands. The storm featured some of the highest recorded wind speeds for a tropical cyclone at landfall, with sustained winds at 170 knots (315 kilometres per hour/196 mph). That's about 32 kilometres per hour (20 mph) faster than Hurricane Katrina, which devastated New Orleans in 2005. Yolanda struck with such force that much of the power, transportation and communications infrastructure was destroyed, and even government-designated storm shelters were swept away. Across both islands at least 6,300 people were killed and many more left homeless.

A tsunami-like storm surge swept through Tacloban, causing about a third of total fatalities and bringing damage and disease. International aid agencies rushed to help but natural disasters on this scale are beyond quick fixes. Power was cut off for months in some areas. Infection and disease spread, partly because seawater, chemicals and sewage reached the surface and groundwater. The impact of ruined crops and polluted farmland was made even worse by an 800,000-litre oil leak from a tanker that ran aground, contaminating local fishing waters. Amid the prolonged chaos, survivors looted stores and fought for food and supplies. In one incident on Leyte, eight people died when a huge crowd stormed a government-owned rice warehouse, causing a wall to collapse.

More than a decade on, other colossal storms have raked the eastern Philippines, notably Super Typhoon Rai (known locally as Odette) in December 2021. Odette resulted in far fewer fatalities than Yolanda – 400 people killed – partly because the government had instituted a warning service, sending emergency text message updates to all cell phones well in advance of the storm. The system helped people prepare and speeded up evacuation of the most exposed areas.

It's hard to figure out which typhoon caused what damage, but the scars are still evident everywhere. Walking around the centre of Tacloban on my first night, there were plenty of buildings that looked long since abandoned by some combination of uninsured damage and business failure. Some of the gloomy relics lined the route to the harbour area, where the crew of a commercial fishing boat was busy working under bright deck lights. A few market stalls still twinkled in the warm, fragrant dark, traders selling hot street food. But most vendors had either gone home or were setting up for a night's sleep behind their stalls.

The next day, on the short drive south to Palo, location of the MacArthur Landing Memorial, I passed a wooden sign with faded red lettering marking 'Evacuation Centre', which was immediately evocative of disaster movies and post-apocalyptic landscapes. Further on, in the coastal barangay of Anibong, the bow of the MV *Eva Jocelyn*, a cargo ship which washed up during Yolanda, has been transformed into a memorial and tourist stop.

When the heavens finally opened at Palo and I decided to leave Red Beach and the MacArthur memorial, I stopped to ask the security guard if she'd been on Leyte when Yolanda hit. 'Oh yes', she recalled. Motioning at the plaza all around us, a place for family strolls and civic parades during better weather, she said, 'All this was covered in seawater – and dead people.'

Walking around Tacloban in daylight, the city's scars of pothole-ridden streets and the weathered facades of empty buildings were muddled in with pockets of progress – new developments, sporadic efforts to modernise, and a sense of bustle. The hotel where I stayed, the Xyz, had the stylish, contemporary and generic feel of international hospitality. It was on the same block as the Price Mansion, the building of most interest to me, where MacArthur based himself during the fight for Leyte. This colonial-style house had been built in the centre of town by Walter Scott Price, a native of Philadelphia. Price was one of twelve US Army engineers assigned to the Philippines at the beginning of the Spanish-American War. He married a Filipino woman and stayed in the country, having a large family and making his fortune from founding the Leyte Transportation Company. When the Japanese arrived in early 1942, Price was rounded up with other expats and sent to the University of Santo Tomás internment camp in Manila. He did not survive captivity.

The Japanese used his twelve bedroomed mansion as an officers' club. MacArthur also appreciated its neoclassical design, with large white pillars outside, and elegant interiors. The Japanese knew exactly where the general was staying, with the Price Mansion even mentioned in a goading Radio Tokyo broadcast, but MacArthur still refused to be cowed. There was a period where Japanese fighters routinely came in low to strafe and bomb the compound. William Manchester's biography describes MacArthur particularly appreciating the mansion's wide veranda, where he could pace up and down, as was his habit. US Army engineers had patched up the house but on taking up residence, MacArthur asked about a mound of earth in the garden. One of them explained that it was an elaborate bomb shelter, built underground and furnished with lounge chairs, electricity and ventilating fans. 'The General said: "Level it off and fill the thing in. It spoils the look of the lawn."'[26]

Today, the Price Mansion is sometimes called the CAP Building, named after the College Assurance Plan, a savings fund which used it as a headquarters for some years. CAP acquired the mansion from the Philippine government, who had seized it from the Romuáldez family after the People Power Revolution – but Imelda's clan seemed to have reclaimed it following a legal wrangle and after CAP went out of business. The mansion has apparently not suffered any major alterations since the war. The various owners have even preserved a hole about the size of an American football where a stray American anti-aircraft shell once lodged in an exterior wall above MacArthur's bedroom but did not explode. Sadly, the mansion was closed without explanation during my stay, so I had to content myself with viewing the exterior. The building sits on the corner of a busy downtown junction and has the wrought iron grills and opaque Capiz shell windows that are a hallmark of Spanish-inspired homes in the Philippines. The grounds include a statue of MacArthur and Sergio Osmeña standing together.

None of the big brand car rental companies operated in Leyte during my stay but the little car I'd reserved with a local firm, Haven's Tourist Transport, was at least inexpensive. It had over 230,000 kilometres (142,915 miles) on the clock, no radio or music player and lacked a functioning air con. It was the most beaten-up rental car I'd ever seen, much less contemplated driving. Yet the manager was efficient and helpful, and the brakes seemed to work, which allowed me to leave town with at least some hope of avoiding mechanical issues in the outback. There weren't enough roads to worry about a Sat Nav. Tacloban, with its lingering sense of hard work, disrepair, and vulnerability, faded in the rear-view mirror.

I headed north to the San Juanico Bridge, crossing over its 2-kilometre (1.2-mile) span to Samar. A thing of engineering beauty, the road bridge is formed of an elegant matrix of steel girders and arches standing on concrete piers. The bridge was commissioned near the end of the 1960s at the behest of Imelda Marcos, who wanted Leyte better connected. When it opened in 1974 the sceptics had no time for the impressive aesthetics. The San Juanico Bridge was a white elephant, they said, over-built given that it links two rural islands. It was just another example of the Marcos' 'edifice complex' where the family saddled the Philippines with billions in foreign debt on vanity construction projects that suggested progress.

Some forty years on, there was still not much evidence of traffic. It was easy to pull over and walk back to take in the sweeping views of the San Juanico Strait. I stared at the great expanse of blue-black water stretching to the north and south, merging with the horizon. The surface was textured like hammered metal, save for a few places where glassy channels glinted as if an invisible current were polishing the surface. Tiny whirlpools spiralled into existence before dissolving into the depths. Rocky islets stood in wistful isolation, dwarfed by the restless waters surrounding them.

I had no plans to go any further. The roads on Samar are by reputation narrow, difficult, and painfully slow, especially during the wet season. In terms of international visitors, it's only surfers seriously intent on getting off the beaten track that tend to brave the route to reach a 150 kilometre (93 mile) long pristine coastline where the big swells come crashing into shore. In 1944 the US Navy created a base with a warehouse complex at Guiuan, on a peninsular near the southern tip of Samar but whatever is left of the depot today, I decided to stay focused on the Leyte landing beaches. I drove back across the bridge and down the east coast to where four divisions of the US Sixth Army stormed ashore.

* * *

The final hurdle before MacArthur could fulfil his vow to return to the Philippines had been the capture of Morotai, a small island at the northeastern edge of Japanese-held Dutch East Indies. On 15 September 1944, American and Australian forces landed there, facing a garrison of about 500 Japanese troops. Within two weeks, the Allies had secured enough ground for Morotai to serve as an operational base.

By this stage of the war, Admiral Nimitz had the US Navy driving west across the Central Pacific with a vastly expanded fleet, seizing the Caroline, Marshall, and Mariana Islands. At the same time, MacArthur's forces were pushing north from Australia through New Guinea. Their paths were converging.

Once the Nimitz-led thrust had seen US forces prevail in the bloody struggles for Peleliu, Saipan, and other islands in the Western Pacific, the stage was set for the next major objective: the liberation of the Philippines. On 20 October 1944, the two great advances finally met at Leyte. MacArthur commanded the overall operation, while Nimitz directed naval support from Pearl Harbor through his admirals aboard the invasion fleet.

Rather than assault the main island of Luzon, where at least 180,000 Japanese troops were located, they went for Leyte as it was only defended by about 20,000 Japanese, part of a larger group defending the Visayas. Victory for the Allies would create a powerful base and springboard for strikes against the other big Philippine islands.

Just prior to the invasion, a number of large-scale softening up and diversionary carrier-based air attacks were launched. These included raids over the Ryukyu Islands (including Okinawa), northern Luzon, and Formosa.

The air strikes over Formosa were devastatingly effective. Much of the land-based air power that Japan retained in the region was massed at two bases located on the south of the island. Yet over three days of air combat these generally inexperienced pilots were routed and some 600 aircraft lost, vastly depleting air capability. Vice Admiral Shigeru Fukudome, watching one of the dogfights from a cave at Takao Air Base, where he and his staff had taken refuge, later wrote: 'Our fighters were nothing but so many eggs thrown at the stone wall of the indomitable enemy formation.'[27] Given that the IJN's carrier-based air arm had suffered a similarly debilitating set back while trying to tackle the Saipan invasion fleet four months previously, military planners would soon have to consider how to counter a vast American armada without mobile air cover.

The Leyte landing force was formidable. It was formed around 738 ships of the US Seventh Fleet crewed by 50,000 sailors, and over 165,000 troops at his disposal under Lieutenant General Walter Krueger, commander of the US Sixth Army.

The invasion ships were supported by the US Third Fleet, which provided cover and featured a breathtaking array of sixteen aircraft carriers, six battleships, plus a litany of cruisers and destroyers.

The assault focused on sites along Leyte's east coast – but especially just below Palo, location of Red Beach, and Blue Beach, some 25 kilometres (15 miles) to the south, above the small town of Dulag. Red Beach was assigned to the Sixth Army's 10th Corps, with 26th Corps tackling Blue Beach.

The landings began at 10.00 hours on 20 October. The assault was mostly uncontested, although there were more enemy aircraft than had been expected, menacing the incoming troop-carrying craft. The Japanese had chosen to defend Leyte from positions on land beyond the easy reach of battleship firepower. By the end of the first day, some 130,000 American troops were ready to push out from two east coast bridgeheads. MacArthur strode onto Red Beach halfway through the operation at 13.30 hours. Tacloban was soon taken, and both of the corps began to make steady progress inland, coming up against fierce opposition, but nothing that would break the momentum of the advance.

My journey to Blue Beach was mostly about a steady drive down the east coast highway with only a sparse flow of traffic for company. After Tanauan, a decent sized town, small villages came and went in flurries of tricycles, houses and shacks. To one side, Leyte Gulf slipped past, a drab expanse of grey only given character by the coconut trees lining the road here and there.

Inland, the plains extended as far as the eye could see. The Americans had hoped to establish a network of major air and supply bases on a square-shaped area of flat terrain here, ready for the assault on Luzon and Mindanao. Along the northern edge it was bordered by a 16-kilometre (10-mile) stretch of east-to-west road. It linked Tanauan with Dagami, a settlement in the rural interior. The bottom of the square was a line drawn from Dulag, the location of Blue Beach, to Burauen, another small agricultural town amidst rice paddies and a series of rivers flowing down from the higher ground further inland.

Tolosa, the next small east coast town I passed through, was the location of a locked up 100-acre beachside estate owned by the Steel Butterfly. The property featured a series of buildings: a seven room residential mansion, a fourteen room room guest mansion, and a pavilion that could accommodate 1,000 people. There was also a nine-hole golf course designed by a legend of the sport, Jack Nicklaus. Much of the work had been commissioned by Ferdinand Marcos. From the highway there was nothing to mark the entrance other than an unremarkable block wall along the road and a 'Private Property' sign. Yet YouTubers have freely roamed the grounds, where the main house is shuttered and the gardens overgrown. The footage shows rainwater and algae despoiling the once pristine Olympic-sized outdoor pool. One of fifty estates owned by the Marcos family across the Philippines, this one features on lists that detail the wanton spending and excess. For all that, Imelda Marcos always maintained the land had belonged to her family for generations. Philippine courts eventually accepted her argument that the government had no right to sequester the Tolosa property, the place where her parents are buried, and returned ownership. The estate was later ransacked by Yolanda but there were reports of it being restored and opening as another Marcos-era museum.

On reaching my destination, Blue Beach just north of Dulag, I managed to miss the tribute that commemorates the American landings and had to back up to find it. An overgrown sign by the roadside marked the bottom of what the Americans called Hill 120 – the only high ground for some distance around, and a place that was robustly defended by the IJA. The tribute read:

> Atop the height of this Hill 120 … at 10:42 a.m. 20 October 1944, only 42 minutes had elapsed since the first assault troops … had landed. 1st Lt. Clifford W. Mills raised the American flag in Philippine soil [for the first time] after it had been lowered at Bataan on 9 April 1942. Floating high and proud [the flag] was tangible proof that the Americans had made good their promise to the Filipinos.

Reaching the top involved walking up 120 concrete steps winding through trees and overgrown bush. On the way a kind of life-sized diorama recreated the moment the Americans re-planted the Stars and Stripes. One figure depicted a soldier climbing a coconut tree to display the flag. A couple of other life-sized models of GIs held radios. At the top, the Hill 120 commemorative site was completely overgrown with tall grass and weeds. A couple of concrete mannequin GIs, the paint flaking off their plaster faces, stood guard, neglected in the bush. A giant US Army helmet, about the size of a garden shed, continued the 1960s theme park kitsch. A tribute to the 96th Infantry Division, part of 26th Corps, it turned out to be full of trash and weeds. Apparently, they clean-up the summit once a year for Liberation Day events. The ceremonial element happens back down in an area by the roadside, lost in the overgrowth during my visit. Local dignitaries sing the Dulag hymn while soldiers from the Philippine Army offer a salute. It all happens a few steps from a Japanese memorial which strikes a remorseful tone. 'To console all souls of Filipinos, Japanese, Americans who passed away in Leyte during World War II. Sworn that the same tragedy and mistake should never be repeated. Prayer for the true world peace and friendship forever.'

I found another gesture of reconciliation in Dulag proper, where there is a roadside tribute to the Japanese officer who oversaw the town in 1943. Captain Isao Yamazoe is remembered for the concern he showed towards civilians. At that time, there were so many Japanese stationed in Dulag it was dubbed Little Tokyo. Yamazoe ordered his men to not abuse the Filipinos and encouraged villagers to plant root crops and vegetables as it was clear food would be scarce. Yamazoe even made efforts to foster friendly ties between locals and the Japanese. This went as far as initiating morning callisthenics, basketball, and cultural shows. His regard for the people reached a zenith when the 32-year-old officer learnt of an impending Filipino guerrilla raid on Dulag. Yamazoe managed to open negotiations via intermediaries and asked to conduct the battle outside of the town to avoid unnecessary civilian deaths. Yamazoe was on his way to this area, called Del Pilar today, when the guerrillas set upon him and his men. On learning of the Japanese officer's death, the citizens of Dulag rang the church bell all day in mourning. The roadside tribute was paid for by local businesspeople. It features a portrait photograph of Yamazoe in uniform, donated by one of his descendants, and an account of his actions. I studied the image, probably taken on a proud soldierly day somewhere in Japan. Nothing stern or cruel could be seen in Yamazoe's gaze; in posterity, he appeared fresh faced and ready for life.

Heading inland, I took the 16-kilometre (10-mile) road from Dulag across to Burauen, the farming town which serves as the last stop before the plains abruptly end at Mahagnao, a dormant volcano carpeted with lush jungle and surrounded by rivers and small lakes. Mahagnao was a brooding presence on the skyline, its higher elevations draped in a mystery of clouds. The US Army soldiers who fought across this easily saturated terrain came to consider themselves mud rats; the land was better for rice than airfields. In 1944 the Dulag-Burauen road formed part of a key cross-country supply route but keeping it open posed on-going challenges for US Army engineers. The road was not designed to take the combination of military traffic and heavy rain. It soon became impassable for about 3 kilometres (1.9 miles) on each side of Burauen. They kept it usable, just about, by dumping a thick layer of gravel over the surface and restricting some sections to one-way traffic.

I was looking for a disused Japanese airfield, one of three built close to Burauen. I could see no sign of anything that might lead to the first of these sites when passing through the hamlet of San Pablo, where an airfield was marked as parallel to the old road on a wartime map. The next two, Bayug and, close-by to the north, Buri, were inconclusive. A minor road towards Bayug that appeared as though it might take me to the disused airfield was overgrown and discouraging in my jalopy. A better option seemed to be at a junction further along, but when I got to an opening for what may have been the entry to the Buri airstrip, an enormous mound of dirt and rubble, as high as a two-storey house, had been dumped, barring the way amid a surrounding quagmire of mud.

Heavy fighting took place in and around the Burauen airfields in the week after the American landings – and two months later when the Japanese launched a major counteroffensive. The town was liberated by 26th Corps on 28 October. Freedom could not come soon enough. Burauen had been one of the hubs of organised sexual slavery across the Philippines. The town featured one of the Japanese 'Comfort Houses' where women were systematically raped. There is a small Japanese memorial to the combatants of both sides but nothing to acknowledge the women's suffering in the rural town.

Given the three airfields and Burauen's importance as a supply route, retaking the area was a priority for the Japanese. The counterattack began on 6 December and included a rarity – a Japanese paratrooper assault. About 300 men were dropped on two of the three airfields, but the force was wiped out by US Army soldiers within 48 hours.

Leaving Burauen, I headed back towards the east coast and turned towards southern Leyte. The road soon passed the area where the Japanese had built another airfield, Dulag aerodrome, in 1943, just above an L-shaped turn in the Daguitan River. It was later used by American bombers and fighters. Today it is agricultural land, but there's a memorial featuring a large model of a Wildcat fighter.

Wanting a break, I came off the highway and headed down a narrow road that led to the shores of Leyte Gulf. I had a picnic lunch here before a grey vista once crossed by opposing naval fleets. Staring at a map, the lure of pressing on to the bottom of the island got the better of me. Back behind the wheel, but without much of a coherent plan, I continued south of the invasion beaches for a time before cutting inland again. The route rose to higher ground and the highway narrowed as it threaded south through heavily forested hills. The ever-present telegraph poles and wires seemed to disappear, perhaps taking a more direct route, which I took as a sign that I was properly in the Leyte outback.

* * *

Japanese military planners were wrong-footed by the American landings, having expected an attack on Luzon or Formosa. Yet they soon resolved to make Leyte the first line of defence in the Philippines. The plan set in motion was called Sho-Go (Victory Operation) and involved three main naval groups converging on Leyte Gulf. Two of them were tasked with engaging and destroying the Allied landing fleet. The third was a ruse to tempt the covering element of the American force, the US Third Fleet, out of Leyte Gulf and far to the north of Samar.

The decoy fleet was led by Vice Admiral Jisaburō Ozawa – nicknamed 'The Gargoyle' by his subordinates who felt sure he was the ugliest admiral in the IJN. His Northern Force operated from Kure, Japan, and approached the Philippines from the north-east. It was formed around his flagship, *Zuikaku*, the IJN's last remaining fleet carrier. *Zuikaku* was a veteran of the attack on Pearl Harbor and the major battles at Coral Sea, Guadalcanal, and four months previously, the Philippine Sea off Saipan.

Zuikaku steamed with three light carriers and two partially converted First World War battleships, where the aft turrets had been replaced by an aircraft hangar and catapult. The Northern Force had no more than 108 planes between the ships – a pitiful number given the strength of the opposition they faced. If the decoy worked, the almost empty carriers would be sacrificed to allow the main strike force of battleships steaming from Singapore to engage the US fleet conducting the Leyte landings. Ozawa fully expected to be annihilated, trading his life, men and ships to give others a chance to destroy the American invasion ships.

The two other Japanese taskforces heading for Leyte Gulf would ultimately have to thread through the only two channels that provide access to the body of water if coming from the east – the San Bernardino Strait to the north of Leyte, and the Surigao Strait to the south. The IJN ships departed from naval bases in the Singapore and the Dutch East Indies, staging and refuelling in Brunei Bay off northern Borneo. From here they steamed through the South China Sea into the Sulu Sea of the southwestern Philippines, an area today considered a pirate-infested backwater best avoided by mariners.

The most important element, the Centre Force, was commanded by Vice Admiral Takeo Kurita. His wartime experience included Guadalcanal, where he commanded the cruiser that inflicted the most intense of the bombardments that wrecked Henderson Field, the main US air base. Regarded as a taciturn old sea dog, who preferred action to words, Kurita was too cautious for some in the IJN and considered an odd choice to lead the attack on the Leyte invasion fleet.

The Centre Force was formed around the pride of the Japanese navy, the two super battleships, *Yamato* and *Musashi*. They moved as part of an armada made up of the older battleships *Nagato*, *Kongō*, and *Haruna*, ten cruisers and thirteen destroyers.

The strategists who commissioned these two behemoths in the 1930s did so with the knowledge that Japan could not keep pace economically with the United States in any prolonged war. If they could not compete for volume, the reasoning was that they may be able to develop a lead in firepower. So the IJN went down the route of designing super battleships whose strength was so great that even the most powerful industrial nations would struggle to match the performance for a few years.

Yamato and *Musashi* were about the same length as the US Navy's four biggest battleships, the Iowa-class, which covered some 263 metres (862 feet 10 inches) – but displaced 63,000 tons, compared to 58,000 tons. They could deliver a broadside that was about 20 per cent more powerful than any Allied warship. Amid conditions of secrecy, construction began on *Yamato* in 1937 at the Kure Naval Arsenal on the edge of Hiroshima Bay. The keel for *Musashi* was laid down the following year at Mitsubishi's navy yard in Nagasaki. As the epitome of Imperial Japan's military prestige, the super battleships had a 16-inch-thick armour belt at the waterline. The principal armament was nine, 18.1-inch 'Type 45' guns, mounted in three triple gun turrets. These colossal weapons presented significant technical challenges in design and operation. Yet the Japanese persisted as the mere 2-inch difference in gun diameter did not adequately describe the step up in destructive power. The weight of a 16-inch US Navy projectile was about 2,200 pounds; for an 18-inch super-battleship shell it jumped to 3,200 pounds. They were the most powerful guns ever fitted to a warship. The turrets could hurl armour-piercing shells more than 40 kilometres (25 miles) at forty-second intervals, with dire consequences for whatever they struck.

On leaving the South China Sea, Centre Force would pass through the strait between Palawan, the most westerly of the Philippine islands, and underneath it, northern Borneo. Tracking east across the expanse of Sulu Sea they would reach the Sibuyan Sea a couple of days later, roughly in the centre of the watery Philippine jigsaw. The final leg meant heading east over the top of the island of Samar and through the San Bernardino Strait, a channel separating northern Samar from the southern extreme of Luzon. Centre Force would then turn south and head down the coast for Leyte Gulf itself.

The third element, the smaller Southern Force, was a collection of seven older warships that also sailed from oil-rich Brunei under the command of Admiral Shōji Nishimura. It would also approach Leyte Gulf from the east, by passing through the Surigao Strait, the channel between southern Leyte and northern Mindanao. On exiting this relatively narrow channel it would turn north and complete a pincer movement against the Allied ships conducting the landings. The Southern Force consisted of an attack group plus a smaller reinforcement squadron sailing some distance behind it that, in the event, never caught up and did not feature directly in the exchange of shock and awe that followed.

If the plan sounded like a rational three-pronged advance on paper, Sho-Go is regarded as fatuous by a number of historians. However mighty some of the IJN battleships were, they lacked the air cover required for survival in the new era of carrier warfare. The last major engagement, during the battle for Saipan, had decimated Japan's naval air arm. The four months since had not allowed enough time to replenish the lost pilots and aircraft, while the land-based force had also been seriously degraded by the air battles over Formosa.

All three Japanese fleets heading towards Leyte Gulf would face swarms of Hellcats, Avengers and Helldivers from sixteen US carriers, and were outnumbered in terms of battleships, cruisers, submarines, and destroyers. In the event, the IJN was also five days too late to prevent MacArthur's forces getting ashore, the principal objective. For all that, while Operation Desperate Gamble may have been a more fitting description, it was also apparent that the Japanese fleet retained enough punching power to inflict death and disaster in Leyte Gulf.

The US Seventh Fleet that would conduct the landings was led by Vice Admiral Thomas Kinkaid. His counterpart in the Third Fleet, Admiral William 'Bull' Halsey, was there to provide cover but also under orders to seize the initiative and destroy whatever forces the IJN brought into the Leyte conflict if circumstances allowed. Halsey, born into a naval family in New Jersey, was renowned as an aggressive commander with a short temper. His biggest disappointment in his career to date was missing the Battle of Midway two years previously, having become seriously ill with psoriasis, which covered a great deal of his body in a rash and caused unbearable itching. Halsey had recovered to take over naval operations in the battle around Guadalcanal and never lost the desire for retribution that was born of witnessing the aftermath of the destruction of Pearl Harbor. 'Before we're through with them, the Japanese language will be spoken only in hell,' he once said.[28]

The first shots were fired faraway when the Centre Force left the South China Sea and was attacked by two US submarines in the Palawan Strait on the night of 22–23 October. Two of the Japanese cruisers, Vice Admiral

Kurita's flagship *Atago*, and *Maya* were struck by torpedoes and quickly sank. A third, *Takao* was so badly damaged it had to leave the battle area, escorted by two destroyers. Vice Admiral Kurita had the chastening experience of having to jump over the side of *Atago* and swim for his life before being rescued by a destroyer.

The following day, Japanese aircraft based on Luzon, launched strikes against the most northerly element of the Halsey's immense Third Fleet, Task Force 38.3. It was operating about 160 kilometres (100 miles) off the coast of southern Luzon. Four of the American carriers in this group had been pounding Luzon airfields in support of the Leyte landings – *Essex*, *Lexington*, *Princeton* and *Langley*. The three waves of Japanese fighters and bombers, each containing between fifty and sixty aircraft, were intercepted by Hellcats. Most were destroyed or driven off. One Hellcat pilot, Captain David McCampbell, shot down a record nine enemy aircraft in this single action. His wingman downed another six. When McCampbell landed, his six machine guns had just two rounds remaining, and his Hellcat had to be manually released from the arrestor wire due to complete fuel exhaustion.

Yet for all the ruthless combat prowess against raw Japanese pilots, one Yokosuka D4Y 'Judy' dive bomber did slip past the fighters and through the screen of anti-aircraft fire. At 09.38 hours, it planted a 250-kilogram bomb on *Princeton*'s flight deck, just aft of amidships. The bomb exploded in the crew's galley, killing cooks, bakers, and other crewmen. The flames shot up through the hole the bomb had created, reaching a hangar deck where between six and ten Avengers, each fully loaded with gasoline and torpedoes, were parked. Some combination of the flames, the concussive effect of the blast or the Japanese bomb striking one of the Avengers on its downward path, ignited an inferno. The blaze raged through *Princeton* for almost six hours and caused a series of secondary explosions. The desperate efforts to get the conflagration under control included the light cruiser *Birmingham* coming alongside to use its fire hoses. The *Princeton* was unable to manoeuvre, and ships were so close they bumped and crashed together on the swell, badly damaging the cruiser. By mid-afternoon the flames reached *Princeton*'s bomb storage area. The explosion that followed put the carrier beyond all hope of salvation and caused extensive damage to *Birmingham*. Given the number of blasts throughout the day and the intensity of fires, the butcher's bill was still relatively light on *Princeton*, with 108 dead and 1,361 rescued. *Birmingham*'s heroic fire-fighting efforts came at the cost of 233 fatalities and 426 wounded from the secondary explosions aboard *Princeton*.

The same morning, Kurita's ships, already mauled by submarines in the Palawan Strait, were transiting the Sibuyan Sea when set upon by aircraft from other elements of Halsey's Third Fleet. In all, aircraft from six US Navy carriers flew 259 sorties against the Centre Force. As if to puncture the bravado that super battleships were unsinkable, most of the effort went into pummelling *Musashi*. With no air cover, the mighty vessel was ravaged in five successive raids. Navy pilots scored approximately nineteen torpedo and seventeen bomb hits. *Musashi*'s hull eventually succumbed, and the ship slipped beneath the surface about four hours after the last strike, taking about 1,000 of her complement of 2,500 sailors to the bottom with her. The cruiser *Myōkō* was also crippled by an aerial torpedo and had to withdraw.

Centre Force was then sighted apparently retiring to the west, giving Halsey reason to believe that his rival Kurita was finished. Yet the reports of the damage inflicted on the Japanese fleet were somewhat overstated. The focus on sinking *Musashi* had in fact left the rest of the fleet relatively unscathed. Kurita did turn away from the charge towards the San Bernardino Strait for a time, but that did not stop him from heading back and resuming the original route once the air attacks had abated.

The effort put into attacking the Centre Force meant Halsey's search aircraft did not detect the Northern Force, the bait the Japanese were dangling in the waters north of Samar, until late afternoon on 24 October. Halsey, like the rest of the US Navy's top brass, had been frustrated by the remnants of Ozawa's fleet slipping away from the Battle of the Philippine Sea off Saipan in the summer. The absolute priority given to taking the Mariana Islands had meant 'The Gargoyle' could not be pursued beyond a desperate air strike at the range-limit of his fighters.

Believing the Centre Force no longer presented a dire threat to the Seventh Fleet conducting the landings, Halsey fell for the decoy and steamed north with everything he had to intercept the mostly empty Japanese carriers. Remarkably poor and ambiguous communications accompanied his momentous decision. Aided by the overly complicated command structure within the Allied invasion forces, the doors to calamity suddenly swung open.

Kinkaid, in charge of the Seventh Fleet, believed that Halsey had left a taskforce in position to cover any incursion from the San Bernardino Strait. In fact, the channel was unguarded and the northern route into Leyte Gulf was wide open.

Several intelligence reports reached Halsey and his staff officers that night to inform them that the Centre Force had resumed its course for Leyte Gulf, but the blood was up and they took no action, believing that Kinkaid's ships should be able to cope with whatever Kurita had left in his battered fleet. For Halsey, the greater threat came from the carriers of the Northern Force; he could not assume that Ozawa's fleet had been denuded of strike aircraft.

In fact, the Seventh Fleet had other concerns. The IJN Southern Force had been detected on its approach to Leyte Gulf via the Surigao Strait between Leyte and Mindanao. Kinkaid set a trap that night by dispatching six battleships, four heavy cruisers, four light cruisers, and twenty-eight destroyers to lay in wait for the Japanese ships. This move considerably weakened the Allied naval presence in Leyte Gulf.

Five of the six American battleships dispatched south had been refloated, repaired and rebuilt after Pearl Harbor. Two of the warships were from the Royal Australian Navy. Some thirty-nine PT boats were arranged in three groups and positioned at the western entrance to Surigao Strait, ready to launch harassing torpedo attacks and to act as an early warning system.

The Southern Force duly steamed into passage in the early hours of 25 October. Given the lack of width in the strait, the seven ships under the command of Admiral Nishimura were forced to arrange in a single-file column, which he knew would place the warships at a disadvantage in any engagement. Nishimura was aware of his likely fate and radioed a final message: 'We proceed to Leyte for *gyokusai*' – a term that translated as 'shattered jewel' and reflected the reality that he expected his force to inflict as much damage as possible before meeting an honourable death. Nishimura's group was formed around two First World War vintage battleships, his flagship *Yamashiro*, and her sister ship, *Fuso*. They were at the back of a column led by four destroyers and the heavy cruiser *Mogami*. The first decisive blows came when the ships were besieged in the darkness and struck by torpedoes and shells from American and Australian destroyers. *Fuso* sank along with the destroyers *Asagumo*, *Michishio*, and *Yamagumo*.

Fuso's death toll was particularly brutal – the old dreadnought split open, spewing oil, which caught fire and incinerated the survivors floating in the water. All but 10 men of 1,630 crew aboard burned to death or drowned. The flagship *Yamashiro* was hit too, and started talking on water, which slowed its forward speed. Despite having already lost four of his seven warships, Nishimura ploughed on, accompanied by *Mogami* and a single destroyer, *Shigure*. As they exited the Surigao Strait they entered what proved to be the last battleship-to-battleship engagement in naval history.

The waiting ambush fleet conducted the classic crossing the 'T' manoeuvre. The repaired Pearl Harbor battleships sailed across the line of Nishimura's depleted armada. Moving perpendicular to the Japanese column leaving the strait allowed the veteran battlewagons to bring all their big guns to bear while only receiving fire from only the forward guns of Nishimura's bedraggled force. A devastating cavalcade of explosions from shells and torpedo hits lit up the black night. Nishimura went down with his flagship, one of at least 4,000 Japanese officers and crewmen to die in the Surigao Strait alone. *Mogami* was badly damaged – struck four times by 8-inch shells from the heavy cruiser *Portland*, including one that destroyed the bridge, killing the captain and the executive officer. *Mogami* limped back towards the strait, but her reprieve did not last long and the cruiser was later scuttled. A single destroyer, *Shigure*, did escape but the threat of the Southern Force had been extinguished.

In all this, Kurita's Centre Force remained battle worthy and had advanced towards the northern entrance to Leyte Gulf. During the same black night the imperious column of IJN warships, 16 kilometres (10 miles) long, passed unchallenged through the San Bernardino Strait. It was heading south down the coast of Samar, about 80 kilometres (50 miles) offshore. Halsey's rush north to engage Ozawa's carriers and the failure of effective communications across all Allied operations was about to create astonishment amongst the US Navy commanders still in Leyte Gulf, who all assumed Halsey's had left a capable force to guard the strait.

The Allied ships that remained in the gulf were adjacent to the beachhead and had been tasked with providing direct support for MacArthur's amphibious landings. This element of the Seventh Fleet under Vice Admiral Kinkaid did not feature any fleet carriers and now lacked the major component of battleships and cruisers sent south to cover the incursion from the Surigao Strait. Kinkaid was left with a group of destroyers and eighteen escort carriers – slow merchant freighters converted to carry and launch a limited number of aircraft.

Built quickly and to civilian standards, which meant lower quality steel and fewer safety features, escort carriers were dubbed 'buckets' in the navy. They lacked some of the engineering that protected fully-fledged warships. Fewer bulkheads and less compartmentalisation meant damage control was harder to achieve. In combat operations, the escorts carried about 21 Avengers and Wildcat fighters, which were smaller and lighter than the state-of-the-art Hellcats that operated from Essex-class fleet carriers, where the air groups could be 100-strong. With a top speed of only 18 knots, the escorts would need ingenious defensive tactics to evade the mighty warships in Kurita's fleet, many of which were twice as fast.

Offensively, none of the US vessels had guns larger than 5 inches, which would bounce off the armour of the biggest Japanese battleships and cruisers. The guns were also limited to a range of 11 kilometres (7 miles). It meant the most powerful IJN warships could fire at them from at least twice that distance away.

By the rain-swept morning of 25 October, Kinkaid's eighteen escort carriers were evenly distributed into three taskforces – Taffies. Each group of six was supported by a group of screening destroyers. The most north-westerly of the groups, Taffy 3, was off Samar when, at 06.47 hours, its commanding officer, Rear Admiral Clifton Sprague received a message from one of his Avenger pilots on anti-submarine patrol: 'Enemy surface force of four battleships, seven cruisers, and 11 destroyers sighted 20 miles northwest of your task group and closing in on you at 30 knots.' As this made no apparent sense, Sprague believed that the sighting was a case of mistaken identity. The 'enemy surface force' was probably just part of Halsey's fleet providing defensive cover. Exasperated, Sprague shouted into the squawk box, 'Air plot, tell him to check his identification,' and went back to work. His six escort carriers, screened by three destroyers and four destroyer escorts, were preparing to conduct more missions in support of the Leyte landings.

Three minutes after the first report, Sprague received another message from the pilot, Junior Ensign William C. Brooks. 'Identification of enemy force confirmed,' he radioed. 'I can see pagoda masts. I see the biggest meatball flag on the biggest battleship I ever saw.'[29]

Within minutes the splashes of large-calibre shells from Kurita's Centre Force began erupting all around Taffy 3, confirming Brooks's astonishing message, and the start of the naval Battle of Samar. The Japanese targeted the biggest US ships which Kurita, unfamiliar with the whole concept of merchant freighters converted for aircraft operations, mistook to be the Essex-class titans of Halsey's Third Fleet.

Taffy 3's escort carriers fled in a tight formation for the cover of rain squalls and launched all their aircraft in defence – Wildcats and Avengers equipped with whatever armament that had already been loaded – generally rockets and bombs for runs against ground targets or depth charges for attacking submarines. Very few carried anti-ship bombs or aerial torpedoes best suited to engaging enemies wrapped in heavy armour. In response, the Kurita's twenty-two-strong force divided itself, with single ships or small groups pursuing the escort carriers.

Kurita believed they had caught Halsey's Third Fleet off guard and needed to rush into attack before its vast complement of aircraft was launched against his taskforce. As his cruisers were the fastest, they were the first to engage, followed by the battleships and destroyers. Heavily outgunned and outnumbered, the prospects for Taffy 3's humble destroyers were especially bleak. The three Fletcher-class warships in the group were dubbed 'tin cans' because they lacked belt armour – supported by one destroyer escort, which had better armament, but fewer torpedoes. Undaunted, they did not turn and run but instead charged directly towards the looming armada. Lieutenant Commander Robert Copeland, aboard the destroyer escort *Samuel B. Roberts* – known to all as the *Sammy B.* – left his men in no doubt as to what they faced. From the loudspeaker, he announced that this would be 'a fight against overwhelming odds from which survival could not be expected, during which time we would do what damage we could.'

In a confused running battle, the best hopes of the tin can sailors rested with launching torpedoes while dodging counter-fire with smoke screens and zig-zagging manoeuvres. The most audacious took turns making runs at the Kurita's armada, creating the incredible spectacle of small destroyers trading salvos with vastly bigger battleships and cruisers, trying to draw fire, buy time, and protect the escort carriers. The destroyers' 5-inch guns had excellent rapid-fire capability but could only damage deck superstructures.

Perhaps the most brazen was Lieutenant Commander Ernest E. Evans, the 36-year-old officer in charge of the tin can destroyer *Johnston*. Evans, who was born in Oklahoma and had native American ancestry (his mother was Cherokee, his father was half White and half Creek Indian) rushed ahead of the other two Fletcher-class destroyers, *Hoel*, and *Heerman*, without waiting for orders. Evans, perhaps not expecting *Johnston* to last long, launched all 10 torpedoes and unleashed a barrage of nearly 200 rounds from the ship's 5-inch battery, which badly damaged the Japanese cruiser *Kumano*.

Only the mistaken assumption that it was facing a well-armoured cruiser and not a destroyer saved *Johnston* when *Yamato*'s mighty 18-inch guns took aim. At 07.30 hours, and from 20,300 yards (18,600 metres), the super battleship let rip with a single, full nine-gun broadside. *Yamato* fired armour-piercing shells, which passed through *Johnston*'s unarmoured hull without exploding. Seconds later, three 6.1-inch-high explosive shells from *Yamato*'s secondary battery did make their mark, smashed into superstructure and wreaking havoc. *Johnston* continued to take hits during this opening duel, which knocked out the power to the main steering and aft guns. One of the explosions peppered Evans with shrapnel, blew off two fingers of his left hand and shredded his shirt. Evans took *Johnston* into a nearby rainstorm, where his crew set about making emergency repairs.

The speed, lack of size, manoeuvrability and use of smoke combined with the poor weather made Taffy 3's destroyers awkward targets. But as the melee stretched towards 09.00 hours the odds shortened. During the two-hour battle, the tin can destroyers endured multiple strikes, with crews trying to cope with crippling damage and raging fires. *Hoel* actually went head-to-head against *Yamato*, causing one of her crew to quip, 'What we need is a bugler to sound the charge.' The destroyer took a series of catastrophic blows and was listing badly when, at 08.30 hours, the abandon ship order was finally given. Just before 09.00 hours, *Hoel* rolled over and sank. Only 86 of her complement survived; 253 officers and men went down with the ship.

No less fearless, *Sammy B.* was taking on the cruisers *Chōkai* and *Chikuma*. The destroyer escort moved so close that the enemy guns could not be depressed enough to hit her. One of the three torpedoes they launched blew off *Chōkai*'s stern. The crew engaged with the Japanese ships for a further hour, firing 608 of her 650 shells and even launching star shells and anti-aircraft rounds while manoeuvring. Their luck ran out when a 14-inch shell blew a massive hole in the aft side of the engine room. At 09.35 hours, the order to abandon ship was given, by which time ninety of the crew were dead. Some 120 survivors made it to life rafts.

Despite having run out of torpedoes, and operating on reduced engine power, the destroyer *Johnston* had by now returned to the fray. Lieutenant Commander Evans saw that the escort carrier *Gambier Bay* was taking heavy fire from a Japanese cruiser. He directed *Johnston*'s guns to open up against the cruiser to draw her attention away from *Gambier Bay*, but it was to no avail – the carrier was dead in the water and soon sinking. An approaching force of Japanese destroyers then tried to add to the carnage by attacking the other escorts, but they launched torpedoes from too great a distance to reach their targets and then, miraculously, turned and withdrew, as if discouraged, which led Evans to comment, 'Now I've seen everything.'

His own ship was riddled with hits and going down. *Johnston*'s crew kept firing until her 5-inch guns were submerged. One of the last sightings of Evans saw him bare chested and bloodied on the fantail, shouting instructions. At 09.45 hours he finally gave the order to abandon ship. As the Japanese destroyer *Yukikaze* closed to point blank range, the survivors expected to be machine-gunned in the water, but *Yukikaze*'s captain saluted and ordered his crew to stand at attention. *Johnston* rolled over and sank at 10.10 hours. Of her complement of 327 men, 141 would survive. Evans was not amongst them. He was observed heading for a life raft but was never seen again. Posthumously, he became the first native American to be awarded a Medal of Honor.

Gambier Bay was the only US Navy carrier sunk by enemy surface gunfire during the Second World War. She went down with the loss of 109 men, and some 800 survivors were later rescued by landing craft. A second carrier, the *St Lo*, foundered later in the morning after a Luzon-based formation of Japanese aircraft passed along her starboard side. Anti-aircraft fire poured upwards, but a single Zero peeled off and made a sudden looping turn down towards the carrier. The aircraft disintegrated into a ball of fire on striking a glancing blow to the deck but two of its bombs punched through to the hangar below. The explosions ignited fuel and the munitions storage area, engulfing the carrier in secondary blasts and towering flames. *St Lo* sank 30 minutes later, taking 126 crew with her to the bottom. About 750 men survived what was recorded as the first major warship lost to an organised kamikaze attack.

Kurita's Centre Force had lost three cruisers to air attacks, and another three others were badly damaged during the chaotic engagement. The Japanese ships continued to be besieged by air attacks. Taffy 2's complement of planes had joined the fray, and other American aircraft were refuelling at Tacloban airfield before returning to harass the fleet. Low on fuel and unable to cut off the retreating escort carriers, Kurita ordered his ships to make for its assigned target – the anchorage at Leyte Gulf. They steamed south until, around 12.30 hours, Kurita unexpectedly ordered them to turn around. Aboard the *Yamato* word passed that an enemy fleet sighted to the north and they were moving to engage.

In fact, the decision baffled some members of his senior staff and was debated by scholars on both sides long afterwards, including no less a figure than Winston Churchill who, in the last volume of his books about the Second World War, suggested: 'It may well be that [his] mind had become confused by the pressure of events … Those who have endured a similar ordeal may judge him.'

Kurita had been on *Yamato*'s bridge for almost forty-eight hours straight. To those who viewed his decision to withdraw favourably, the old sea dog had probably calculated that by continuing on he would sacrifice what remained of the fleet and their crews for little gain. By this point, Kurita would have learnt that the Southern Fleet had been destroyed. As the landings had taken place five days before, they would be racing to sink empty transport ships. Doing so would keep his ships within range of American air attacks from land and sea, and Allied naval reinforcements would surely arrive from the north and south, which meant being trapped in a duel in the gulf with no route back east. Convinced his ships had already delivered a significant blow, he duly pulled back. To those who judged his decision negatively, Kurita acted dishonourably, if not cowardly. He had not completed his mission and by withdrawing the Northern and Southern Fleets had sacrificed themselves in vain.

Kurita's ships were subjected to further air attacks for the rest of the day but escaped back down the San Bernardino Strait before Halsey's forces could get to them. The bulk of the Third Fleet remained preoccupied with sinking Ozawa's carriers. The battle took place the following day off Cape Engaño, a peninsula at the north-west tip of Luzon. From first light to early afternoon, the Northern Fleet was decimated by 527 American sorties that had sent all the carriers, including *Zuikaku*, to the bottom, along with a number of destroyers. Ozawa did evade Halsey again and escaped back towards Japan aboard one of two converted First World War dreadnoughts, but the Battle of Leyte Gulf was over.

In all, Allied losses amounted to seven warships, including the light carrier *Princeton* and two escort carriers, *Gambier Bay* and *St Lo*. Over the 3 days of fighting some 1,000 Americans died, a heavy toll comparable to the combined fatalities of American men and ships at the Battle of the Coral Sea and Midway. The IJN had suffered its greatest defeat – twenty-eight warships, including one fleet and three smaller aircraft carriers, three battleships (including *Musashi*), ten cruisers and eleven destroyers. Around 10,500 IJN sailors were killed. The fighting had not ended Japan's resistance in the Philippines, but it had finally broken the back of its navy as an offensive force in the Pacific War.

* * *

Near the southern tip of Leyte, the jungle highway divides ahead of where the island becomes two fingers of land. Glad to be leaving the outback, I took the right side and headed in the direction of Sogod Bay. The road ran parallel to a winding river and down through forested hills towards sea level. Once out of the bush a long body of water stretched out before me and the telegraph poles and wires reappeared. Bay side villages of tin roof houses, roadside stores and parked-up tricycles slipped past. My destination was Southern Leyte Divers, at the end of my chosen tip, and where the bay opens out to the ocean.

The dive centre was on its own at a beachfront site just before the small town of San Roque, and down an elevated single-track road that led across mangroves. Parked up and, with no one around, I wandered inside. The resort was formed of one white painted main building and a small collection of native-styled bungalows, all set peacefully amongst mature coconut trees and either side of a concrete courtyard. The hallmarks of adventure were immediately at hand. Work areas for scuba diving, including rinsing tanks to remove seawater and sand, storage for air cylinders, and hanging rails for drying gear all looked in pleasingly good order.

The beach front bungalows were simple, single-story and square, but raised up from sea level, with steps leading up to a veranda. A low wall separated the front of the resort from a narrow ribbon of shoreline lined by lazy coconut trees with trunks that slouched over the sand. To one side, sun loungers awaited on a raised concrete area. I made a plan to crash out there and watch the sun go down.

To enter the main building was to step inside a tropical world of wood furniture, rattan panels and bamboo joists in an open plan area. It served as the reception and bar/dining room. I looked across at ten empty dining tables where there was space for about thirty people. The skull of a decent-sized barracuda decorated the rattan wall behind the bar, with some rather less fearsome shark jaws for company. The entrance side of the room had more of a lounge feel, with a small library and a dart board set on the wall. A large wooden model of a white-painted dive expedition boat, *Mind Games*, had pride of place in the space where, in other parts of the world, you might see a fireplace.

Günter Mosch, the owner, appeared and welcomed me with a steady, unhurried bearing of someone who has owned a business in an out of the way place for much of his adult life. Grey, bearded and somewhere in his sixties, he asked lightly about my travels, and we sat down to go over the diving options. It soon became clear there were no other guests – a reality that, along with a forecast of more bad weather, turned out to drastically limit the possibilities for some unscheduled exploring. There weren't any wartime wrecks within reach, so I asked about a trip out to Limasawa, an island about two hours south by boat. Günter shrugged: the sea conditions were poor and there was no one else around, even at the two other dive resorts in Sogod Bay, so it was not feasible to put a trip together. My hopes of diving in the company of whale sharks fared no better. I was about a month early, he said. They pass through these waters from November and, in a good season, are in the area until the end of May. The best he could do was organise a couple of shore dives in the protected waters of Sogod Bay. Having driven all day, more in hope than planned good judgement, I signed the papers and set myself up for a couple of nights in one of the beach bungalows while I considered my next move.

I had managed to be in Leyte in the same month that the 1944 Allied invasion took place – October, which is peak rainy season. Nothing about the lack of out of season options was hugely surprising, but I had to make peace with the part of me that did not want to miss anything. I lay on my bed in the bungalow, staring at the ceiling fan as it turned, doing my own *Apocalypse Now* Captain Willard-style reckoning. The practical restrictions of time, budget, weather, seasons, and foreign languages were all making their presence felt. Whale sharks would have been wonderful to see but are not exclusive to southern Leyte. Limasawa, however, felt like a blow. I had learned that it was the second island (after Suluan in Eastern Samar) that Magellan visited in 1521 – and the first place in the Philippines where a Catholic mass was held. All this before the great navigator headed west to Cebu, upset the locals, and met a grisly end. As much as I wanted to physically connect with the history, I could not face the idea of being fed-up in somewhere as wild and off the beaten track as southern Leyte, which was special in itself, so after an hour or so, I resolved to make the best of it.

The next day I did two relaxed shore dives in Sogod Bay and spent my final evening at the bar, chatting with Günter and a Filipino dive guide from another resort, Pedro Batesi, who had no guests and was making a social call with his neighbour. With no TV or music playing, the only background noise was the cicadas doing their thing. In this laid-back, outback atmosphere, we began with the usual dive talk – where have you been, the whale sharks, favourite sites, and so on.

Raising the topic of the Second World War with a German host felt surprisingly awkward – beyond asking about wrecks, which made for a short conversation. Nothing had been found in southern Leyte within recreational diving range. We were also some distance from the shores of the Surigao Strait, where a handful of Japanese survivors from Nishimura's sunken Southern Force made it to land – only to be shot or hacked to death by Filipino guerrillas. Sogod Bay, by contrast, was a peaceful place that had escaped the worst of the fighting.

So I shared some of my overall impressions of the Philippines with Günter – it struck me as a nation of toil, where everything bustled and nothing came easily. Was it a hard-work Asian culture like Japan or Korea?

'The hardest workers,' he countered, 'are the ones who go overseas and send money back home. People here – one day of hard work, and they want to party.'

I'd read that the country remains, in many ways, rooted in feudalism – especially on islands like Leyte, where agriculture dominates the economy. Most farmers don't own the land they work and are often forced to labour for landlords who profit from rent, high-interest loans, and low crop prices. In such a system, it was simply the way of things that local bosses called all the shots.

Günter turned up his face at the mention of politics. 'What I don't like is the authorities. They give you a hard time. It's nothing to do with that Philippine friendliness. As a foreigner, it's just your money they want.'

He paused for a beat, then softened the thought. 'I'm still happy here. I like the sea – I'm a diver. I still love the weather apart from typhoons. Even on the days it rains, it's something special.'

On and on we went, over cold San Miguels and beneath the slow-turning ceiling fans. Günter was originally from Karlsruhe, a small German city near the French border. He started diving in 1978 and, after working in the Maldives, Egypt, and Palawan, set out in search of more pristine, untouched dive locations.

It was in Palawan that he met Alona, who came from southern Leyte – a place that, in its own way, felt more remote than anywhere he'd travelled. They got married in Germany, had two sons, and hatched a plan to set up a business near San Roque, her hometown. They started running dive tours in 1997 and were steadily building a successful resort until, late on the afternoon of 16 December 2021, Typhoon Odette did its best to level their dream.

'At the start, you stay calm and make preparations,' said Günter. 'The emergency warning system worked well.'

At least a week out, text alerts – still the most reliable way to reach islanders – had raised the prospect of a super typhoon hitting the Visayas, giving communities time to lock down or evacuate. Alert levels ran from 1 to 5, with 5 representing extreme danger.

'The day the typhoon came in, the warning was at level 3. It escalated to level 5 within two hours,' he said.

By the time Odette made landfall, the Mosch family was camped inside the resort. The sea state was so rough that it was impossible to get their dive boats at anchor any further from harm's way by hauling them out onto the shore.

'It started getting dark at 4pm, and the first branches came down,' Günter recalled. 'Roof sheets were flying. Around 7pm, we were in one of the downstairs rooms when my son said, "Papa – flood!" All of a sudden, a storm surge came through the whole resort. Water everywhere. It was rising up the steps of the elevated bungalows.'

He paused. 'I was thinking, is this the first or second stage of the typhoon? I said, "Let's go upstairs," because there was no more chance to go outside – too much flying debris. The roof was already gone, so it was pouring.' Then came silence.

'All of a sudden, quiet. People were happy – "It's over!" But then … shit. We'd been in the eye. And then came the worst.' He shook his head slightly. 'Before the eye, the wind came from the west. After that, it came from all directions. Like a tornado. It sounded like a roaring train.'

The storm raged for over four appalling hours. They held out in one of the other resort rooms that could still provide cover. By the time it was over, Günter's pride and joy, the dive expedition boat *Mind Games*, was smashed to pieces. The resort's second dive boat, which had been under construction, fared only marginally better. None of the damage was insured.

Günter spoke with the dry, even tone of a project manager and it was hard to imagine him being emotional. Yet the storm left him bereft, a howling vortex that tore his life's work apart, in its own way echoing the roar of wartime history itself: indiscriminate, unrelenting, swallowing old certainties. 'In the morning I was crying. All the work, 15 years, gone. At this point I had not even seen the full damage to the resort, I just knew the boats were gone. I took a walk around, the air cons were 30 metres away in the mangroves, debris everywhere. I didn't go there for the next seven or eight days. I just couldn't stand it. We had no electricity for seven to eight days. Fortunately, we had water, we fixed the lines. Then I was sitting down, without even estimating, I was thinking, is it worth it to rebuild? But what else can you do?'

* * *

The most compelling of Leyte's artefacts may be beyond the scope of battlefield tourism, but that does not mean they are completely out of reach. The world's most extreme expeditionist, Victor Vescovo, has chalked up a list of travels and accomplishments that might seem far-fetched to an adventure novelist. Finding and diving on the wrecks of *Samuel B. Roberts* and *Johnston*, two of the defiant heroes of Taffy 3, and the world's deepest shipwrecks discovered to date, would not even top the list.

Vescovo, a private equity investor from Texas, was the first person in history to have climbed to the summit of all the world's continents, visited both poles, as well as descended to the deepest parts of all five oceans. Primarily a mountaineering enthusiast, his on-land achievements took fifteen years to complete. They required reaching the highest seven peaks, including Mount Everest, and skiing over 100 kilometres (62 miles) to both the North and South Poles.

Vescovo, who served as an intelligence officer in the US Navy Reserve for twenty years, then tackled the maritime challenges in a titanium submersible that he helped fund and develop. He descended to the abyssal trenches in the Atlantic Ocean (Puerto Rico Trench); the Indian Ocean (Java Trench); the Southern Ocean (South Sandwich Trench); the Pacific Ocean (Mariana Trench); and the Arctic Ocean (Molloy Deep). The fact Vescovo made the first solo submersible dive to the wreck of *Titanic* barely gets a mention.

To literally and figuratively top it all, in June 2022 Vescovo flew into space aboard Blue Origin's reusable suborbital launch vehicle, *New Shepard*, which is being developed for space tourism by Amazon mogul Jeff Bezos.

His undersea expeditions demonstrate how cutting-edge exploration technology can recover fragments of history from the planet's most inaccessible places. In tracing the wrecks of Taffy 3, he proved that even in the hardest to reach, most hostile corners of the planet, echoes of the Second World War still wait to be discovered.

In 2021, a deep ocean expedition led by Vescovo confirmed the identity of some large pieces of wreckage as belonging to *Johnston.* The artefacts had been located in 2019 by the Vulcan group, backed by the estate of the late Paul Allen of Microsoft fame.

Vulcan's team used an unmanned remotely operated vehicle (ROV) that had a depth limit of 6,000 metres (19,685 feet). They discovered a deck gun, a propeller shaft, and some miscellaneous debris that they felt sure belonged to *Johnston.* Yet Vulcan's researchers saw nothing to conclusively prove wreckage came from one of Taffy 3's destroyers. Although they pushed past their depth limit and risked losing the ROV, the Vulcan team could not get deep enough to confirm the origin of the wreckage. Vescovo's search was conducted in a two-person submersible, *Limiting Factor*, which was built for him by the Florida-based Triton Submarines. The pressure hull is a titanium sphere and, together with the support system around it, represents one of the world's most exotic pieces of maritime hardware. It is rated to full ocean depth, 11,000 metres (36,000 feet). They actually pressure tested *Limiting Factor* far beyond that limit, taking it to 14,000 metres (46,000 feet) at a scientific facility in Russia. On the third attempt to find *Johnston*, Vescovo and his co-pilot descended to the seabed at 6,468 metres (21,222 feet). They arrived at the debris previously filmed by the Vulcan ROV. After following a V-shaped gouge in the seafloor, the submersible's lights fell upon the front two thirds of the destroyer. *Johnston*'s naval identification number, 557, was still resplendent in white paint on the grey hull.

The footage put the warship into the *Guinness Book of Records* as the world's deepest discovered shipwreck. The following year, Vescovo returned to the same area off Samar and found the *Sammy B. Roberts* lying almost 400 metres (1,300 feet) deeper at 6,865 metres (22,523 feet), setting a new record.

The destroyers had come to rest in the hadal zone. It starts some 6,000 metres (19,685 feet) below the surface. *Johnston* was so full of holes from battle damage that any trapped air could escape which meant the hull did not rupture on the long fall to the bottom. *Sammy B.* met a different fate, the stern blown off on the way down – either because the hull could not equalise the air trapped inside or due to one of the depth charges exploding.

The hadal zone exists along the boundary where the Earth's vast tectonic plates collide and converge, one inexorably dragged beneath the other by gravity and immense geological forces. This relentless movement carves abyssal scars – long, narrow V-shaped chasms of eternal darkness. The trenches stretch across thousands of kilometres of ocean, rendering the odds of finding a broken-up destroyer that tumbled into the abyss vanishingly small.

Hades, the Ancient Greek god of the underworld, was a strange fish to rule in this kingdom: it has a darkness so absolute that no plants or phytoplankton have ever existed. The water temperature hovers just about freezing, and the pressure is around 1,000 times that at sea level. There is so little oxygen and aquatic life that the wartime wrecks have been spared corrosion and are considered pristine time capsules.

Johnston has very little of the decay evident on, say, *Titanic*. The ill-fated White Star liner resides at 'only' half the depth, some 3,800 metres (12,500) feet. It is gradually disintegrating, a process speeded up by bacteria that have colonised its metal hull, producing reddish-brown stalactites of rust that hang down like icicles from the superstructure.

The images filmed by the Vescovo expeditions show the forward two thirds of *Johnston* still sat upright. The hull is buried in the sand up to the waterline. Her forward 5-inch guns are trained to the right, as though the ship was still targeting an enemy. The impact points where Kurita's 18.1-inch shells riddled the hull, punching into the sides and wrecking her superstructure are clearly evident. *Johnston* is believed to have split in two at some point on the descent in the area where she took one of these hammer blows, leaving the destroyer's back third undiscovered. Nevertheless, the bridge is still intact and recognisable. Blast damage is clearly visible from a smaller 6.1-inch shell fired by *Yamato* that tore a hole beneath the bridge where Evans, commanding the ship, had his fingers and shirt blown off.

Vescovo, who describes himself as a military history buff, invested $51 million of his own money in developing *Limiting Factor* and running the ultra-deep ocean expeditions. After these and other record-breaking dives he sold off his controlling stake and business interests in maritime exploration. That may mean the wrecks of the escort carrier *Gambier Bay*, the tin can destroyer *Hoel* and the Japanese ships lost during the Battle of Leyte Gulf are not discovered any time soon. They are thought to rest in even deeper water, perhaps as far down as 8,000 metres (26,246 feet) but the new owners of the submersible and its surface mother ship apparently have no interest in wartime wrecks.

Vescovo's endeavours put him in an elite club. The most prolific explorer of Second World War deep ocean wrecks, Paul Allen/Vulcan, discovered and surveyed twenty-six major warships. These include the IJN fleet carriers *Akagi*, and *Kaga*, and the super battleship *Musashi*; and three American carriers, *Wasp*, *Hornet* and *Lexington*, along with three heavy cruisers – *Indianapolis*, *Vincennes*, *Astoria*, and two light cruisers, *Helena*, and *Juneau*.

Vescovo was not content to merely discover what happened to these ships. That could be achieved with unmanned submersibles, as per the Vulcan expeditions. Vescovo wanted to risk it all by personally venturing down into the eternal darkness. The level of danger, cost and technical challenge, when put together with all his other outlandish achievements contributed to my own oddly unsympathetic first reading of the adventurer. Are the peaks and troughs of the Earth really just a numbers game, notches on a travel belt? The language used to describe some of his expeditions does not help. Vescovo may object to any form of words that suggests a mastery of nature, but you still must get past a wealth of material about him which uses terms such as 'conquering' Everest.

Further investigation suggested someone more sympathetic and well-intentioned. Tall and rangy, Vescovo has a presence one journalist who has spent time with him described as 'more warm than imposing.' When interviewed by *D Magazine* for a cover story called 'The Most Interesting Man in Dallas',[30] Vescovo was happy to talk about himself as a nerd and as someone who, despite his highly public global adventures, is an introvert by nature. Born in 1966, Vescovo talked of his love of scientific fiction and historical non-fiction over other literature. His parents split when he was 16. Vescovo's father worked in commercial real estate; his mother was a nurse. He spoke of following her much more reserved, cerebral, and methodical approach to life.

Vescovo studied at Stanford University, double majoring in economics and political science. He then earned a degree from Massachusetts Institute of Technology in defence and arms control and followed this with an MBA from Harvard Business School. He made his fortune in private equity, following stints on Wall Street and at Bain Consulting. Along with his former boss at Bain, he left to form his own company, Insight Equity, which focuses on industrial and defence turnarounds. Somewhere in all this, Vescovo found the time to take his passion for mountaineering to extremes before going to the deepest places on Earth.

The Texan keeps his faded auburn hair pulled into a faintly counter-cultural ponytail and sports a pointy white beard. Others have observed that while Vescovo is wealthy by any conventional measure, and one of the handful of people to have so far defined the limits of twenty-first century experiential tourism, he has relatively humble means compared to his extremely adventurous peers. His own personal wealth is dwarfed by the handful of movers and shakers in this billionaires' travellers club. They are led of course by Elon Musk, who is focused on Mars. Following closely behind is Bezos, who is periodically the richest individual on Earth. Bezos created Blue Origin as a step towards making astro tourism real and the commercialisation of the heavens possible, envisioning a time 'when people can tap into the limitless resources of space and enable the movement of damaging industries into space to preserve [the] Earth, humanity's blue origin.'

Vescovo was one of the six people on the fifth manned Blue Origin flight in June 2022. A ticket cost $1.25 million and the journey lasted for ten minutes. They launched from Blue Origin's facility in west Texas, reached a peak of 347,538 feet (106 kilometres) above ground level, before the vessel parachuted safely into the nearby desert. The Kármán line, generally considered the dividing line between Earth's atmosphere and space, is about 100 kilometres (328,084 feet) above the planet. One of the other passengers was the British billionaire Hamish Harding, who was to perish twelve months later in the OceanGate *Titan* submersible that imploded on the way down to visit *Titanic*.

Vescovo knew Hamish Harding well and considered him a friend, as he did the French deep sea explorer Paul-Henri Nargeolet, who died in the same incident. The OceanGate *Titan* saga waved a giant red flag about the extremes of tourism, whatever it seeks to discover. As the expedition took place in international waters, the vessel's designer, Stockton Rush, was able to avoid certification and use untested carbon fibre instead of proven steel or titanium for the pressure hull. Together with his choice of a cylinder as opposed to a sphere, the strongest geometric shape, to make more space for paying passengers, Rush eventually proved what his critics said all along: *Titan* was a death trap.

Vescovo has survived venturing to extremes, he says, by avoiding delusion and de-risking ventures with relentlessly detailed preparation. It includes robustly investigating the pitfalls of any process, realistically appraising potential hazards and by making testing and accreditation paramount. He is acutely aware of what mountaineers' call 'summit fever', pilots classify as 'plan continuation bias', and lesser mortals might describe as 'get there itis'. He prides himself on pulling the plug before any given situation gets out of control. He felt that OceanGate's business model was financially precarious. It meant that cancelling expeditions or even going back to the drawing board when concerns were raised about the technology became insurmountable hurdles in themselves.

Vescovo is not a monosyllabic technologist and, in other interviews, has spoken in relatable ways about the surreal experience of going to the depths where the Leyte wrecks now reside.

He chose the adjectives ancient, quiet and ominous as the best means of describing the sense of the ultra-deep ocean.

> You can't see that far, maybe 20–30 metres with all the lights blasting so it always feels like the deep ocean is hiding its secrets from you. You don't know what is near you until you are almost on top of it, so there is that feeling of being in a huge, dark, quiet house and you know you really shouldn't be there – the outside pressure would kill you instantly. But it is so old, and has amazing and unusual life forms that exist nowhere else on Earth. It has to be as close to exploring another planet as anything else on our world. It is so different from going into space, which is loud and violent with amazing thousand-kilometre views, or climbing Everest with the wind, noise, cold, hypoxia, and raw physical danger. No, the deep oceans are ominous, brooding, and perhaps most of all, mysterious.

* * *

I said my farewells at Southern Leyte Divers, packed up the jalopy and headed north to complete my circuit of the island. Maasin, a workaday hub of ferry terminals and docks, offered no particular reason to stop in the pouring rain. It took all morning to get up the west coast towards Ormoc, a small port that once provided the only means of getting reinforcements and supplies to the increasingly beleaguered Japanese forces in the north-west corner of the island.

Ormoc is best known today for providing a maritime link between Leyte and Cebu. The oldest buildings were constructed in the post-war period as Ormoc was laid to waste in the fighting during 1944. The former city hall, now the People's Museum, was not built until 1947 when it was the centrepiece of the reconstruction. There is a memorial to Filipino resistance in Veterans Park on the waterfront. The neat horseshoe-shaped bay has a peaceful ambience, with barely any shoreline development beyond the central area. The waters are the resting place of several wartime wrecks, but the notable sites are well beyond the reach of scuba diving and Ormoc's tourist facilities did not, in any case, include a dive centre.

Disaster has been one of Ormoc's regular visitors. In 2013, the typhoon winds of Yolanda shredded much of the city's-built infrastructure, badly damaging Ormoc's hospital, cutting power and blocking roads with debris and downed telegraph poles. A storm surge that swept in from Ormoc Bay reached up to the second story of buildings. Yet as lethal as Yolanda proved across all of the Eastern Visayas, it actually caused fewer casualties in Ormoc than 1991's Typhoon Uring (internationally named Thelma), which was about half as powerful.

Uring reached a peak intensity with estimated ten-minute sustained winds of 75 kilometres per hour (45 mph) but the interaction of the typhoon with high terrain above Ormoc produced a three-hour biblical torrent of rain. At the peak of the flooding, rivers broke their banks and waters rose by just over 2 metres (7 feet), according to a 1992 report by the Manila Observatory, a scientific research institution. The flash floods wreaked havoc and buried sections of western plains of the province in water, sediment and debris. At least 4,000 people were killed. When the waters receded, the floods left behind sediment that was a metre-deep in places. Aside from the intense rainfall, the Manila Observatory identified other factors that contributed to the devastation. While the illegal logging and deforestation were to blame for the landslides, geographic conditions in the area also had to be considered. The soil in the Ormoc watershed exceeded its capacity to hold water, while the central part of the island of Leyte, classified as volcanic terrain, has earth that is susceptible to erosion. The problems were also exacerbated by debris from poorly made infrastructure while one of the worst hit areas in Ormoc city centre, Isla Verde, recorded a high death toll because it was a known risk flood area that was allowed to be heavily over-populated.

In the aftermath of the disaster, Ormoc's municipal government set about improving its infrastructure, including reforestation projects in the hills. In this they received support from Japan's International Cooperation Agency, which conducted studies and flood mitigation projects. These included slit dams for landslide reduction, and improvement of the drainage of rivers in the city. The projects did their job when, just over a decade later, Yolanda battered Ormoc and the surrounding hills, limiting the secondary effects of the storm.

The Japanese forces on and around Ormoc in late 1944 had little hope of stopping the flood of American air, sea and land resources closing in on them. All that could be achieved was to draw out the fighting for as long as possible and inflict as many casualties as ammunition and supplies would allow. As elsewhere in Pacific Island warfare, the ability to hold out for a sustained period rested on the arrival of extra combatants, ammunition and food, in this case, dispatched from Manila.

The IJN operation eventually landed some 34,000 troops at Ormoc in destroyer and transport dashes. The new arrivals doubled the size of the defensive force on Leyte, but the convoys suffered terrible losses to marauding US carrier aircraft and warships. US Navy destroyers also intercepted landing ships. The Battle of Ormoc Bay was fought between 11 and 21 November, with the most brutal engagement sending four IJN destroyers, a minesweeper, and five packed transports to the bottom. It represented the last major effort to bolster the forces ashore. Nevertheless, the besieged IJN troops fought on defiantly, even mounting a series of counterattacks, and smaller groups of reinforcements did continue to make it to shore for another month.

The strength of the resistance and difficulty of taking the high ground between Leyte Valley and Ormoc contributed to what was considered a slow American advance, which ultimately delayed MacArthur's plans to advance on Luzon.

After the 20 October landings, 10th Corps pushed up Leyte Valley and past Tacloban to secure the northern coast of the island. At the same time, 26th Corps fought its way inland and sent one division overland to the west coast. The former would fight across the northern highlands to get into the north-west province via Ormoc Valley. The latter could cross the island and work its way up the west coast, completing a pincer movement.

As frustration at the lack of progress grew, a second amphibious landing was ordered by Lieutenant General Krueger to augment the plan. On 7 December, some 8,500 men and equipment of the reserve 77th Infantry Division landed just south of Ormoc, catching the IJN in the area off guard. The US Army landing was unopposed but subjected to kamikaze air attacks. After three days of heavy fighting, some of it street-to-street, the port town was in ruins but under American control.

The second landing prompted an IJN withdrawal and reorganisation. It meant the US Army troops advancing through the mountains in the north suddenly encountered less resistance. The push over the top picked up pace and units began to take hilltop after hilltop. The combination of artillery barrages, flame throwers, and hand-to-hand combat did the rest and eventually wore down Japanese resistance in Ormoc Valley. Though there remained almost two months of 'mopping up' operations, Leyte was officially secured on Christmas Day 1944.

A bleak account of the fate of one Japanese replacement company sent to Leyte during the final weeks is told in the semi-autobiographical Japanese novel, *Fires on the Plain*[31], which was published in 1951 and has twice been made into a film, in 1957 and 2014. It's loosely based on author Shōhei Ōoka's experience fighting on Leyte and made for compelling reading during my time on the island. It is not about the nobility of fighting a lost cause. Instead, the characters are presented as an embodiment of Japan's living death and decay into barbarism.

The protagonist is Private First Class Tamura. His company survived an ocean passage and made it to Ormoc but lost all its artillery on route, sunk on another transport. Tamura is thrown out by his own unit as he is too weak to fight and suffering from tuberculosis. Rejected once by an overflowing field hospital, he's sent back again by his squad leader and told to kill himself if denied care a second time. Tamura wanders aimlessly through the Leyte jungle where remnants of the IJA are gradually being encircled by the American-Filipino forces. Guerrillas, determined to avenge the brutal Japanese occupation, light the signal fires of the title for communication, to report sightings of Japanese on the run.

With every step, Tamura's odyssey becomes bleaker. All of the Japanese troops on Leyte are badly malnourished and spend their days foraging for food. Tamura survives by eating raw grass and leeches. At a seemingly abandoned village he finds rotting corpses of Japanese troops, apparently killed by locals, and piled up like logs. Tamura stabs a starving dog to death with his bayonet before noticing a Filipino man and woman approaching the empty village in a canoe. He follows them into a hut where, on seeing him, the woman screams. Tamura tries to placate her by lowering the gun, but she remains hysterical, so he shoots her dead, while her companion escapes back to the sea. Tamura finds the prize the couple had been seeking – a cache of salt hidden under the floorboards. He flees back into the jungle with his stolen goods before the guerillas can arrive, dropping his rifle in the process.

Tamura then chances upon three soldiers from a different company. He is told that the whole army has orders to withdraw to Palompon, on the coast just above Ormoc Bay. From Palompon they will try to evacuate to Cebu.

The three men are the only survivors from a battle for the Burauen airfields. Like everyone else he meets, they are filthy and suffering from malnutrition. One jokes about having eaten the dead people during a previous campaign in New Guinea and warns Tamura against joining forces with them lest he becomes a meal. In the end Tamura pays in salt, which is treated like a delicacy, for the privilege of accompanying the three men to Palompon.

They link with a larger, bedraggled group with the same plan. It includes two men from his original unit – Nagamatsu and Yasuda. Most of them are then massacred by American tanks and machine guns near the Ormoc Road. In the chaos Tamura slips away alone into the jungle.

Tamura, once a soldier, now becomes a spectre, drifting again through a landscape littered with dead comrades. It is a world stripped of meaning, where the only choices left are to kill, be killed, or be consumed. One starving, delirious, soldier staggers up a hill and dies in front of him, his last words, 'It's been raining forever.'

Later, Tamura finds another deranged soldier propped up against a tree, out of his mind with starvation, and eating his own excrement. The dying rake raises an arm, telling Tamura he should eat the bony limb when he's gone. Our protagonist moves on but collapses soon afterwards. He's found by Nagamatsu, who, it turns out, also escaped the massacre with the injured Yasuda. Tamura is given water and promised food.

If anything, when the three are back together, the two men with food look even worse than Tamura. Both show signs of paranoid delusion. Each privately confides to Tamura that they fear the other will kill them given the opportunity. Nagamatsu shares 'monkey meat' with Tamura, who tries to chew it only for his teeth to fall out. Later, after hearing a shot, Tamura sees Nagamatsu aiming at a Filipino civilian who is running away. He realises that the 'monkeys' his comrade had been hunting were other human beings.

The story ends with the three starving men stalking each other. Nagamatsu kills Yasuda and sets about his corpse with a machete, manically removing slabs of skin and bone. Amid the hellish gore, Tamura shoots the butcher dead. Walking off towards the horizon, Tamura appears to want to try surrendering to local farmers. It is not an act of hope but resignation, the last step in an odyssey where even survival feels like abject defeat, a metaphor for all of Imperial Japan.

An estimated 49,000 Japanese military personnel gave their lives for the emperor in the efforts to defend Leyte. The critical loss of twenty-six IJN warships and hundreds of aircraft in the Battle of Leyte Gulf was made even worse at Ormoc Bay, where another six destroyers, twenty small transport vessels, one submarine, one patrol boat and three escort vessels were eventually sent to the bottom.

The US Navy lost another three destroyers to torpedoes and kamikaze attacks in Ormoc Bay, along with one high-speed transport and two medium landing ships. The overall Leyte campaign cost American forces a total of 15,584 casualties, of which 3,504 were killed in action.

The defeat on land, combined with Japan's catastrophic losses in the Battle of Leyte Gulf, set the stage for MacArthur's next target: Luzon. The difficulty of establishing airfields on rain-soaked Leyte made Mindoro, with its drier climate, the logical alternative for US fighter operations. Securing the island took only three days, and from there, MacArthur's flyers could strike Clark Field, Corregidor, and Manila Bay. With the Luzon invasion countdown on, Halsey's mighty carrier force was once again mustered. They did not face any significant opposition from the IJN but the fleet was not beyond harm's way. Typhoon Cobra, a compact cyclone of monstrous force, was about to tear through Halsey's fleet as if to remind the admirals that theirs was not the only power in the Pacific.

Aircraft from elements of the Third Fleet had been pounding IJA targets on Luzon when the extreme weather closed in. The conditions began to drastically deteriorate on 17 December, making at-sea refuelling operations impossible. Many of Halsey's ships were low on fuel due to the continuous high-tempo combat operations. In the era before weather satellites and computer modelling, avoiding typhoons depended on old school weather forecasting and a 'seaman's eye'. The techniques were far from foolproof and the problem with Typhoon Cobra, which would sweep over Halsey's ships in a matter of hours, was that although it was intensely powerful, its size and movement meant the gravity of the situation was not apparent until the maelstrom was almost upon them.

A handful of images captured during the disaster show the light carriers – built on cruiser hulls and known for their poor sea-keeping qualities – rolling at harrowing angles, some up to 70°. Aircraft were torn from their moorings and washed overboard. Aboard *Monterey* – whose crew included a future US president, Gerald R. Ford – one plane broke loose on the hangar deck, slammed into a bulkhead, and sparked a fire that claimed the lives of three sailors. In all, eighteen aircraft were destroyed – either consumed by flames or swallowed by the sea – while another sixteen were battered as they careened wildly through the hangar bay in the relentless motion.

It got far worse, and the smaller ships faced the gravest danger. *Spence*, a Fletcher-class destroyer, was nearly out of fuel, and all attempts to resupply her failed amid the tumultuous seas. During one of the violent rolls, seawater entered the ship, short-circuiting the electrical system and jamming the rudder hard to starboard. At 11.10 hours, *Spence* rolled deeply to port and righted herself – only to be struck by another monstrous wave moments later, this time capsizing and sinking with 317 of her crew. She became the first US destroyer lost to a typhoon.

A sister ship, *Hull*, faced a similar fate. The destroyer was top heavy as she had over 500 tons of extra weapons and equipment added. *Hull* experienced rolls of 50° that got progressively worse until a blast of wind estimated at 110 knots pinned the ship down on her beam ends, and water poured down the funnels and into the pilothouse. *Hull* capsized and sank a few minutes after midday, with 202 of her crew lost.

Nature – unbound by strategy, deaf to command – took its toll with those towering waves. No valour could anchor a ship; no voice, however resolute, could summon its salvation. In time, the storm passed, as all storms do – indifferent to the names of men it had claimed or the flags they served. And when the sea grew still again, it held its silence, as if nothing had happened at all.

Chapter 5

Scorched Earth

I took a motor tricycle to The Manila Hotel, the rider weaving through the evening rush hour traffic as I crouched in the sidecar. No two tricycles were ever the same. I'd picked one where I had to duck and bend to get inside. Once seated it was too late to back out. The owner, a wiry, spare woman somewhere in her twenties, had unsmiling eyes that peered above a bandana she wore against the fumes. An improvised fairing – a tarpaulin held in place with string – kept some of the rain off her. My sidecar had a canvas roof to guard against the elements, but not the fumes or the noise. I was prepared to put up with a bit of discomfort to watch how she picked through the traffic. Cars, trucks and jeepneys swarmed close-by, competing for every inch of tarmac.

The sidecar had the faintest touch of 1940s nostalgia. Philippine motorised tricycles evolved from motorbikes with sidecars used during the Second World War. The passenger cab is attached to the side, in contrast to tuk-tuks used in African and other Asian countries, which are factory-built three-wheelers. From what I could see, motorised tricycles caused much less chaos in Manila than the pedal-bike variant. They had the power to pull away quickly and weave with serious intent. They were also less likely to block the way by randomly stopping to tout for fares.

Soon we were bumper-to-bumper amid the din of Roxas Boulevard, one of the longest straight roads in the city. It runs parallel to the head of Manila Bay. Low down and boxed in on all sides by grumbling vehicles, mine was not a vantage point to take in the views. Yet I knew exactly where I was. During the war this road was Dewey Boulevard, a kind of Manila version of the Avenue des Champs-Élysées in Paris. It was here that, in May 1942, the Japanese marched starving and bedraggled columns of Allied prisoners from Bataan and Corregidor towards the city's Bilibid Prison. Filipinos risked punishment by throwing them food and trying to give them water.

Photographs taken on this same bomb-blasted boulevard in February 1945 show American GIs taking cover behind Sherman tanks as they closed in on the great walls of Intramuros, a city within a city. My mind also drifted to Muhammad Ali, who went on pre-dawn training runs along Roxas Boulevard in September 1975 before the *Thrilla in Manila*, the most famous heavyweight boxing contest of the twentieth century.

She pulled up beside The Manila Hotel and I clambered out. There had been no possibility to ask about her day; I'd read that some riders work eighteen-hour shifts, making perhaps thirty paid journeys. No time for questions: the pesos handed over, she acknowledged me with a slight nod and pulled away, heading back into the staccato city.

Standing before the hotel's five story white facade, I suddenly felt underdressed in walking shorts, well-worn trainers and a safari shirt that I had been hand washing for days. Bell men in pristine white uniforms recalled the colonial era. During the hotel's heyday dignitaries stepped out from limousines under the canopy here.

Measured by the US presidents who visited, this era ran from Dwight Eisenhower and through John. F. Kennedy, Lyndon B. Johnson, and Richard Nixon before the streak ended with Bill Clinton. Nelson Mandela, when he was president of South Africa, stayed in the MacArthur Suite on the hotel's top floor.

From the grand opening on 4 July 1912 and onwards, the building was a glitzy symbol of colonial wealth and its divides, the Haves and Have Nots of Asia. The glory days drew an eclectic cast of luminaries and featured global figures from entertainment such as Douglas Fairbanks Junior, Marlon Brando, Liza Minnelli, and Sammy Davis Junior.

I had been particularly drawn to a photograph from April 1941 of Ernest Hemingway, taken in a sunny spot somewhere in the grounds. The author is wearing a plain white T-shirt and shorts, sat back in a chair, an easy smile one of contentment, with what looked like a rum and coke at his side. This was peak Hemingway – 42 years old, handsome, still in good shape, and on a professional and personal honeymoon of sorts. His Spanish Civil War novel *For Whom the Bell Tolls* had been published in 1940. A few months later he'd married his third wife, the war correspondent Martha Gellhorn. He was accompanying her while she completed an assignment to cover the

Sino-Japanese War. The photo was taken during an extended stopover in Manila. On the spot where I now stood, Hemingway had been mobbed by admiring Filipino journalists and authors from the Philippine Writers League.

The Manila Hotel was built a decade after the end of the American-Filipino colonial war. It was one of the centrepieces of a vision to sanitise, modernise and effectively Americanise the waterfront area by creating new parks, streets, and railways. One of the programme leaders was the architect and urban planner Daniel Hudson Burnham. He recognised that a luxury hotel was necessary to host foreign investors and dignitaries. He allowed for one at the north end of a wide, tree-lined boulevard at the edge of the bay. The hotel was constructed on reclaimed land. Burnham used the same idea to good effect elsewhere in the city, filling in the mosquito-ridden moats to establish gardens around the nearby old Spanish colonial centre, Intramuros, where I was staying. These gardens gave way to Luneta Park – today known as Rizal Park, one of Manila's most welcome escapes from its concrete and glass high rise jungles.

Another architect, William Parsons, won the commission for the hotel itself. The California Mission-inspired design he came up with was based around an 'H' shape – with 129 guest bedrooms in the parallel wings, and the connecting central section housing public spaces, all beneath a green tiled roof. The mission style had boomed in California in the late nineteenth century, marking a shift away from the heavier-set and blocky East Coast architectural traditions. Parsons opted for a look that evoked Spanish colonial heritage. He gave The Manila Hotel clean, minimalist lines and a frontage of five unadorned decks of white plaster walls. The hotel was arranged so that the left side of the H formed the grand frontage and main entrance, with the doors positioned at the centre of that wing. It still looked refined and pleasing to me, despite the addition of a tower at the back of the plot in the 1970s.

In the early days The Manila Hotel had a rooftop garden but this was lost to stately ambition. The change was a direct result of President Quezón asking his old friend MacArthur to become the nation's defence consultant in 1935. One of the conditions attached to the agreement was that MacArthur would have accommodations that rivalled the president's own quarters in Malacañang Palace. So the rooftop garden was built-over to become a seven-bedroom penthouse for the general, his wife, Jean, and Arthur IV. It came complete with a drawing room and a dining room to entertain guests, along with study and a library to contain his collection of military books. By moving into The Manila Hotel, MacArthur presided over the meeting point for the social elite, a world of upscale cultural fusion, where the Philippines' first steps towards self-confidence and twentieth century modernisation were taking place.

The building also has a footnote in the more recent history of change. One of the keynote moments on the way to the People Power Revolution came in January 1986 when the widowed Cory Aquino gave a speech about democracy in the hotel's Heritage Room; one of the sparks that lit the flame that burnt down the Ferdinand Marcos dictatorship later the same year. 'My political program is simple,'[32] she told the audience of supporters.

> I propose to dismantle the dictatorial edifice Mr. Marcos has built. In its place I propose to build for our people a genuine democracy. I am first to admit that it will not be easy. The dictatorial edifice is strong. I am first to admit that the Marcos dictatorship has been cleverly crafted by an evil genius. And I am first to admit that the evil genius, allowed to run amuck for 20 years, succeeded in foisting on the nation a grim constitutional joke built on deceit and manipulation. The deception should not be allowed to last one minute longer.

I cleared a metal detector check, showed my vaccination pass and entered a high, grand, and echoey lobby of old-world luxury. Glittering chandeliers made from brass, crystal, and seashell hung from dark wood panelled ceilings. The marble floor was adorned with plush lobby furniture. Three sides of the space were framed with decorative colonnades. A double grand staircase led up to a mezzanine floor that once included a music room and a children's dining area (a leftover convenience from the Victorian age for wealthy parents). I knew well that the entire building is a reconstruction of the one where MacArthur and his family lived, which was left in ruins by the fighting around Manila Bay in 1945. Yet it remains a landmark site for wartime history.

At once there was a glimpse of Filipino high society: a young woman in a ball gown being photographed on the grand stairs. It turned out she was having her debut – a traditional coming-of-age celebration that occurs when a young woman turns 18. She beamed for the camera, a princess for the day. At a party held in her honour later she would receive a rose from eighteen of the most important men in her life. Dances and speeches would also mark the occasion, and eighteen candles lit to symbolise the light of love the debutante will take on her journey to adulthood.

As much as I liked the idea of crashing the party, if only to see the historic function room, there was of course no prospect of this happening. So I became a scruffy resident in one corner of The Tap Room, an upscale ground floor bar which was all deep red armchairs, discrete lighting, lush carpets and yet more dark wood panelling. The hotel website described The Tap Room as reminiscent of an English pub but I could not recall being in a hostelry so fine. The sprinkling of other guests grew by two when an upscale English couple, perhaps in their mid-thirties, arrived. Almost as soon as they sat down they began arguing. Unexpectedly, the woman stood up, her voice rising to a controlled timbre of anger and masked hurt. 'You need to grow up,' she said, and walked out.

When he left too, I was back at peace. Craving familiar food, I waited for a pizza while sitting with a cold San Miguel, free peanuts, all the while luxuriating in the air con. Prior to the trip I had not been able to find any feature films set in or around the pre-war Manila Hotel, but I was trying to match up the interior in my head with *They Were Expendable*, the well-regarded 1945 John Ford film, that I had at home on DVD.

White-uniformed naval officers are enjoying some R&R at a Manila bar. John Wayne is among them, playing PT boat commander Lieutenant 'Rusty' Ryan, who wants a transfer, believing that serving in an Asiatic backwater will get him passed over for promotion. The wooden boats, after all, are considered 'expendable'. Rusty argues the point with his sombre commander, John Brickley, played by Robert Montgomery – a bigger star than Wayne at the time, and a real-life PT boat captain with a distinguished wartime record. The band stops playing, and the evening ends abruptly with an announcement from the stage. The men are being recalled to base: there has been a surprise attack on Pearl Harbor.

Aware that The Manila Hotel has a Heritage Room to showcase its history – and that it's sometimes possible to view the $8,000-a-night MacArthur

Suite – I later presented myself at the lobby reception and asked if I might have a look around. I had no idea whether any of this was open to non-residents. When my status wasn't challenged, I could barely contain my glee. A duty manager was duly summoned. A locked room on the ground floor turned out to be a treasure trove, lined wall-to-wall with photographs from the hotel's VIP years. Astronaut Neil Armstrong and bandleader Glenn Miller were among the faces looking back.

A wooden chair apparently used by MacArthur was positioned as a kind of altar, with his khaki-coloured gold braided peaked cap hat placed on the seat. The hat was vintage MacArthur, a one-off that speaks of his authority and individualism. It was also key to his legend, often in surprising ways. The example of show dates back to his pre-war appointment as field marshal of the Philippine Army – at that point more of an honorary title as the Philippine Army had still to be properly formed. MacArthur certainly enjoyed presenting himself as a field marshal, the highest military rank that can be achieved. The US Army does not have field marshals but this did not stop MacArthur wearing the cap throughout the war. He styled it up by adding bling in the form of a row of embroidered gold leaf that circled around the hat and a row across the black visor. He also preferred a gold embroidered US insignia over the standard brass badge.

MacArthur, it has to be said, led where others followed in terms of style. He had long been known for his appearance which was described by another of his eminent biographers, Arthur Herman, as 'unorthodox to an almost insolent degree.'[33]

This was first noted during the First World War, when he served as colonel in France. Rejecting the standard olive drab tunic of an army officer, MacArthur wore his grey West Point military academy sweater, a memento of his baseball days at the institution. Instead of carrying standard gas mask, plus a sword or pistol, he sported a riding crop, which he said reminded him of his time on the American plains. The regulation steel helmet, worn by officers and men alike for obvious safety reasons, also had to go.

Herman explained:

> He wore a barracks cap, tipped at a rakish angle, with the steel liner removed, so that it crumpled like someone had sat on it. And as the war went on, he

> never changed the MacArthur look, even when leading troops under fire or during a gas attack. The look got some laughs, and the feelings of more buttoned down officers can be imagined, but it also drew the news cameras, as he knew it would. Interviews with Colonel MacArthur accompanied by photos of him featuring his hat and his riding crop began to dot newspapers around the country.

There were others in the army who found the look refreshing and took to imitating him. One of them was his long-time friend, airman Billy Mitchell, who served in France in 1918 and eventually became an American icon as a pioneer of combat aviation (which included being the first American aviator to cross enemy lines). 'When he met MacArthur at the front, he was so impressed by the hat minus the steel liner that he pulled his own out and wore his own the same way for the rest of the war. From Mitchell it would become the classic headgear of bombers pilots in World War Two, immortalised in films like *Twelve O'Clock High*.'[34]

It must also be pointed out that MacArthur was not alone in carefully considering presentation – and that fashion and its accessories did have a place on the battlefields of the Second World War. General George S. Patton, for example, was famous for carrying his own ivory handled single action cowboy six-shooters in Europe, while Japanese generals carried Japanese *katana* swords typically associated with samurai warriors. German generals arguably had the most professional and disciplined appearance. It is well-documented that some of the uniforms were produced by Hugo Ferdinand Boss, founder of the iconic fashion brand. The company has since apologised for his past association with the Nazi Party and its treatment of slave labourers. Yes the uniforms and the full-length leather greatcoats were sharp and well-tailored but saying so remains a delicate topic to this day; I knew of an editor at British *GQ* who was forced to resign over a feature that pictured Erwin Rommel in full uniform and described him as 'stylish in the face of true adversity.'[35]

Up on the top floor, the MacArthur Suite was immediately persuasive that I had stepped into a cool and contemporary take on upscale 1941. I had read so many negative descriptions of MacArthur as a narcissist. Yet stepping into this simulacra of where he lived for six years, a qualified admiration seemed the more natural response.

The suite has been refurbished to replicate the original design. Some of the furniture may or may not have been used by the general and his family (I recognised one mirror) but the first impression was simply of rooms that have a kind of beautiful restraint, a dialled down art deco that is anything but pompous. Bowled over by the unexpected sense of style, seemingly at odds with everything that is functional and military, I took it all as a nod to MacArthur's interest in image. A glass cabinet displayed copies of his decorations and medals. His wood-panelled office was smaller than I expected, but his main headquarters were across the street from the hotel at No. 1 Calle Victoria.

Every morning a ceremony involving father and 3-year-old son was conducted in the bedroom. MacArthur tended to work seven days a week but the routine was that Arthur IV would come into his father's bedroom about 07.30 hours, clutching a favourite soft toy, a rabbit which he called 'Old Friend'.

'MacArthur would instantly bound out of bed and snap to attention,' wrote William Manchester in *American Caesar*.

> Then the General would march around the room while his son counted cadence: 'Boom! Boom! Boom! *Boom*!' After they passed the bed a few times the child would cover his eyes while MacArthur produced that day's present: a piece of candy, or a crayon, or a colouring book. The ritual would end in the bathroom, where MacArthur would shave while Arthur watched and both sang duets.

The most evocative formal space was the dining room, with a long table for ten and tall windows overlooking the bay. By this point in my private tour it was the blue hour – that brief spell before sunset when the sky turns a soft, velvety indigo. Beyond the floor-to-ceiling glass doors, ship and crane lights had begun to twinkle against the darkening waters of Manila Bay. It seemed impossibly glamorous, and yet a place where I had no trouble imagining the last night in the tropics before the Philippines, along with the rest of east Asia and the Western Pacific tumbled into war.

MacArthur's Chief of Staff, the priggish Dick Sutherland, and a few of the general's other lackeys have just left after a late meeting. The Japanese have yet to strike at Pearl Harbor. Pan Am's China Clipper is moored out in the bay, a symbol of the early days of trans-Pacific flight, a fleeting golden age before the time when the only people crossing borders were combatants and refugees. MacArthur is still leafing through memos, thinking only of routine military matters, unaware that the world is about to change. Downstairs, a jazz band is striking up in the open-air Fiesta Ballroom, where Rusty and the PT boat boys are still grumbling about their lot. The dance floor is loaded with American officers and expat women in all their finery.

* * *

Manila was a graveyard. Wrapped in a shroud of biting dust, its gaunt grey shell-scarred fire blackened walls and torn twisted girders reached mutely to the sky. The pungent stench of charred bodies filled the air. So wrote MacArthur's stenographer, Lieutenant Paul Rogers, who, like the other American officers who had served in Manila before the war, mourned the spectacle of the shattered 'Pearl of the Orient.'

MacArthur stepped through the ruins at his beloved Manila Hotel. A dead Japanese colonel lay at the front door of his suite. He had followed a unit that fought its way upstairs, the corpses getting warmer on each floor. Inside the suite, most of his books and family's belongings that had been abandoned in the hasty escape to Corregidor three years before had either been torched or were missing. Decades in the past, when America's relationship with Japan was still cordial, Emperor Meiji, the grandfather of Hirohito, had gifted an exquisite Japanese vase to MacArthur's father as a token of goodwill between nations. The offering had been left in a prominent place when the MacArthur family fled on Christmas Eve 1941 in the hope that whoever came afterwards would respect what had been their home. It was smashed to pieces.

The race to liberate Manila had begun on 9 January 1945. Another colossal invasion fleet disgorged some 175,000 troops from the US Sixth Army onto the shores of Luzon. The armada had endured multiple kamikaze strikes but only faced light opposition when landing on the same beaches of Lingayen

Gulf north-west of Manila that Lieutenant General Masaharu Homma had used in December 1941. Once it was considered safe, MacArthur repeated his 'I have returned' walk through the surf for the cameras and newsreels.

The Sixth Army was under the direct command of Lieutenant General Walter Krueger. His cautious, methodical approach had frustrated MacArthur during the Leyte campaign – and Krueger stayed true to type on Luzon. He led a painstakingly deliberate advance south, always wary of over-extending and leaving his flanks exposed. In the opening exchanges his force engaged Japanese troops in the hills to the north and east of Lingayen Gulf. It took two weeks to get south to the first of his objectives – Clark Field – before Manila made it to the top of the agenda.

Nothing was happening fast enough for MacArthur. His concerns were based on the safety of hundreds of Allied prisoners of war and circa 4,000 civilians held at two internment camps – the biggest of which was at the University of Santo Tomás in Manila. Reports from Filipino guerrillas and one escaping American soldier had already relayed harrowing details. A group of 139 POWs had been murdered on the island of Palawan in the western Philippines on 15 December 1944. When the local Japanese commander thought an American fleet was approaching, the prisoners were herded into three small underground bunkers, doused in aviation fuel and burnt to death. The diary of a Japanese sergeant major who witnessed the massacre had only the faintest trace of conscience. He noted that although they had been POWs (and therefore presumably worthless), 'They truly died a pitiful death.'

A daring mission behind enemy lines on 30 January 1945 did liberate 489 Allied POWs and 33 civilians held at Cabanatuan, 100 kilometres (62 miles) north of Manila. It was the first and most audacious of four rescues within a month.

Grasslands around the Cabanatuan camp had been cleared by the Japanese guards who feared attacks from Filipino guerrillas. At dusk, troops from the US 6th Ranger Battalion risked everything by crawling on their bellies across flat, exposed land towards the perimeter fences. Their hopes of avoiding detection rested on the distraction provided by a single American aircraft passing over at a pre-arranged time, faking engine trouble and creating the impression that it was able to crash land on the other side of the camp. The

US Rangers suddenly stormed the fences, killed the guards and liberated the prisoners.

The POWs were mostly Americans, but with British, Dutch, Norwegians, and a Canadian also amongst the starving and enfeebled survivors. As most of the inmates were in a desperate state from three years of disease, beatings and little food, it was a mission of the finest margins. Some 7,000 IJA soldiers occupied the nearby town. Yet the rescue party got away to American lines undetected, which allowed the prisoners to tell of the Bataan and Corregidor atrocities in detail for the first time.

* * *

MacArthur's demands to speed up the assault eventually produced a kind of race to Manila from points in north, west and south of Luzon. In all cases, getting across bridges before the Japanese could blow them up became the overriding concern.

There were two further amphibious landings. The first was led by Robert Eichelberger at the head of the US Eighth Army, the general whose previous triumphs included breaking the deadlock amid the Buna-Gona- Sananda quagmire of New Guinea. On 29 January, his forces took Subic Bay west of Manila and quickly sealed off the Bataan peninsula from the Japanese units retreating from Krueger's army to the north-west. A further landing on 31 January at Nasugbu, 72 kilometres (45 miles) south-west of Manila, amphibiously deployed 6,462 glider troopers of the 11th Airborne Division. They would be supported by 1,792 soldiers parachuting in during major sorties farther inland a few days later. The combined forces joined-up and headed for the capital. They made rapid progress only to become bogged down in fighting around the heavily defended southern edge of the city limits.

The second part of MacArthur's rapid advance sent elements of the US Sixth Army charging towards Manila from the north, effectively putting the capital within the closing jaws of a gigantic US Army vice, while American aircraft roamed the skies, unchallenged.

Still frustrated, on 30 January MacArthur drove to Guimba, 32 kilometres (20 miles) south of Lingayen, where the 1st Cavalry Division had just arrived from Leyte. He left Major General Verne Mudge in no doubt as to what was expected.

'Go to Manila,' MacArthur said, according to Mudge's subordinate, Brigadier General William Chase, who observed the meeting. 'Go round the Nips, bounce off the Nips, but go to Manila. Free the internees at Santo Tomás. Take Malacañang Palace and the Legislative Building.'[36]

Within thirty-six hours, a Manila advance force was mustered and ready to go under Brigadier General Chase. The division was broken down into three mobile columns mainly made up of a tank company, artillery, engineers, and a medical squadron. In true cavalry fashion, they carried only what they needed. Some 1,900 men began setting off at 10-minute intervals. No one was on foot – they moved in armed jeeps and trucks, accompanied by sixteen Sherman tanks, artillery squads, and engineers with bulldozers.

Guided by American aircraft, the advance units took a zig-zag route to avoid blown bridges and enemy strong points, dodging firefights where possible. As they approached some villages they were met by Filipinos shouting '*Mabuhay*' – hooray – and offered bananas and papayas. No cheering locals suggested the IJN was probably around. The charge took seventy hours to cover 160 kilometres (100 miles) to the outskirts of Manila.

General Tomoyuki Yamashita, the 'Tiger of Malaya' who first outwitted the British on the Malaysian peninsula and then successfully bluffed them into surrender during the battle for Singapore, was in charge of the defence of the Philippines. His most noted predecessor, Homma, had long since been exiled for apparently showing a lack of aggression in overcoming the defenders of Bataan and Corregidor back in 1942.

Yamashita, regarded by some historians as the IJA's finest commander, had suffered an even worse fall from grace that same year. Despite his famous victory over the British Army, Yamashita was then dispatched to guard the border with Russia. Taller and heavier set than the average Japanese soldier, and possibly lacking political guile, his mistake may have been, falling foul of the jealousy of Prime Minister Tōjō, who was wary of him as a rival for army leadership. Tōjō's resignation following the seismic fall of Saipan in July 1944 allowed Yamashita to return from the wilderness.

Yamashita still had some 262,000 troops on Luzon, but the loss of air and naval support during the defence of Leyte had so narrowed his options that he now decided to fight a delaying action. To avoid the massive bombardment power of the invasion fleet, the American landings were allowed to be conducted largely unopposed. Yamashita instead withdrew the bulk of his forces into three widely separated mountain strongholds and settled down for a long battle of attrition.

He saw his job as tying up the Allies for as long as possible, doing what he could to keep the supply lines from the East Indies open and sapping strength that would otherwise be directed against the home islands.

The largest force, the Shobu group, was under his direct command in northern Luzon with about 152,000 troops. The Kembu group, with 30,000 troops, controlled Clark Field, Bataan, and Corregidor. The Shimbu group, based in southern Luzon, had around 80,000 soldiers.

Yamashita considered Manila indefensible. The terrain was too flat and most of the buildings outside of the old Spanish colonial core of Intramuros were highly flammable. He also wanted to avoid the problem of managing its 800,000-plus besieged population. The city had suffered increasingly severe deprivations during Japan's three years of occupation. With everything of value long since looted from stores and warehouses, and agricultural fields left to rot, the Manila economy had collapsed and social fabric was coming apart. By 1945 death by starvation claimed hundreds of lives each week. Destitute people even resorted to plundering graves in search of anything that could be bartered or sold food.

Yamashita wanted out of the capital but other Japanese officers had a different agenda. As the army withdrew to hold up in the distant Luzon hills, Rear Admiral Sanji Iwabuchi moved into the city with a patched together force of somewhere between 14,000 and 20,000 sailors and assorted service personnel. Iwabuchi had been directed to withdraw once his force had blown up all the piers, warehouses and other port facilities that might be useful to the Americans. In the event, the 49-year-old disregarded the order to leave and mandated his men to hold the city. 'If we run out of bullets, we will use grenades; if we run out of grenades, we will cut down the enemy with swords; if we break our swords, we will kill them by sinking our teeth deep in their throats,'[37] he decreed.

The sailors knew little about infantry tactics or street fighting but were well armed and erected strong points. Pillboxes, anti-tank and anti-personnel mines were used extensively in the city centre. Troops constructed barricades out of cars and trucks at major intersections. They also filled windows with reinforced concrete, bored shooting holes and made gun slits in walls, and stashed ammunition in strategic places. Scout-snipers perched in high buildings made the approaches to the defensive positions even more deadly. In 1942, Iwabuchi had been publicly disgraced and his career side-lined for surviving the sinking of the battleship *Kirishima* that he commanded during the Battle of Guadalcanal. This time he was going down with the 'ship' and determined to die with 'honour'.

The American breakthrough came on 3 February when a fast-moving armoured column from the US 1st Cavalry Division pushed into Manila. The last remaining barrier to the city proper was the steep-sided Tullahan River in the northern suburbs. One squadron reached the bridge just as Japanese soldiers were getting ready to set off demolition charges. As the two sides opened fire on one another, the Japanese lit the fuse. Despite the palpable risk to himself, Lieutenant (Junior Grade) James P. Sutton ran on to the bridge and cut the burning cord.

After three years of a war on beaches and in the fevered outback, the Americans had to adjust to a different set of hard realities – street fighting. But as dusk approached, the armoured cavalrymen continued on through the northern district. The route took them by the Bonifacio Monument, a towering column that today sits in the centre of an enormous cloverleaf-shaped traffic interchange. They headed on past the sprawling Chinese cemetery, from where snipers took potshots at the column of American tanks and jeeps. Against an ominous red sky, the unit made it to the University of Santo Tomás at dusk, where some 3,700 mostly American internees were being held captive by a relatively small number of guards.

* * *

If rivers were the life-giving starting point of our first civilisations – the Nile in Egypt, the Ganges in India, China's Yellow River and the Tigris and Euphrates of Mesopotamia – this one said nothing encouraging about how we live today. The Pasig threads through Manila from Laguna de Bay to the east, the largest body of inland water in the Philippines, to Manila Bay and the open sea in the west. It's crossed by twenty-four bridges linking the capital north to south along its 27-kilometre (17-mile) length. Just looking at the water made me feel dirty. Decades of intense urbanisation without meaningful pollution controls and proper waste management facilities have transformed the waterway into a bacterial nightmare. On its passage through the city the freshwater from Laguna de Bay becomes a medium for transporting untreated sewage, industrial waste and garbage out to the sea. People stopped swimming in the Pasig during the 1950s. By the 1990s the river was declared biologically dead. Despite rehabilitation efforts, it remains one of the world's most polluted rivers and, according to the American Association for the Advancement of Science, is the single biggest source of plastic waste that ends up in the ocean.

Mine was supposed to be a straightforward journey to the University of Santo Tomás but my tricycle rider only got as far as the south bank of the Pasig.

'How old do you think I am?' he asked with a smile as he pedalled us away from Intramuros. He was missing all but one of his front teeth but was not out of breath. Before I could answer he said, '70', a little amused with himself.

The deal was he'd take me all the way to Sampaloc, the university district, but he stopped after about ten minutes. It might have been that it was too far for him or there was some restriction on tricycles using the crossing. I accepted the change in our agreement and went on my way on foot.

Only four bridges crossed the Pasig in 1945. They were all blown up by the Japanese at the start of the battle for Manila as the Americans entered the north of the city. I walked across a replacement of the Jones Bridge – named after William Atkinson Jones, who authored the Philippine independence legislation. The original was built in 1920 and graced with four statues that are collectively known as *La Madre Filipina* (The Philippine Motherland). They celebrate aspects of Philippine nationhood in its transition from being a US colony – Gratitude, Democracy, Progress and Justice. Three of the four original statues have been reinstated, reclaimed and restored from wartime damage. I made my way to the north side of the Pasig and then on through an intense maze of city blocks, traffic and overhead telegraph wires, heading for the former internment camp.

In aerial reconnaissance photographs from 1945 Santo Tomás is set in its own grounds at the semi-rural edge of the city. A 3.6-metre (12-foot) stone wall surrounded the campus with only a sprinkling of other less grand institutional buildings as neighbours. The university occupies the same 22-hectare (55-acre) plot of land today but the site is now bordered by the intense bricks and mortar expansion of Metro Manila, with much of the campus obscured at street level by walls, buildings and fences.

I walked to España Boulevard on the south side, assuming I could find an entry point. It was down this road that the first US forces approached Santo Tomás. At the head of a column of six tanks, a Sherman named *Battlin' Basic* rumbled toward a reckoning with the Japanese garrison inside the university – much less enter the campus. The crew of *Battlin' Basic* had no such trouble, pushing through gates I had yet to find, and into an empty courtyard. There was no sign of the internees, but they were confronted by a single guard. Before being shot dead, he threw a grenade that mortally wounded Manuel Colayco, a Filipino newspaperman and clandestine intelligence officer acting as a guide.

Perplexed by unmanned, locked gates, I hiked several sweaty blocks to reach the opposite side of the university on Lacson Avenue. There, it was security guards, barriers, and paperwork that barred in the way. I eventually talked my way past the bureaucracy and, after registering my details, made for the central plaza – the focal point of the campus.

Solemn and imposing, the weathered four-story Main Building stood in relative isolation. It appeared taller than it was, its time-worn façade of renaissance revival architecture calling to mind a more pristine *Hôtel de Ville* in Paris. Elsewhere in Manila, buildings tend to crowd each other out with reckless indifference. Here, I could stand back and take in the palatial symmetry: the grand entrance, the roofline crowned by a clock tower, and statues of theologians, writers, and historians flanking it like sentinels of learning.

The stone academics on high looked out beyond the plaza to some gardens and a bronze statue of Miguel de Benavides, the university's seventeenth century founder. Further on, the Arch of the Centuries, which once served as an entrance gate, stood as an eighteenth century architectural treasure. To one side of the gardens and the plaza, a large open sports field with a small grandstand beckoned me, wholesome and uncluttered. It gave me the odd sense of being on a university campus from another time. Only the tower blocks beyond the high perimeter walls on España Boulevard intruded from the outside world.

The original campus was founded by the Spanish in 1611 – some twenty-five years before America's first university, Harvard, was established. Santo Tomás remains a Catholic institution run by the Order of Preachers, more simply known as the Dominicans. A post-war growth in student numbers prompted the move from Intramuros to the current site in Sampaloc during the 1920s.

The Main Building was designed by Father Roque Ruaño, a priest and head of the university's Faculty of Engineering. He began work in 1922 on a rectangular structure with a 40-metre (131-foot) frontage and a 28-metre (92-foot) depth, enclosing two large interior courtyards filled with gardens. Construction wasn't completed until 1927, partly because Ruaño spent time in Japan studying seismic resistance. His design produced the first large-scale building in Asia engineered specifically to withstand earthquakes: forty independent structures, separated by 1-inch gaps filled with loose cement, allowing them to shift independently during tremors.

Sitting on a bench beside the mostly empty sports field, I realised I could have stayed there all day – with a book, or with nothing at all – simply absorbing the campus atmosphere and its unspoken history. It felt like the kind of pause academics dream of when pushing back against deadlines, metrics, and performance targets. Movements like Slow Scholarship call for just that today: a more reflective pace, room for ideas to take their time, and space to think about the common good rather than personal gain. Maybe it could catch on – on campuses with the same peaceful ambience – though I doubted that moment was anywhere near in Manila. There were no signs that Santo Tomás embraced radicalism in any form. Everything I saw spoke of deference to tradition and the steady machinery of institutional life. And beyond the walls, Metropolitan Manila – like so many cities now – pulsed with a kind of manic capitalism that left little room for lofty alternatives.

I sat watching a sprinkling of Thomasians going about their day. Figuratively, they walked in the footsteps of former students who once helped shape the nation's destiny. The university's alumni include national heroes like José Rizal, Emilio Jacinto, and Marcelo H. del Pilar – to say nothing of presidents, chief justices, senators, scientists, architects, engineers, and writers.

Closing my eyes and slipping back in time, I imagined the plaza where I now sat as it had been – a crowded parking lot filled with US Army tanks, trucks, and jeeps. In February 1945, the advance column arrived here and brought an end to three years of internment. For that long stretch, the campus grounds had served as a kind of shanty town, populated by foreign nationals trapped by war.

Photographs taken in the first days after liberation show painfully malnourished internees, their bodies wasted to little more than skin and bone. One of the most affecting images captures an American, Bernard Herzog, holding a cigarette and speaking with the crew of a Sherman tank. Herzog, wearing only shorts and shoes, appears chronically underweight. Starvation has left him with sunken cheeks, skeletal arms, pronounced ribs, and a hollowed-out stomach. His legs are swollen from beriberi – the result of a vitamin deficiency brought on by a diet of little more than white rice. The tankers beside him are healthy young American men, broad-shouldered and physically robust. In comparison, they seem to glow with abundance.

The Japanese began rounding up enemy aliens and transporting them to Santo Tomás in January 1942. The internees were guarded by a garrison of around seventy soldiers – mostly captured Chinese nationals operating under often brutal Japanese overseers. The prisoners were a mix of expatriate businesspeople and their families: executives, engineers, bankers, plantation owners, hotel staff, and missionaries. The group also included about seventy US Army nurses captured after the fall of Bataan and Corregidor.

By February 1942, the camp's roll call included 3,200 Americans, 900 British (including Canadians and Australians), 40 Poles, 30 Dutch, and smaller numbers from Spain, Mexico, Nicaragua, Cuba, Russia, Belgium, Sweden, Denmark, China, and Burma. About 100 of the total were Filipino or part-Filipino – often the spouses and children of American citizens. Of the 3,200 Americans, 2,000 were men and 1,200 women, including 450 married couples and around 400 children. The imbalance reflected earlier decisions by many expat families to send wives and children back to the US in 1940 as relations with Japan deteriorated. Some internees arrived at the university with pockets full of money; others had only the clothes they wore.

Within days of confinement, a peculiar wartime community began to take shape. The Japanese appointed Earl Carroll – a Manila-based insurance executive from Alabama – as camp head. Ernest Stanley, a British missionary who had lived in Japan and spoke the language fluently, served as interpreter. Both reported directly to the camp commandant.

The Japanese were particularly concerned about sexual relationships between internees and tried to enforce a ban on physical affection. Sleeping arrangements were strictly segregated, and a nightly roll call was held at 19.30 hours. Internees were required to stay in their assigned rooms overnight, with monitors appointed to ensure compliance. Yet once an Executive Committee and various sub-groups were established, Santo Tomás was largely left to manage its own affairs – within the limits of Japanese rule.

Those with money could buy extra food and construct simple huts in the open grounds – makeshift shelters of bamboo and palm fronds where they might find some privacy during the day. The Japanese suspected these shacks were used for 'inappropriate' relations between men and women, but they were not dismantled.

The first show of brutal force was enough to dissuade any thoughts of escape. In February 1942, three young internees – two British and one Australian – climbed over the wall, hoping to join guerrilla forces still fighting on Bataan. They were recaptured, tortured, and executed four days later. Carroll, Stanley, and the monitors from the rooms where the men had slept were forced to witness their deaths.

In the early weeks, many internees believed their imprisonment would be brief. They expected MacArthur and the US Navy to repel the Japanese advance and reclaim the city. Yet once word of the surrender at Bataan and Corregidor reached Santo Tomás, the grim reality of a long internment began to settle over the compound.

When the population passed 5,000, the Japanese opened a second camp at Los Baños – an agricultural college about 64 kilometres (40 miles) south of Manila, near the shores of Laguna de Bay – which would eventually hold just over 2,000 internees.

Though numbers at Santo Tomás dropped back to around 4,000, overcrowding remained a serious problem. The Sanitation and Health Committee worked constantly to stave off squalor, assigning scores of internees to construct additional toilets and showers, manage garbage disposal, and control the mosquitoes and vermin that infested the compound. The nurses organised public health talks to stem outbreaks of sickness and the spread of tropical disease.

The Main Building was not a dormitory but people had been instructed to stake out living and sleeping quarters on three floors of classrooms and offices. Today it is once again an all teaching and administrative space. I wanted to see inside but could not blag my way past the guard and had to be content with reading the plaque outside.

THROUGH THESE PORTALS PASSED UP
TO TEN THOUSAND AMERICANS AND
OTHER NATIONALS OF THE FREE WORLD
WHO WERE INTERNED WITHIN THESE
WALLS BY THE JAPANESE MILITARY,
SUFFERING GREAT PHYSICAL PRIVATION
AND NATIONAL HUMILIATION FROM
JANUARY 4, 1942, UNTIL LIBERATED FEBRUARY
3, 1945, BY THE AMERICAN FORCES
UNDER GENERAL DOUGLAS MACARTHUR.

A couple of blocks away across campus, and beside the security gate where I had entered, the Education Building also housed internees. About 200 men and boys slept on the third floor. The two lower floors were occupied by the Japanese garrison. During the liberation the building became a focal point of Japanese resistance. Today it serves as a teaching hospital; there was no chance to wander around inside its halls.

One of the British contingent in 1942 was Rupert Wilkinson, a four-year resident of the Education Building. He wrote of his experiences in *Surviving a Japanese Internment Camp: Life and Liberation at Santo Tomás.* His father Gerald ran a Manila-based sugar company but also spied on Japanese movements for the British intelligence services. Wilkinson senior was on Corregidor when the Japanese invaded and later, like MacArthur, was evacuated to Australia. The rest of the Wilkinson family – Rupert, his mother Lorna and older sister Mary Jane – ended up confined at Santo Tomás.

'At first, camp life was not that bad,' Rupert Wilkinson explained in one article recounting his experiences. 'Our daytime shanty home was cosy, if crude. Resembling a one-room Filipino peasant hut on stilts, it had as furnishings a table, a cupboard, and a few chairs. Friends on the outside could send food and other aid.'[38]

After two years of relative stability the internees' plight became more precarious as the Allies drew closer to the Philippines. 'Again and again the Japanese army cut our rations. Guards and soldiers pilfered camp stores. By January 1945, each of us was living on 900 calories or less a day, and every day at least one resident – usually an older man – died. The dead got a quick prayer before burial in a mass grave outside the grounds.' The camp's most senior doctor, an American, was placed into solitary confinement after refusing to take 'malnutrition' off death certificates he was issuing.

The desperate attempts to avoid starving to death included cooking and eating hibiscus leaves until the internees discovered they were poisonous. The boiled roots of the banana plant were more palatable as were leafy weeds, which they consumed while trying to find a source of vitamin B1.

For those who had something to trade, the guards willingly accepted jewellery for small quantities of food. 'The woman living next to me traded a $700 ring for ten pounds of rice for her little girl and boy,' one internee, Jean Hick, told the UPI news agency after liberation. 'One had to be a very rich person to buy food outside. If you could get someone in camp to cash a check you were likely charged 200 percent interest – a $3,000 check would get you $100 in cash and could buy one kilo (nearly two pounds) of sugar or two kilos of rice.' She recalled rare occasions when they ate camp specials such as cornmeal mush or tough carabao meat 'which was wonderful.'

From 1944 the camp guards had a Japanese overseer, Lieutenant Nanakazu Abiko, who enjoyed humiliating internees. 'At roll call Abiko would force residents of a dormitory to practise bowing for half an hour or more,' wrote Rupert Wilkinson. 'On top of that, the secret police, the Kempeitai, would raid Santo Tomás to grab and torture internees suspected of contact with Filipino guerrillas and ransack dorms and shanties in search of illicit radios, which they never were able to find.'

Disbelief was the overriding emotion when American GIs finally rolled up to the gates. Rupert Wilkinson was in his dorm in the Education Building late on 3 February.

> We had grown accustomed to night time gunfire, but the shooting that evening seemed louder and nearer. I tried not to hope too much, but when we heard cheering erupt in other rooms, I and the other boys on the third floor rushed to the windows, joining men shouting, 'They're here!' As we watched, headlights crept onto campus. A flare went up, illuminating American tanks with G.Is walking alongside.

The hated Abiko was mortally wounded when he approached the Americans brandishing his samurai sword – shot when seemingly reaching for a grenade. As he fell to the ground, a group of camp inmates recognised him in the tank headlights. Rushing from the Main Building, they kicked and spat at him, and two women burned him with cigarettes. Others tried to use Abiko's own sword to slice off his ear before American soldiers intervened and took Abiko into the Main Building, where he soon died from his gunshot injuries.

While the Main Building was quickly liberated, the rest of the camp garrison had yet to show itself. The Japanese officer in overall charge, Lieutenant Colonel Toshio Hayashi and his remaining men held up in the Education Building – somewhere between fifty and sixty guards. 'An American voice yelled through a megaphone for everyone in the building to get down,' recalled Rupert Wilkinson. 'Machine guns began firing. I told myself I would not die. When the shooting stopped, guards came into our room to peer out windows and grab our mattresses, which they used to barricade the stairs. They also commandeered our beds, leaving us to sleep on the floor.'

Hayashi regarded the 200 internees in the Education Building as hostages. The following day was marked by an informal truce and a standoff that ultimately led to negotiation. It was agreed Hayashi and his forces would be escorted out of the university and under American guard and allowed to rejoin their lines elsewhere in the north of the city, in return for the hostages remaining unmolested – an extremely rare parley in the Pacific War.

Walking the same streets today it was still possible to ignore Manila's urban din and imagine the tension between the enemies. With each step away from the campus Hayashi's men became more concerned they would be shot in the back, while the Americans remained wary of an ambush. Any Filipinos who jeered the Japanese along the route were hushed or waved

Inside the ruined Manila Hotel. (*US National Archives*)

The lobby at The Manila Hotel, 1945. (*US National Archives*)

An American soldier looks at a huge shell hole in San Agustín Church, Manila. (*US National Archives*)

The Legislative Building, Manila, March 1945. (*US National Archives*)

An American soldier views ruined central Manila, 1945. A different view of the Legislative Building. (*US National Archives*)

Ruins of Colegio de San Juan de Letran, 1945. (*US National Archives*)

Escolta Street, Manila, 1945. (*US National Archives*)

Bomb damaged Cavite naval base. (*US National Archives*)

Wrecked Manila Post Office, 1945. (*US National Archives*)

Destroyed area around Pier 7, Manila, 1945. (*US National Archives*)

Ruins of Manila Cathedral. (*US National Archives*)

Shell blasted building in Manila. (*US National Archives*)

The Agriculture Building, Manila, 1945. (*US National Archives*)

The destroyed Ayala Bridge, Manila, 1945. (*US National Archives*)

The remains of the Cathedral of Saint Mary and Saint John, Manila, 1945. (*US National Archives*)

Dead civilians imprisoned at Intramuros. (*US National Archives*)

Filipinos tied up and shot dead in Manila. (*US National Archives*)

GIs firing on the Japanese in Intramuros. (*US National Archives*)

Woman and child murdered by Japanese. (*US National Archives*)

American tank in Intramuros, 1945. (*US National Archives*)

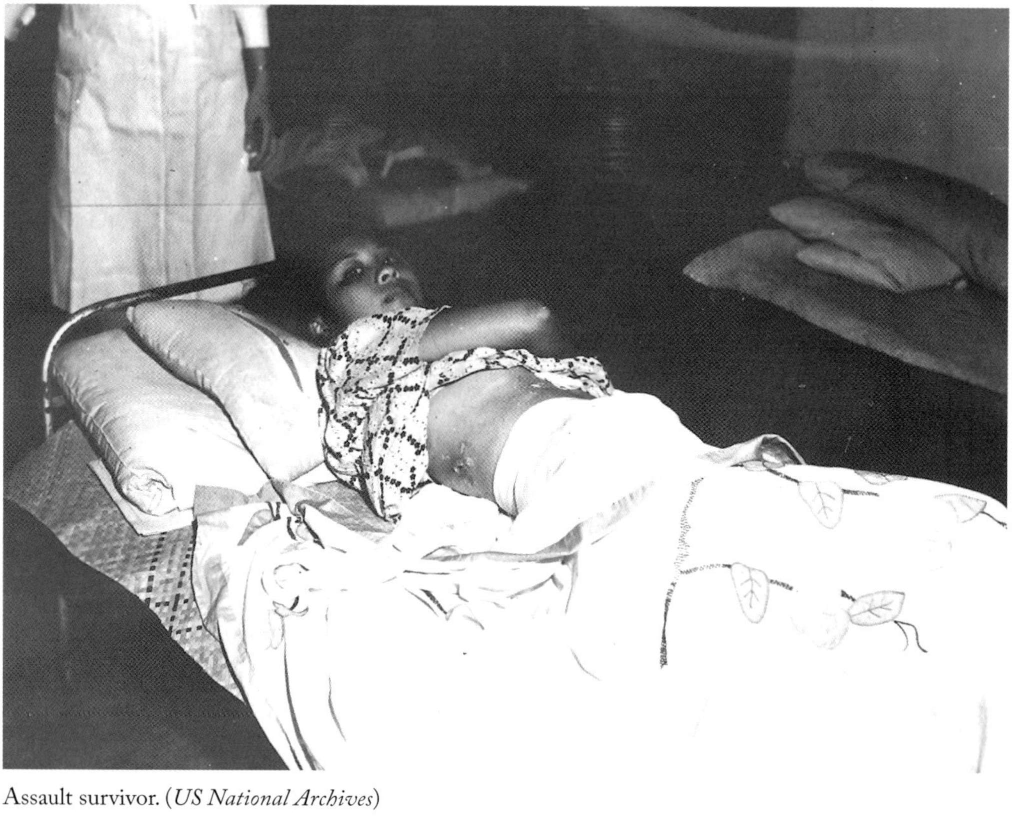
Assault survivor. (*US National Archives*)

Internees liberated at Santo Tomás, 1945. (*US National Archives*)

The Tablets of the Missing. (*iStock*)

The Manila American Military Cemetery and Memorial. (*Chris Hulme*)

MacArthur greets Major General Jonathan Wainwright in Yokohama; their first meeting since they parted in embattled Corregidor in the Philippines. (*US National Archives*)

Douglas MacArthur and his wife Jean. (*US National Archives*)

away. It was only towards the end of the march that some of the Japanese soldiers lost their discipline and ran ahead in fear, seeking cover, much to the fury of Hayashi. Yet no shots were fired and the agreement was respected by both sides.

It is not clear which route they took back towards Japanese lines. I headed from Santo Tomás to the site of Bilibid Prison, a few blocks south and closer to the Pasig River. It is still in service today as Manila City Jail – one of the world's most notorious prisons, with around 5,000 inmates crammed into a space that would be overcrowded with 1,000 inside. In 1945, the cell blocks were arranged like the spokes of a wagon wheel. The layout remains in the same configuration but I got no further than staring at the unprepossessing entrance at the end of a cramped little street. The steel gates were set within a drab block facade with castellations, a knock-off version of a grander and more forbidding approach to the correctional facility the Spanish built in the 1800s.

The Philippines periodically tops the list of countries with the most overcrowded jails, with a prison population exceeding 600 per cent capacity. There are very long waits for trials. The ratio of guards to prisoners is about 1 to 200 – far below international guidelines that recommend a ratio of 1 to 7. Given the tropical climate and the intense overcrowding, Manila City Jail is renowned as a skin-on-skin hell-hole where inmates must sleep in shifts and fights over personal space have turned into full scale riots. Yet about 90 per cent of the inmates have not actually been convicted of anything and are simply awaiting trial – typically for drug offences.

Manila City Jail echoes some of the conditions that marked out the Santo Tomás internment camp. Illnesses like tuberculosis and skin diseases are a huge problem and there's an element of the inmates governing themselves. Each of the cell blocks have 'mayors', who appoint their own deputies and marshals to help maintain order. 'We have a system where we share the governance,' Jayrex Bustinera, the jail's chief records officer, told one Al Jazeera journalist who spent two weeks filming inside. 'We delegate some of the authority to the inmate leaders where inmates can police co-inmates ... They help us institute peace and order.'[39]

Bilibid Prison was liberated without a fight in 1944. Before withdrawing on 4 February, its Japanese commander, a Major Ebiko, gathered the internees together and told them that his men were leaving as they had been assigned to other duties. In an all too rare act of humanity and common decency, Ebiko left food and medicine and warned the 800 POWs and 500 civilian internees of the dangers of stepping outside into what was now a war zone. Ebiko also posted a clear notice on the gates informing other Japanese troops that they should not molest the prisoners and internees as they had been lawfully released. Yet the war and its savage extremes was not done with any of them.

On 6 February, MacArthur issued one of his premature communiques, announcing the imminent recapture of Manila and began receiving public accolades from Allied leaders while his staff planned a victory parade for Roxas Boulevard. In fact, the battle for Manila had barely begun. As more American units arrived in the northern districts, Iwabuchi upped the systematic destruction of the capital, with incendiary squads sweeping through the streets. The north of Manila boomed to the sound of buildings, bridges and other infrastructure being blown apart by dynamite. Fires raged out of control; there was no one to contain the blazes.

Two American divisions eventually secured a couple of crossing points from the north banks of the Pasig, with the 37th Division on the right and the 1st Cavalry on the left as they pushed south. Under heavy fire, the 37th Division got over the river in assault boats near Malacañang Palace and then turned west and moved towards Intramuros. The 1st Cavalry crossed the Pasig further out towards the eastern city limits, then also drove at the bay in a thrust that paralleled the 37th Division.

The 11th Airborne Division had closed in from the south of Manila but ran into a well-prepared defence known as the Genko Line. This stretched across the narrow isthmus just south of where Ninoy Aquino International Airport stands today, from Manila Bay to Laguna de Bay, with what was the former American airfield, Nichols Field at its centre. The line was fortified with 5-inch naval guns relocated from Japanese ships, along with anti-aircraft guns and scores of concrete pillboxes, machine gun nests and mines. In many cases, the only way through the maze of deadly hazards and the interlocking fields of fire was by entering buildings, clearing them room by room, and then blowing out a wall to allow the troops to find a route to get behind a pillbox before attacking it.

Progress slowed to a crawl and, for many across the city, the liberation did not come soon enough. Iwabuchi's troops began massacring Filipinos within hours of the Americans entering the northern districts. War crimes investigators later identified twenty-seven major atrocities committed inside Manila to go alongside scores of other crimes inflicted on the population throughout the Philippine islands. Men, women and children were burned and butchered. Some streets echoed with terrified screams while in others, the victims raised no more than quiet sobs and mute acceptance.

One of the first incidents took place in a field by Dy Pac Lumber Yard, between Juan Luna and Morga streets in Tondo, a district close to the northern section of the port of Manila. Within hours of American forces breaking through the gates at Santo Tomás, Japanese troops had rounded up and confined more than 100 suspected guerrillas and their families at the lumber yard. By torchlight the troops began beheading the men in what author James M. Scott described as a 'production line of horror.' When they thought all the men were dead, the troops bayoneted the women, children and infants.

Scott's account, *Rampage*, is one of the toughest reads on the Pacific War. It is packed with horrific testimony of survivors and others who witnessed the organised depravity and barbarism across the city. The statements were used as part of war crimes trials and included an account from the GIs who discovered the aftermath of the lumber yard massacre.

'Over the course of the war, the seasoned 37th Infantry Division soldiers had grown accustomed to witnessing battlefield violence,' Scott wrote. 'But there amid the towering weeds, the troops found that the dead did not wear helmets and camouflage fatigues but rather flower-print dresses, nightgowns, and even infant sleep suits.' A squad surveyed the grounds on the morning of 7 February. 'They counted 115 dead civilians, the adults with their hands tied behind their backs. It appeared whole families had been killed, Private First Class Claude Higdon Jr. reported in an affidavit.'

Tondo was used as an artillery base by the Americans for shelling Japanese positions on the southside of the Pasig. The district was completely levelled in the subsequent exchanges of fire. Large parts of Tondo have never recovered from the devastation, with the wasteland being claimed and retained by Manila's most impoverished citizens after the war. At the heart of Tondo today stands Manila's largest and most notorious slum, an epic, sprawling mass of failed public policy and disenfranchisement, where generations of families have lived in abject poverty. The most destitute occupy Barangay 105, also known as 'Happyland' where some 12,000 people exist on a dumpsite surrounded by piles of garbage, either living on what passes for streets or in small, improvised shacks. The word '*Hapilan*' originates from a local Visayan-dialect and translates to 'smelly trash'. The warnings for visitors to stay away start with bag snatching, chain grabbing and pick-pocketing, and it's not on any formal tourism itineraries. 'Do not ever go there alone at dusk or your body will be on a sea shore full of garbage the next morning,' was fairly typical of the travel advice I encountered.

At the outset of the battle for his beloved Manila, MacArthur had refused to allow planes to bomb the city for fear of killing civilians and wrecking infrastructure and historic buildings. He relented when it came to pinpoint artillery after American soldiers suffered badly while traversing the Pasig. For the Filipinos trapped in the city, the chances of surviving were dramatically decreased by the shelling and they sought refuge in robust public buildings and private homes. Tragically, by taking shelter it only made it easier for the Japanese to find and slaughter them.

* * *

By 9 February, Rear Admiral Iwabuchi, sensing there was not long left, upped the ante again in the districts south of the Pasig. Written orders recovered as part of the war crimes case made it clear the killings were not random acts of extreme violence. A series of Iwabuchi edicts declared that anyone still in Manila who was not part of the Japanese military was a guerrilla, including women and children. He provided advice to his own men about how best to dispose of guerrillas without expending too much ammunition or creating a problem of corpses littering the city – essentially, round up people en masse, burn them, or consider throwing bodies in the river.

Ermita and Malate, the two cosmopolitan bayside districts connected to the old Spanish core, were both put to the torch while Paco, a working-class area by the Pasig, was visited by death squads. One of the most harrowing atrocities occurred on 10 February at The German Club, a site today occupied by Torre de Manila, a forty-two-story tower of luxury condominiums that overlook Rizal Park and the National Museum of Natural History. The German Club was a classic colonial outpost from 1930s Manila – with a large veranda fronting the entrance, a restaurant and bar, a billiard hall, an in-house bowling alley and a tennis court set amid gardens. The second floor had nine rooms rented out as bachelor units to male members. As nominal allies of the Nazis, Germans in Manila had been largely left alone during the Japanese occupation – despite the fact most of its members distanced themselves from Hitler's regime and refused to cut ties with prominent members of Manila's Jewish community. Manila Germans were neutral enough for the club's managers to be denounced as enemies of the Third Reich by one disgruntled Nazi who resigned his membership. Yet nationality was no protection from the orgy of violence that followed. Some 500-plus Filipinos, Spaniards, and Germans had taken shelter in an area beneath the club. At about noon, a platoon of Japanese Marines cordoned off the premises and started killing 'everyone in sight', according to Edgar Krohn Junior, a German national hiding inside.

At least twenty Japanese Marines raped a young girl outside the entrance before slicing her breasts off – after which a Japanese soldier placed them on his chest to amuse his comrades. Two other women were raped and murdered in the same area as a prelude to more systematic killing. When the club's manager Martin Ohaus came outside to protest, presenting his German passport, he was bayoneted to death. The same fate met others who stepped forward to ask the soldiers to stop the violence. The Japanese then doused the dead in gasoline and set them on fire. The building and its fixtures and furniture were next to be covered with petrol. The smell of it reached the basement where a large group was still hiding. The Japanese sailors then found some small windows to the sub-floor and started shooting indiscriminately inside before igniting the blaze. Anyone who tried to escape being burnt to death was gunned down or bayoneted. Several days later American soldiers found the bloated corpses of the civilians who made it outside. They also found the body of Martin Ohaus, whose dead hand still clutched his German passport.

The Japanese death squads worked through the bayside districts, ordering hundreds of civilians into the dining hall at another Catholic campus, Saint

Paul's College. The high-ceilinged building was rigged with explosives which, when detonated, blew the roof off and left a gaping hole in one of the side walls. Any survivors who stumbled outside were murdered. In all, about 360 people perished. The Saint Paul's chapel was also shelled but its facade, dominated by a statue of Jesus on the cross, remained standing amid the broken ruins. To some the mournful spectacle spoke of a miracle, evidence that Christianity can endure anything. The image made me think of the 9/11 terror attacks on New York where a four-pronged strand of the South Tower's steel facade remained standing after the collapse of the World Trade Centre; rescue workers called it Four Fingers. The Saint Paul's facade is back where it belongs today, fronting a restored chapel amid a reconstructed campus.

No one was safe as Manila was defiled. The same day as the attack on Saint Paul's, Japanese troops also forced their way into the Philippine Red Cross headquarters. A modest two-story building, it served as an emergency hospital and stood on Isaac Peral Street (now UN Avenue) at the corner Taft Avenue. Modesto Farolan, the general manager, was in his office, when Japanese Marines entered the dispensary and began shooting and bayoneting patients and staff in what became the first of three hospital massacres.

'My father ducked underneath his desk and luckily was partially covered by the falling body of one of the doctors who got hit in the first volley of fire,' his son, Ramon Farolan, later recalled.[40, 41, 42] The Japanese shot under the desk but failed to hit Modesto before continuing on with a room by room killing spree. Amid the desperate screams and pleas for mercy, one of the victims was Corazon Noble, a filmstar of the pre-war era. She was stabbed multiple times in the chest, abdomen, back and other parts of her body while trying in vain to prevent the murder of her 10-month-old daughter Maria in her arms. At least fifty civilians were slaughtered. James M. Scott recounted the fate of John Lewy, a Jew who had fled Germany, and who survived by pretending to be dead. His fiancée was not so lucky. 'When I came to my senses, I thought it was a dream,' he later told war crimes investigators, 'but everybody was dead.'

There is an historical marker today outside the Chapel of the Most Blessed at De La Salle College on Taft Avenue. It acknowledges the killings that took place on 12 February when around twenty Japanese forced their way inside. The chapel was being used as refuge from the shelling by about seventy people, including thirty women and girls, and sixteen Christian Brothers. The college's Director-Brother Egbert Xavier had been forcibly taken by a group of Japanese soldiers two days previously and was never seen again. This time, troops shot, slashed, and bayoneted the people inside, with some bodies thrown into a nearby tributary of the Pasig. The chapel was then set on fire and only a handful of victims would escape the inferno.

A supermarket now stands on a site once occupied by a house in the central district of Paco, part of an unremarkable road of apartments and small shops beneath the ever-present lines of telegraph wires. Yet in 1945, the address, 1195 Singalong Street, served as a decapitation chamber. 'Troops cut a hole in an upstairs floor and then marched everyone from blindfolded teenagers to grandfathers inside and forced them to kneel,' wrote James M. Scott. 'A Japanese marine then slashed each man's neck with a sword before kicking the body into the hole. Two hundred men died this way, though nine ultimately survived, watching as body after body tumbled down the hole, forming a pyramid of tangled arms, heads, legs, and torsos.'

The American-Filipino Romero family were in a group of about 2,000 foreign nationals rounded up at dusk on 10 February. They lived at 12 Plaza Ferguson, the other side of Dewey/Roxas Boulevard from where the US Embassy stands today. 'The visible city surrounding our house was ablaze,'[43] recalled Joseph J. Romero, who was 11 years old at the time. His mother was an American Caucasian married to a Filipino.

> Glowing bits of paper were sailing like leaves against the orange-black sky. We left the house and directly ahead of us on the plaza were hundreds of people. Japanese troops were shouting and assembling the crew into some sort of order. (They had passed the word that they were going to shelter us because our city was afire). We were being shoved around by soldiers. The men to the left and women and children to the right. The Jap shoved me to the left, my Dad knowing something was going to happen pushed me into the side with the women and children.

The men were divided up and escorted to different buildings in the area – including The Manila Hotel, where they were taken out in groups of about thirty and slaughtered in the grounds, their bodies then set on fire. The women and children were marched towards a short distance to the Bay View Hotel, which was occupied by Japanese troops. The civilians marched along a route lined with soldiers brandishing guns with fixed bayonets, shouting at the frightened herd.

According to testimony at war crimes trials, about 400 women and girls who had been captured during the round up of Ermita and Malate were submitted to a selection board at the Bay View Hotel that picked out the 25 women considered most beautiful. Over the following week these women and girls, many of them 12 to 14 years old, were raped by officers and enlisted men.

With his mother, sister and brother, Joseph Romero remained trapped in the nine-story building throughout this period. '[The hotel] was empty of all furniture [and] we were shoved into rooms,' recounted Romero. 'Sat on the floor all night, the American artillery continuously pounded against the outside walls. The building shook, noise deafening, flashes of light all night. The building stood thanks to pre-war American earthquake construction.'

Early on, his mother had faked derangement brought on by lack of water and was left alone by the troops. 'Before long the Japanese started taking the young girls out of the rooms to rape them,' wrote Romero.

> The older women would cross themselves and lament 'She is such an innocent girl. She has never missed a day of mass.' The process was unrelenting. My sister hid, laying down behind my mother, my seven-year-old brother, Mike and myself. With my mother acting crazy, the Japanese did not go near us and did not see her. In time some of the people, who had been scrounging for food said they saw a soldier raping the corpse of a dead girl.

Romero accepted that he would probably die soon. 'I was no longer frightened. All that mattered was that I die quickly. Given the choices of being burned alive, shot with a rifle or bayoneted, I wanted a mortar shell explosion in the back – not a dud. This would be final. No shell, no Joe in an instant.'

Eventually the Bay View Hotel caught fire, and smoke filled its stairways and halls. 'I am certain that this was set off by the Japanese, since mortar and howitzer fire could not put a dent in the walls of this building,' recalled Romero. The Japanese would not let anyone leave but his mother, who was in her thirties at the time, tried some psychology. 'She spotted the Japanese officer in charge. Said to him "Number one man say no can go." Whatever his reason, I presume it was to save face, this officer said. "I number one man, go!" And without any further ado we started streaming out of the building into the shelling outside. The entire Ermita section was now rubble.'

They made it to American lines but all across the districts south of the Pasig, Filipinos were being shot, bayoneted, beheaded, blown up or burnt alive. The Japanese did not discriminate. 'They slaughtered Russians, Spaniards, Germans, and Indians,'[44] wrote James M. Scott. 'Troops killed men and women, the old and the young, the strong and the infirm. The butchered victims included two Philippine Supreme Court justices, the family of a Philippine senator, and scores of priests.'

The civilians who did manage to pick their way through this manic deathscape came under the gaze of war correspondents as they finally got to American lines. 'All morning we had seen the long files of people walking mutely rearward past advancing infantry,' wrote *Life* magazine photographer Carl Mydans in a diary entry featured by Scott. 'Some of them limped with improvised wound dressings. Many of them walked, heaven knows how, with open wounds.' Internee Robert Wygle described the parade of wounded who came to Santo Tomás in search of help. 'They are so far beyond recognition,' he wrote, 'that, in many cases, one can't tell whether they are men or women, boys or girls, dead or alive.'

* * *

The White Knight hotel was well within the walled city. I was having trouble sorting out access to Corregidor and eventually arranged to meet a tour guide who said he could help. Glad to get out of my decrepit room, I made the short walk along a cobbled street to Barbara's – a restaurant and wedding venue set over two floors that trades on its heritage.

Intramuros is something less than 1.6 kilometres (1-mile) long and about a third of that wide. What it lacks in size it makes up for in density. The district has a high concentration of historic buildings and sites surrounded by a ring of thick, centuries-old defensive walls that, at about 6 metres (20-foot) high in places, are never far from view. The walls are punctuated at intervals by roads and seven city gates. Barbara's stood next to Casa Manila, a restored upscale Spanish-era mansion. Both are staples of Manila tourism and like much of Intramuros, with its Catholic churches and old colonial architecture, heavily dial down the feeling of being in Asia. Pleased to arrive before the tour groups, I found a seat amid islands of white tablecloths and old-world elegance. Sat by a window, I had a cold drink as the guide explained what to do given that my calls and emails attempting to register my visit had not been returned by the Corregidor Foundation Inc. He would contact them on my behalf and also handed over a number for Villa Carmen on Bataan, from where I could arrange my own boat crossing. I paid for the advice and he accepted that, as I had read Scott's *Rampage*, and was focused on 1945, a standard visitor tour of Intramuros might not add much.

The morning deluge had eased off by the time I stepped back outside. I was ultimately heading for Fort Santiago, a public park and museum where the district of Intramuros overlooks the Pasig. The first stop was immediately opposite: the San Agustín Church. During the final stages of the battle for Manila, artillery bombardment destroyed six of the seven churches in the old Spanish core, along with government buildings and most of the houses. Made from locally quarried adobe stone, San Agustín somehow survived, albeit dotted and chipped by impacts from bullets and shrapnel. It is the oldest standing church in the Philippines and a UNESCO World Heritage Site.

The current structure was completed in 1607. It has remained unchanged through multiple wars, typhoons and earthquakes – with one obvious exception. The church facade is dominated by neoclassical columns and huge wooden entrance doors. This central section of its frontage was flanked by a bell tower on either side until a series of earthquakes in 1880 produced almighty vertical cracks in the tower to the left. Photos taken at the time captured gaping black fissures in the stone. Despite being repaired, the left tower was later removed, leaving the facade part-stunted and asymmetrical.

I stepped from the small plaza into the cooler air of the interior to appreciate what is one of the Philippines' cultural and artistic gems. Designed in a baroque style, the most impressive feature was the barrel-shaped ceiling, painted by two Italians who succeeded in producing a *trompe l'oeil* – French for an optical illusion of three-dimensional space and objects on a two-dimensional surface. With a forced perspective that creates the impression of mouldings and carvings, the ceiling was decorated with religious symbols in the Old and New Testaments, pillars, angels, animals, floral motifs and rosettes. Work began in 1875 and took fifteen months. The painting was completed by Cesare Alberoni and Giovanni Dibella, two artists more typically employed to paint backdrops for operas. The splendour continued with sixteen chandeliers hanging over the pews, a dramatic pulpit, a grand pipe organ, paintings and dark wood choir seats intricately carved from local molave trees with ivory inlays. Several wooden confessionals set throughout the interior brought a sense of human frailty amid the grandeur.

San Agustín was used as both a prison and a strong point as the street fighting reached its climax in 1945. Japanese troops removed the lower portion of the right front door and placed sandbags at the opening, turning the entrance into a makeshift machine gun post covering General Luna Street. Scores of Intramuros residents and clergy had been held hostage inside the church. The son of one of them, Jose Maria Zabaleta, later reported that 'my father was killed by the Japanese, together with over a hundred Spaniards. They were marched from the church to be shot and bombarded with grenades.'[45] At one point, the Japanese did release over 1,000 hostages from San Agustín and the Delmonico Hotel, a block away, a move intended to complicate and slow down the American advance. As far as I could tell, the building that was the Delmonico still stands today at the junction of Santa Potenciana and General Luna Street, with a Starbucks on the ground floor.

Further on, Manila Cathedral was levelled to the ground during the shelling but completely rebuilt to the old design in 1958. It stands grandly before Plaza Roma, a public square that was called Plaza Mayor during the Spanish colonial era, then Plaza McKinley from 1901 to 1960 under the American occupation, and Plaza Malaki when the Japanese were calling the shots. Its present name Plaza Roma was given in 1960 in honour of the College of Cardinals in Rome, after the elevation of Archbishop Rufino Santos of Manila as the first Filipino cardinal.

The cathedral remains the seat of the Roman Catholic Archdiocese of Manila. The impressive facade and wooden doors led into a huge but less spectacularly ornate interior, where the stained glass was the most striking feature. A church has stood on this site since the late sixteenth century when construction of the walled city was well underway under orders originally given by Miguel López de Legazpi, the Spanish conquistador who led the first wave of European colonisation in the Philippines.

Fort Santiago, a couple of blocks beyond the cathedral, served as the military headquarters of four successive colonial rulers. It is the centrepiece of a fortified settlement where the southern banks of the Pasig meet Manila Bay. Construction started in 1571 once López de Legazpi and his men battled and overcame Rajah Sulayman, the Filipino-Muslim leader who originally controlled the land. The conquistador, who was from the Basque region of Spain, did not live long to enjoy his victory or see his base transformed from a wooden fortress into a stone citadel. López de Legazpi died of heart failure the following year and was eventually laid to rest at San Agustín. (Monks re-buried his remains in the church after they were ruthlessly exhumed in 1762 by the British while searching for golden treasures during a two-year period when they occupied and plundered Manila.)

Towards the end of the Spanish colonial era and during the three decades of grand American modernisation that followed, ambitious land reclamation projects actually moved the coastline. The works separated the old western flank of Intramuros from the shores of Manila Bay by creating a wide strip of land where twentieth century signature buildings such as The Manila Hotel and everything along Dewey Boulevard were constructed.

I walked from Plaza Roma into another park, the larger and more linear Plaza Moriones, where its granite paving stones were still wet from the morning downpour. Beyond the ticket office an official guide was selling tours of the fortress just up ahead. Around the fringes of the plaza, frangipani trees, statues of historic figures and formal gardens filled out the space once reserved for military drills and parades. Plaza Moriones is the product of a 2017 plan to establish a Mediterranean-style park in front of Fort Santiago. It is now hired out in the evenings for weddings, with a fountain in the middle of the plaza a favoured backdrop for formal portrait photographs. The transformation from the old colonial grounds was not met with universal approval. One Filipino cultural critic complained that the re-landscaping had 'paved over his heart' and had nothing to do with Intramuros' character or history.

Yet history still abounds. On the left side of the plaza, a structure known as the Baluartillo de San Francisco Javier was built on to the side of the district's defensive wall and originally served as a military storage area. It now houses the Intramuros Visitors Centre, alongside an art gallery, souvenir shop, and café. Next door, the remains of the Royal Warehouses back up against the defensive wall. First built in the sixteenth century, these buildings were used as a secure storehouse for goods unloaded by ships at the river gate during the Manila-Acapulco galleon trade. A little further on again, the two-story shell of what once served as the American barracks in 1898 added another layer of history. Bullet holes from the firefights with the Japanese in 1945 can still be seen in what is today used as an open-air exhibition space.

Fort Santiago proper does not begin until you cross a bridge above a moat and approach a gate set amid the thick walls. On each side, a few paces away, the entrance is guarded by two huge ramparts – the Baluarte de San Miguel to the left and the Medio Baluarte de San Francisco to the right. Above the entrance gate there's a royal seal of Spain and a wooden relief sculpture of Santiago Matamoros (St James the Moor-slayer), crushing Rajah Sulayman's Muslim natives under his horse's hooves. The main entrance gate was largely destroyed during 1945 and has been reconstructed. One of the most compelling photographs from the battle for Manila features a Sherman squeezing through the same half-ruined opening.

I followed the path of the tank into Fort Santiago's inner sanctum, the Plaza de Armas. It was smaller and somehow more reverent than I expected in bustling Manila, a manicured grass area surrounded by walls and ruins of barracks and storehouses. In the centre stood a statue of José Rizal, a heroic figure who campaigned for Philippine independence before being imprisoned here by the Spanish in 1896. One of the barracks has been restored to serve as a small and evocative museum devoted to Rizal and all that he lived and died for; I was completely engrossed. The 35-year-old had trained in ophthalmology before his political writings and activism inspired revolt. A series of bronze footprints led out from Fort Santiago to a gate that exited Intramuros to Bagumbayan Field (the site of today's Rizal Park), the place where the rebel leader's life was ended by a Spanish firing squad.

During the Japanese occupation the cells and tunnels underneath Fort Santiago were used by the kempeitai to deal with anyone who they were even vaguely concerned might be a guerrilla. The darkest history awaited a few steps on and beneath the Baluarte de Santa Barbara, a defensive position set at the extreme north-west of the fortress, overlooking the Pasig. The former ammunition stores beneath this gun platform here were used by the Japanese as both an execution chamber and dungeon.

The documents presented at war crimes trials included the diary of a Japanese soldier, identified only as 'Member 9th Shipping Engineer Regiment, Japanese Army' whose belongings were recovered by American troops. The entries matter-of-factly recount the daily horrors. An entry for 7 February said simply: '150 guerrillas were disposed of tonight. I personally stabbed and killed 10.'[46] On 9 February it got far worse: 'Burned 1,000 guerrillas to death tonight.'

When US Army troops finally fought their way into Intramuros, they forced open the iron doors of a dungeon – and were met with a horrific sight. Inside the stifling darkness lay the decomposing bodies of 600 Filipinos, left to die without food or water.

I stood before a single grainy black-and-white photograph on a faded tourist sign: bodies upon bodies, tangled in death. The horror lay in the accumulation of lives taken slowly, breath by breath, in the cramped dark. There was outrage too, as if the dead, long past crying out, still demanded to be seen. This was not history in the abstract. These were not numbers. They were people – with names, families, plans, and dreams.

Today, the 600 rest in a mass grave just steps away, beneath a tall cross and a plain marble stone set into the earth. It is a place for reflection, a stone ledger of unimaginable suffering. Even now, decades later, visitors can and do weep when confronted by the evidence of such cruelty – its scale, its profound silence, its inhumanity.

In a daze, I wandered up to the ramparts, which look out over the unlovely Pasig. My mind drifted back to the Manila of the 1920s – a fledgling global capital where East met West in trade. Steamers tied up along the river wall. Launches and *bancas* moved back and forth, ferrying people, chickens, pigs, fruit, and vegetables to market. A trip upstream toward Laguna de Bay would have threaded through the city's past. Grand colonial boulevards and rising construction projects would slowly give way to the old Philippines – meadows, high riverbanks fringed with feathery bamboo. Here and there, clusters of nipa houses and coconut groves would appear – a reminder of a simpler world, and one, perhaps, without quite so much hate.

Chapter 6

The Tablets of the Missing

Corregidor was retaken in February 1945 with a plan so bold that even MacArthur took some convincing it was worth the risk. The combined airborne and amphibious assault saw 2,050 American paratroopers dropped onto the parade ground on the Topside of the island ahead of the landing craft hitting the southern shoreline with tanks and troops.

The idea was simple enough: the paratroopers would surprise and distract the enemy defences while the larger amphibious assault got ashore at Black Beach, near the Malinta Tunnel. Yet its execution required pin-point accuracy, with any paratroopers missing the comparatively miniscule landing area at risk of going over a cliff near the southern end of the parade ground and/or ending up in the sea.

The airborne element was led by the Third Battalion, 503rd Parachute Regimental Combat Team – an experienced unit, which had seen action in New Guinea. The landing area they were trying to hit was about the size of an American football pitch. The transport planes, at 100 mph (160 kilometres per hour), would have roughly ten seconds over the drop zone to get the men out.

At 08.30 hours on 16 February, two long columns of C-47s approached Corregidor from the south-west. To reduce the time in the air and therefore the amount of drift, the men initially jumped from just 183 metres (600 feet). This was lowered to 152 metres (500 feet) once the first few sticks of men got away and missed the parade ground, going over the cliff, but still making it to terra firma, from where they had to fight their way inland. The plan worked as the Japanese, expecting an amphibious assault, were taken completely by surprise. Ground fire was fairly light up until the end of the first wave.

Don Abbott, one of the jumpers, later spoke of his short, but electrifying drop.

> While the time in the air could not have been more than a few seconds, I vividly recall several observations. The first thing a jumper does is to look up and check his canopy. The canopy was fully open so the chute would be doing the job it was designed to do. Then I looked in the direction we had come, the south, to see where the cliff was. Battery Wheeler stood out very clearly 200 or 300 yards away but, being so large, it seemed closer. Beyond the Battery the drop-off of the cliff was very evident because PT boats in Manila Bay were coming into view.[47]

He watched a flight of Douglas A-20 medium bombers dropping ordnance and strafing near Malinta Hill. 'I landed amid rubble of a burned and blasted building floor and bounced and was dragged another 20 or 30 yards. The parachute was still full and dragging me further. Fortunately, a couple of men who had been on the ground from the first pass lent a hand in collapsing the chute.'

Eight men were lost to enemy fire either in the air or before they were able to get free of their chutes. Three others died as a result of parachute malfunctions, and two were killed when they hit buildings. Yet once the first jumpers fought their way off the parade ground, they began to create a perimeter, and the nearby Corregidor lighthouse was earmarked for the American command post.

The amphibious assault was led by the 34th Infantry Regiment. As it set out to cross Manila Bay in landing craft, a flight of B-24 Liberator heavy bombers flew over Corregidor and dropped 500-pound bombs on Japanese positions away from Topside, covering the island with a cloud of dust and smoke. The troops and tanks from the 34th hit the shore at 10.33 hours, between the two morning parachute drops. The first wave featured twenty-five landing craft. Each was full to capacity with troops and one vehicle.

In the first hours, the fortunes of war twice favoured the Americans. A group of jumpers who overshot the parade ground landed in an area where they came into contact with Captain Akira Itagaki, commander of the 6,000 Japanese troops on the island. Itagaki and his senior officers were at the time attempting to observe the American amphibious landings getting underway across the water. The paratroopers proceeded to wipe out the whole group except an orderly, who was taken prisoner.

A different group of American paratroopers who had landed in the wrong place spotted Corregidor's telephone exchange near the Mile Long Barracks. This key facility was only lightly defended – and both the exchange and the troops defending it were promptly destroyed. With the commanding officer dead and communications disrupted, the Japanese, with a few exceptions, struggled to launch large, coordinated attacks on the invaders.

The 34th suffered casualties from landmines on the beach but secured a bridgehead by the end of the first day. Two weeks of fighting were still required to secure positions around the rest of Corregidor. The longest holdouts were in the besieged Malinta Tunnel. Large numbers of Japanese committed suicide in its dark recesses with grenades when it was clear their position was hopeless.

The most destructive blast at Malinta was caused inadvertently when a Sherman fired a shell into one sealed tunnel suspected of harbouring Japanese soldiers, but which instead contained tons of stored ammunition. The colossal explosion threw the tank several dozen feet, killing its crew and 48 US Army soldiers nearby, and wounded more than 100 others in the immediate area.

Fighting continued until 1 March, when Manila Bay finally reopened to Allied shipping. In the end, the American assault to recapture Corregidor left the 503rd Parachute Regimental Combat Team with 169 dead and 531 wounded parachutists. The beach landings and push inland cost the 34th Infantry Regiment: 38 killed and 153 wounded.

* * *

By the end of February 1945, street fighting, tanks, and heavy shelling had shrunk the Japanese perimeter within Intramuros and isolated remaining pockets of resistance south of the Pasig to a handful of well-built institutional structures. The Legislative Building – grand enough for Rome, and only recently completed under Daniel Hudson Burnham's master plan – was an apocalyptic ruin. By the time it was 'liberated' on 28 February, the neoclassical columns had collapsed in on themselves. It was later painstakingly restored, but mostly from memory, as few original blueprints survived. Today it stands as the National Museum of Fine Arts.

By 3 March, Manila was finally free from gunfire and artillery – and a terrible reckoning began. An estimated 100,000 civilians lay dead. Somewhere between 30 and 40 per cent of Manila's wartime population is believed to have perished, many from American shelling, the rest at the hands of Japanese forces rampaging through the shattered city. Countless others were maimed, traumatised, or left destitute. Around 200,000 people were homeless.

The physical devastation was as breathtaking as it was complete. Some 613 city blocks had been flattened. Much of what remained was so damaged it had to be bulldozed. Books, artworks, cultural artefacts – gone in the flames. Generations of public records and scientific data vanished with them. As William Manchester put it: 'The destruction of Manila was one of the greatest tragedies of World War Two. Of Allied capitals in those war years, only Warsaw suffered more. Seventy percent of the utilities, 75 percent of the factories, 80 percent of the southern residential district, and 100 percent of the business district was razed.'[48]

Roughly 1,000 GIs were killed in the street fighting, with many more of MacArthur's attacking force – 35,000 US troops and 3,000 Filipino guerrillas – wounded. With few exceptions, the 16,000 Japanese sailors, marines, and army units fought to the death, defending each position – as one GI put it – 'as if the emperor himself was in one of the buildings.'

The cost of liberation both confirmed the wisdom of MacArthur's 1942 decision to declare Manila an open city, sparing it then, and also raised questions about the urgency to retake the capital and the scale of artillery use in densely populated areas. There are no definitive answers. Only the knowledge that war is an appalling taskmaster.

What is clear is that the twenty-nine days of fighting revealed not just desperation but genocidal intent. Rear Admiral Sanji Iwabuchi, the hard-line Japanese commander, did not merely lose control of his men – he issued specific orders to systematically exterminate civilians, aiming to do so with minimal use of ammunition.

Iwabuchi took his own life with a grenade on 26 February, just days before the inevitable defeat. The remaining Japanese forces on Luzon would resist to the bitter end. General Tomoyuki Yamashita, commanding some 50,000 troops from his mountain base in Kiangan in northern Luzon, held out until after Emperor Hirohito's surrender on 15 August – drawing the curtain down on the Second World War.

Despite the diligence of investigators, not all the war crimes committed in Manila – or elsewhere – could be fully documented. 'In some cases, entire families had been slain, leaving no one to report the massacre,' wrote James M. Scott. 'Other times survivors, whose homes were burned and families killed, chose to abandon the city. At times, victims broke down, which was dutifully noted in each statement. "The witness appeared too grief-stricken to testify at more length," one investigator observed.'

The war crimes trials recounted acts of barbarism as sickening as anything in modern history – babies skewered on Japanese bayonets, deaths by torture, corpses mutilated for sport. Newsreel footage from General Yamashita's trial opened with the testimony of a 10-year-old girl, who told the court how she had been stabbed once in the arm and three times in the back with a bayonet.

And then came testimony that defied even the grimmest expectations of the court. Her evidence was followed by Francisco Lopez, an executive with Metro-Goldwyn-Mayer, who described what he had witnessed during The German Club massacre: Japanese sailors raping women outside the club, then pouring petrol on their hair and setting them on fire. The newsreel narrator warned that the rest of Lopez's statement was too graphic to broadcast. He was referring to an incident in which a woman was nearly decapitated – and then her corpse raped by a Japanese sailor still wielding the knife.

These and other unspeakable horrors left Filipinos and other survivors struggling to understand how such extreme violence could have been unleashed against them. 'Even American investigators were at a loss to fathom the widespread butchery, exhausting the thesaurus for adjectives like "diabolical," "inhuman," and "savage,"' Scott wrote. 'The numerous atrocity reports often included commentary by investigators about how humans could commit such barbarities. "This orgy of looting, raping, and murder defies credence – were it not for the mass of indisputable evidence establishing its commission,"' one report read.

* * *

I spent the final morning of my time in the Philippines exploring the airy halls of the National Museum, located at the edge of Rizal Park. An entire floor was devoted to 'The Longest Journey' exhibition, a retelling of Magellan and humankind's first circumnavigation around the globe. The epic quest took place between 1519 and 1522. It changed our understanding of the Earth's dimensions and especially the vast scale of the Pacific. For the Europeans who had always dreamed about Asia, the Orient was no longer a fantasy as opaque as Capiz. Trade routes would eventually open, firing the starting gun on the centuries of colonisation, empire and our on-going global competition for resources.

Magellan, the great navigator, would have understood my frustration at the hour it took afterwards to cover the 16 kilometres (10 miles) from Rizal Park to Taguig, a district in the south-east of the city. It was hot and humid inside the cab. The driver did not speak as he jostled and jabbed through the traffic.

My destination was the Manila American Military Cemetery and Memorial. It is the United States' largest military overseas cemetery, dwarfing those in Europe, and serves as the final resting place of 16,859 Americans who died during the Pacific War. The remains of a further 3,000 service personnel who could not be identified are also buried here and have headstones marked 'Here lies in honored glory a comrade in arms known but to God.' Most of the dead men and women took part in New Guinea and Philippines campaigns. Among the graves there are twenty-nine Medal of Honor recipients. In twenty instances, two brothers lie side by side in graves.

The cemetery is located on 152 manicured acres within the boundaries of what used to be Fort McKinley in 1940s Manila. The balance of that land is today given over to a Philippine Army base, Fort Bonifacio. The expansion of Metro Manila means both the military base and the cemetery beside it are now overlooked by the soaring sixty-plus floor towers of Manila's new business district, Bonifacio Global City.

On leaving the cab and passing through a security gate house, I stepped over a threshold and into a place of open air and tranquillity. A gently rising grassy plateau stretched out a long way ahead. It was marked by thousands of immaculately aligned white marble crosses. The visual repetition emphasised the vast scale of the loss. A straight path led through the graves, marked here and there with big, mature and graceful mahogany trees. There was no differentiation in rank or status, reflecting equality in death. The route led to a focal point in the distance where a white stone memorial structure stood on higher ground.

Walking through the fields of crosses arranged with such well-ordered symmetry added to an accumulating jumble of emotions. I already understood that any cemetery can have a centring effect – something to do with the fact that whoever you are, whatever you do, all lives come to this. Here, though, the perfect alignment spoke of something more than finality. The precision had its own kind of eloquence, as if nothing was too much trouble for the men and women who gave their lives in the service of their countries. Yet the perfect expanse of the lawns, covered in bone-white crosses, also resembled a public art installation. It's one that delivers a message to the living: this many lives should never have been lost at all.

Stopping here and there, I wondered about the identities of the fallen – where they had lived, how they had died, and who had mourned them. Each headstone is a presence and an absence. I felt mix of reverence and sorrow at the scale of sacrifice but also a direct connection to history, as if close proximity produces a kind of intimacy with loss. I briefly considered what it truly means to 'rest in peace.' If you are not religious can the phrase be used to describe a kind of nothingness? A dreamless calm? No more chatter, no more expectations, never to wake? I imagined a soldier's body, dressed in something simple, hands folded, resting beneath the earth. In the immediate aftermath of a battle, soldiers were often buried in temporary graves near where they fell. In such cases, it was common for the dead to be laid to rest in their combat uniforms, no matter how bloodied and torn, often because there was no time or ability to change them. Here, amid the formality and dignity of a military cemetery, the deceased would generally have been reburied in clean, ceremonial uniforms or other appropriate attire.

Our minds tend to recoil at the starkness of endings and all that is taken from us. The love withheld. The time we never had. Tough enough for civilians to bear in any circumstance – yet there is another dimension to this reckoning in wartime. The soldiers, sailors, and flyers died in service, doing their duty. Their time was not their own to keep. Their last moments belonged to something bigger, to the mission, to the sacrifice that outlived them. All we can do is remember them, standing among graves and reading names carved into stone, but we can never hope to grasp the enormity of all that was committed and lost.

A place that allowed for and encouraged contemplation stood at the centre of the cemetery. A memorial area here featured two semi-circular buildings set around a large courtyard. Together, the two curved and open structures, known as hemicycles, gracefully encircled the open space. The design had a balance that encouraged peaceful reflection. There was also a small chapel to one side.

The hemicycles were compartmentalised into sections by dividing stone walls. They stood like giant dominos and supported the curved flat roofs. When I went into their divisions, some of the walls featured large and colourful glass mosaics depicting maps of the key military campaigns from the Pacific, China, India and Burma. Yet these impressive maps were not what I had come to see.

Most of the other stone walls were inscribed with the names of over 36,286 American and Filipino soldiers for whom there are no known graves – The Tablets of the Missing. I looked for the men whose stories I had followed, whose remains took their place among the elements on the battlefields and oceans where their fight came to an end. The highest profile names included Ernest E. Evans, the officer who led the fearless charge of the tin can destroyer *Johnston* at Leyte Gulf. I went on for a time, wanting to pay homage; so many souls, so many names recorded and acknowledged.

The work of the poet Archibald MacLeish did not feature at the Manila American Military Cemetery and Memorial, but I wished they had found a place on the walls for *The Young Dead Soldiers Do Not Speak* – an elegy to fallen soldiers, which I felt conveyed their posthumous lesson. It features a ticking clock to remind us how time never stops marking us – and asks questions about what it means to honour those who have fallen.

The young dead soldiers do not speak.
Nevertheless, they are heard in the still houses:
who has not heard them?
They have a silence that speaks for them at night
and when the clock counts.

They say: We were young. We have died.
Remember us.
They say: We have done what we could
but until it is finished it is not done.
They say: We have given our lives but until it is finished
no one can know what our lives gave.
They say: Our deaths are not ours: they are yours,
they will mean what you make them.
They say: Whether our lives and our deaths were for
peace and a new hope or for nothing we cannot say,
it is you who must say this.
We leave you our deaths. Give them their meaning.
We were young, they say. We have died; remember us.

Afterword

The two American generals who defended Bataan and Corregidor at the start of the war with no realistic hope of relief both endured over three years of brutal captivity.

Major General Jonathan M. Wainwright was the highest-ranking American officer taken prisoner in the Second World War. Tall and gaunt, and already known as Skinny to his friends, Wainwright was among a group of prisoners transferred by ship from Luzon in August 1943. They were taken to camps in Formosa, before ending up in northeastern China in and around Mukden, a population centre in Manchuria. The area today is Shenyang, the capital city of Liaoning Province which borders North Korea.

Rank was no shield against rough treatment. During his time in captivity Wainwright routinely suffered humiliations such as being paraded before Japanese soldiers as a symbol of defeat. Like other POWs, he had to survive severe malnutrition as food provided was extremely scarce and of poor quality.

Major General Edward P. King Junior, who made the moral choice to surrender on Bataan in violation of Wainwright's direct orders, endured almost identical conditions in captivity. A decorated First World War veteran, King had ordered a cessation of fighting to avoid what he considered a pointless slaughter on Bataan. Beyond resupply, the soldiers in his care were sick, starved, and facing certain defeat after four months in combat. King also had to consider the civilian population under his control, trapped with the troops at the southern end of the peninsular.

Wainwright and King were initially held separately but did spend some time together in various camps. Stalin's Red Army entered Manchuria after the Nagasaki bombing in August 1945 and soon began liberating Allied prisoners. In the chaos of the final days there were fears about the unpredictable conduct of Japanese prison guards and the safety of POWs. Men from the Office of Strategic Service (OSS), a forerunner of the Central

Intelligence Agency, arrived shortly after the Red Army to rescue the missing generals. The OSS officers found Wainwright in a camp at Siam, 160 kilometres (100 miles) to the north of Mukden, along with the most senior British officer held captive during the war – Lieutenant General Arthur Percival, former commander of Allied forces in Malaya and Singapore.

Wainwright's first words on meeting the OSS operatives were 'Are you really Americans?' The greatest fear of a proud soldier, to be considered a coward, soon surfaced. Wainwright asked the officers how he was thought of back home. Given the defeat in the Philippines, he was incredulous when told that he was considered a national hero.

On being liberated by the OSS operatives in Mukden, King wasted no time in declaring what had weighed heavily on him in captivity: he alone bore responsibility for the surrender on Bataan. Like Wainwright, King had endured his imprisonment tormented by guilt, convinced he had failed his country and expecting, if he ever returned home, to be scorned rather than honoured. Yet by holding out for as long as they did, both officers had succeeded in disrupting Japan's timetable for conquering the South West Pacific, buying precious time for the US military and industrial complex to rally itself and cope with the vast distances involved. The five months of resistance through to the fall of Corregidor also played a part in Lieutenant General Masaharu Homma, the foe they faced on Luzon, being relieved of his command.

When Wainwright eventually made it back to the United States he was honoured with a ticker tape parade in New York City. He was promoted to the rank of full general (four stars) by a special act of Congress. This was a significant recognition of his service, due in part to the last man standing circumstances of his surrender in the Philippines. Wainwright also received several prestigious awards including the Medal of Honor, which President Truman personally presented to him in September 1945. MacArthur had relented over his 1942 objection that this ultimate accolade could not be awarded in situations of surrender, regardless of the conditions or level of courage required. The citation spoke of Wainwright's extraordinary heroism in the defence of Corregidor and Bataan.

It is said that for the remainder of his life, Wainwright bore no grudge or malice against MacArthur or any other senior American commander involved in the decision to abandon his command to its fate in the Philippines.

Wainwright was 62 years old at the time of liberation. He retired in 1946 and lived quietly in Texas. He remained a beloved figure in the eyes of the American public, frequently speaking at military and patriotic events. Wainwright died of a stroke on 2 September 1953, aged 70 years old. He is buried at Arlington National Cemetery in Washington DC.

Edward King's post-war path was more subdued, and his legacy remained fragile. His career did not conclude with parades or promotions. Instead, he served on the Secretary of War's Personnel Board before retiring to Georgia. Among veterans, it was widely believed that MacArthur – still unwilling to forgive what he saw as an act of disobedience – refused to receive King in the years that followed.

Wainwright, ever the soldier, was circumspect in his assessment. While he remained personally opposed to King's decision to surrender, he acknowledged that it 'required unusual courage and strength of character.' In the absence of official honours, it was left to the men who had served under King to defend his memory. For them, he was the general who had chosen mercy over martyrdom – and had, in doing so, saved countless lives.

Regarded as a 'soldier's general', King remained revered by his men, many of whom felt that MacArthur, operating from Australia during the final days on Bataan, was out of touch with frontline reality. In 2002, Major Richard M. Gordon, a veteran of the campaign said of King in a speech at the American Cemetery in Manila: 'If General King did not have the courage to surrender, we survivors of Bataan who are here today, would not be here. Today, General King is an ignored figure in history. Had the General not surrendered, it would have been a blood bath on Bataan.' Edward King died peacefully in 1958, aged 74. He is buried at the Cemetery of St John in the Wilderness Episcopal Church in Flat Rock, a village in North Carolina.

The American and British generals who were forced to concede defeat in 1942, Wainwright in the Philippines, and Arthur Percival at Singapore, both attended the formal Japanese surrender ceremony on the teak decks of the battleship *Missouri* on 2 September 1945 in Tokyo Bay. The speeches and signatures drew a line under the bloodiest conflict in human history – and lasted all of twenty-three minutes. It began with a brief address by MacArthur, Supreme Commander of the Allied Forces, and now de facto ruler of Imperial Japan. He called for justice, tolerance, and rebuilding.

The document that closed out the war was no less concise. It had been prepared by the US War Department and approved by President Harry S. Truman. Eight short paragraphs formalised the 'unconditional surrender to the Allied Powers of the Japanese Imperial General Headquarters and of all Japanese armed forces and all armed forces under Japanese control wherever situated.'

What had begun in fire, fury, and produced unimaginable losses now concluded with the quiet scratch of pens. MacArthur signed first. Then came Japanese Foreign Minister Mamoru Shigemitsu and General Yoshijirō Umezu, Chief of the Army General Staff. Delegates from the other Allied nations, including China, the United Kingdom, the USSR, France, Australia, Canada, the Netherlands and New Zealand witnessed the event.

* * *

The Second World War was the first major conflict in history in which the victors carried out trials of persons in the defeated nations for 'crimes against peace' and 'crimes against humanity,' two new and broadly defined categories of international crime. At the conclusion of the war, the Allied powers established three classes of defendants: Class A charges were reserved for Japan's top leaders and alleged crimes against peace. Class B and C charges applied to Japanese personnel of any rank and covered conventional war crimes and crimes against humanity.

Among those called to account was Lieutenant General Masaharu Homma, the Japanese commander who had led the invasion of the Philippines in 1942. Though he succeeded in capturing the archipelago, Homma's progress was deemed too slow by his superiors. Not long after the fall of Corregidor, he was recalled to Tokyo and forced into semi-retirement – an obvious rebuke from the Imperial High Command.

Yet the war had a long memory. In 1946, Homma was extradited to Manila to face forty-eight counts of violating international rules of war. Chief among the charges was his command responsibility for the Bataan Death March. Homma denied direct involvement. His defence argued he had been focused on taking Corregidor and that his forces had been overwhelmed by the sheer number of prisoners. Still, he accepted responsibility and was found guilty.

His wife appealed to MacArthur for clemency, but the request was denied. Homma was granted one concession. In recognition of his comparatively humane treatment of civilians, he was executed by firing squad rather than hanged – a soldier's death as opposed to the ignominy of the criminal gallows.

Another high-ranking officer to face judgement in Manila was General Tomoyuki Yamashita, one of the IJA's most accomplished leaders. His conviction and subsequent execution by hanging became one of the most controversial outcomes of the post-war tribunals and set a lasting precedent for command responsibility.

Known as the 'Tiger of Malaya' for his audacious capture of Singapore in 1942, Yamashita had been sidelined by Prime Minister Tōjō before being recalled in 1944 to lead the defence of Luzon. He withdrew his forces into the hills and played no part in the Manila massacre. He surrendered only in September 1945, after Japan's formal capitulation.

Yamashita was defended by an American soldier and lawyer, Colonel Harry Clarke, who was determined to ensure a fair trial. The prosecution focused on two main events: the 1942 massacre of between 150 and 200 staff and patients at Alexandra Hospital in Singapore, and the atrocities committed against civilians during the fighting on Luzon.

Yamashita conceded that atrocities occurred on Luzon but maintained they were not carried out under his orders and that he was unaware of them. He testified that he had been outraged by the brutal killings at the Alexandra Hospital and had the soldiers responsible executed, as well as offering a personal apology at the time to survivors.

Regarding the Manila massacre, his defence argued that Rear Admiral Iwabuchi and his naval forces had acted independently. Nevertheless, Yamashita was found guilty and hanged in February 1946. His case established what became known as the 'Yamashita Standard': the legal principle that commanders can be held criminally liable for war crimes committed by subordinates, even without direct orders or knowledge.

While Homma and Yamashita were tried under Class B charges, Japan's highest-ranking military and political leaders were brought before the International Military Tribunal for the Far East in Tokyo. In 1946, twenty-six Class A defendants stood trial for crimes against peace, including former

Prime Minister Hideki Tōjō, who had exiled both Homma and Yamashita during the war. Two additional defendants died before proceedings began.

When American soldiers arrived at his Tokyo residence on 11 September 1945 to arrest him, former Prime Minister Hideki Tōjō attempted to escape justice the only way left to him. Drawing a pistol, he shot himself in the chest in a failed act of ritual suicide. The bullet missed his heart. A now-famous black-and-white photograph captures the scene: Tōjō slumped in an armchair, dishevelled and unconscious, his shirt marked by a dark bloom of blood – a fallen warlord caught between defiance and futility. Revived by military doctors, Tōjō reportedly apologised for 'taking so long to die.'

The Tokyo tribunal lasted over two years and heard testimony from 419 witnesses and saw 4,336 pieces of evidence, including depositions and affidavits from 779 individuals. Tōjō, seen by many as the personification of Japanese militarism, was held responsible for launching aggressive war across Asia and the Pacific, and for the deaths of millions of people across the region. When the tribunal concluded, seven defendants, including Tōjō and General Iwane Matsui (found responsible for the 1937 Nanjing Massacre), were sentenced to death by hanging. The remaining defendants received life imprisonment.

One conspicuous absence from the dock was Emperor Hirohito. Despite being a central figure in Japan's wartime leadership, he was not indicted. MacArthur, wielding immense authority during the occupation, used his influence to shield the emperor from prosecution. Hirohito was seen by many Japanese as a divine and unifying figure, and MacArthur believed that trying or removing him could spark unrest or undermine the reconstruction of Japan. It was a controversial but calculated decision, emblematic of the delicate balance between justice and pragmatism in the aftermath of total war.

In the years that followed Hirohito, an enigmatic figure, is said to have wanted to express his regret and remorse over Japan's conduct. Papers discovered in 2019 detailed candid exchanges with his staff over a speech Hirohito was due to make in 1952 at the time Japan regained its sovereignty. Specifically, Hirohito wrote: 'I just think I really need to include the word remorse.' In another memo the same year also quoted Hirohito as saying, 'If we reflect, we have all done bad things, so please write well and include in the upcoming speech the meaning that we must all reflect and not repeat them.' Yet Hirohito ultimately accepted political advice not to use the words 'regret' or 'remorse'. The documents also revealed a sovereign troubled by the path that led to Japan's defeat, saying 'no one could stop the military,' particularly by the time Tōjō was serving as the country's prime minister. To this day, the extent to which Japan has come to terms with its conduct during the Second World War remains a controversial and divisive issue, especially in terms of its relationship with China.

* * *

General Douglas MacArthur remained in military service for six more years following the end of the Pacific War, ultimately dismissed by President Harry Truman in 1951 for insubordination during the Korean War.

When Korea was liberated from thirty-five years of Japanese colonial rule in August 1945, it was – by agreement between the Allies and the Soviet Union – temporarily divided at the 38th parallel. Like Berlin, the peninsula became a front line of Cold War geography: the Soviets occupied the north, and the United States took control of the south.

What began as a temporary arrangement quickly hardened into division. By June 1950, tensions erupted into open war when North Korea, led by communist leader Kim II-sung and supported by the Soviet Union, invaded South Korea, which was backed by the United States and governed under a democratic system.

In response, a United Nations force led by the United States – and by MacArthur in particular – repelled the North Korean invasion and pushed their forces back across the 38th parallel. Yet MacArthur did not want to stop there. He advocated for a wider war against China, which had entered the conflict in September 1950 on the side of North Korea. His public criticism of Truman's more cautious policies and his own desire to escalate the conflict got him fired in April 1951.

MacArthur's return to the United States was anything but peaceful. In every city he passed through – Honolulu, San Francisco, Washington DC, and finally Manhattan – he was met by adoring crowds. When he and his family took up residence in a 10-bedroom suite at the Waldorf Towers, they were greeted by 150,000 letters and 20,000 telegrams from well-wishers.

Speculation about a possible MacArthur bid for the presidency in 1952 surged but ultimately came to nothing. Still, he remained a respected and influential figure in American public life.

MacArthur later became chairman of the Remington Rand Corporation and was frequently called upon as a speaker on matters of defence and international security. In July 1961, he made a final visit to Manila – his beloved wartime post – where he was again honoured as a national hero.

His final major public address came in May 1962 at the US Military Academy at West Point. Pacing the stage and speaking without notes, he delivered a stirring farewell to the Corps of Cadets:

> The shadows are lengthening for me. The twilight is here. My days of old have vanished, tone and tint – they have gone glimmering through the dreams of things that were. Their memory is one of wondrous beauty, watered by tears and coaxed and caressed by the smiles of yesterday… In my dreams I hear again the crash of guns, the rattle of musketry, the strange, mournful mutter of the battlefield. But in the evening of my memory, I always come back to West Point. Always there echoes and re-echoes in my ears – Duty, Honor, Country. Today marks my final roll call with you. But I want you to know that when I cross the river, my last conscious thoughts will be of the Corps, and the Corps, and the Corps. I bid you farewell.

MacArthur died in April 1964, aged 84. He was buried in Norfolk, Virginia – a location that, to some, seemed an unusual final resting place for an army general. Norfolk, after all, was known primarily as a major US Navy base. Yet for MacArthur, the city held personal significance.

His mother, Mary Pinkney Hardy MacArthur, came from a prominent Norfolk family, and his parents were married there in 1875. Norfolk was also the birthplace of his eldest brother, Arthur MacArthur III, who died in 1923 from appendicitis while serving as a captain in the US Navy. There was one other link – his other brother, Malcolm, who passed away in childhood, was buried in a Norfolk churchyard. These family ties gave the city a resonance that few other places could match.

In November 1951, MacArthur returned to Norfolk to speak at the dedication of a new city park on the site where his mother's home, *Riveredge*, had once stood. The park was named in her honour, and its boundary wall was constructed entirely from bricks salvaged from the original house. During the ceremony, MacArthur lightly remarked that, after a lifetime spent on military bases and in transient hotel rooms, it was unusual to find himself somewhere that actually felt like home. Norfolk's mayor never forgot that comment.

A decade later, the city offered MacArthur its old City Hall building as the site for a proposed MacArthur Museum to house his personal library, papers, and memorabilia. The idea appealed to him. On the condition that both he and his wife, Jean MacArthur, could be interred in the museum's rotunda, MacArthur accepted the proposal. Their partnership with the City of Norfolk led to the creation of the MacArthur Memorial, which officially opened in 1964 – the same year the general passed away.

Jean MacArthur lived until she was 101 years old. She passed away in 2000 and is buried alongside him in Norfolk. In her obituary, only their son Arthur and Jean's sister Angie McCarthy are referenced. No grandchildren are mentioned, suggesting there are no descendants from one of America's most decorated military families.

Born in 1938, Arthur MacArthur IV did not set foot on American soil until he was 13-years-old. His was a childhood shaped by war's long shadows and its strange proximities: while other children were evacuated from danger, Arthur remained in the theatre of combat, within sight and sound of destruction, of one thunderous barrage after another.

Few adults are likely to remember their fourth birthday, but it's doubtful Arthur ever forgot his. Deep inside the bomb-blasted hills of Corregidor, a makeshift celebration was arranged in the tunnels. Enough ingredients had been salvaged to bake a cake. The PX – the army's retail outlet – was long gone, blown up during the Japanese air raids, so gifts were improvised. Someone had noticed the boy mimicking his father and his pipe, Arthur puffing thoughtfully on a pencil. So one of the island's besieged residents fashioned a cardboard cigarette holder for him. His nanny, meanwhile, persuaded a Chinese tailor, trapped on the island, to sew a miniature officer's cap. Arthur wore it at once. The next morning, an enlisted man passed him near the tunnel entrance and saluted with a grin: 'Good morning, General.' Without missing a beat, the boy replied, 'I'm not a General – I'm a Sergeant.'

He wanted to be a sergeant because they alone, he'd thought, got to drive the cars.

Arthur not only remained with his parents through the war but also during the long American occupation of Japan, wandering through a world where innocence and grand strategy lived side by side. His surroundings became those of grand halls and quiet isolation. William Manchester wrote of Arthur's persistent solitude, his longing for playmates, and the comfort he ironically found in the company of another child who understood the weight of inheritance – Crown Prince Akihito, the eldest child of Emperor Hirohito.[49] Together, they occupied a rarefied sphere where policemen saluted children and no one else came near.

So singular was Arthur's experience that he is said to have attended part of Tōjō's war crimes trial, seated near the front, small headphones pressed to his ears, the weight of history reaching him in hushed translation.

The public expectation was that Arthur would eventually follow in the family tradition by attending West Point and serving in the US Army, like his father and grandfather before him. Instead, he enrolled at Columbia University, graduating in 1961 with a degree in English. Arthur had a deep interest in literature, music, and the arts. By some accounts, his father had been reluctant to pressure him into a military career – perhaps a reaction to the expectations placed upon him in his own youth to live up to a Medal of Honor-winning officer.

Arthur would go on to live an extraordinarily private life, in stark contrast to the global renown of his father. He never spoke publicly or acknowledged his heritage. At the time of Douglas MacArthur's death in 1964, Arthur was 26. Little has been known of his life since. It's reported he continued to visit his mother at the Waldorf Towers but otherwise shunned the spotlight. According to the *New York Post* he adopted the assumed name 'David Jordan', and by 2004 was living under that identity in an apartment at the Mayflower Hotel, near the southern edge of Central Park in Manhattan. When the building was slated for demolition to make way for 15 Central Park West – now one of New York's most exclusive addresses – 'David Jordan' agreed to a buyout. The developer was reportedly astonished to discover that the elderly tenant was, in fact, General Douglas MacArthur's only child.

Arthur is believed to have purchased a $650,000 condominium nearby. A lawyer involved in the relocation, Michael Grabow, described him as one of four bachelors still living in the Mayflower Hotel – implying Arthur had never married. Another report suggested he had lived as an artist or composer in Greenwich Village.

I've often wondered what memories Arthur and his father might have shared – if not aloud, then in companionable silence. The opulence of pre-war Manila. The smoke-filled tunnels of Corregidor. The midnight escape across hostile waters to Mindanao. A peaceful interlude in wartime Brisbane. The long post-war years in Tokyo and Korea. And just as easily, I can imagine them years later, walking through Central Park with arms folded against the afternoon chill. Not speaking of generals and campaigns, but of music and books, seldom acknowledging the unique weight of their shared history.

By every account, Douglas MacArthur adored his son. The general who had commanded great armies spent his final years in quiet retirement at the Waldorf Towers, his world narrowed to a suite of rooms and the company of those he loved most, his uniforms and medals packed away.

To my mind, Arthur's silence in the years after his father's passing left a troubling vacuum. His life, lived under an assumed name, deepened the mystery. Did Douglas MacArthur retain the love and affection of his only child? Or had the weight of that famous name driven them apart? The silence itself became a kind of answer but one that was interpreted differently by everyone who considered it.

Until, finally, in January 2024, it broke.

That winter, General Douglas MacArthur was posthumously awarded the Order of Military Merit, First Class, by the government of South Korea – a country where his name still carries the weight of deliverance from tyranny and an enduring solidarity with its people.

At the ceremony, a simple, dignified statement was read. It was Arthur MacArthur IV's first public comment in more than sixty years: 'On behalf of the General Douglas MacArthur Foundation and the MacArthur Memorial, please accept my thanks for the issue of the Order of Military Merit, First Class, to my father. The award is a testament to my father's legacy and an honour that forever binds him to the people of Korea.'

A little over a year later, he issued another acknowledgement to mark the eightieth anniversary of the Battle of Manila, recalling the Philippines fondly as 'the land of my birth.' Then, in September 2025, during the seventy-fifth anniversary of the Korean War's Incheon Landing Operation, he spoke of his father's impact again, saying: 'As a result of the Incheon Landing Operation, the Republic of Korea has become a shining beacon to all free people around the world today. I sincerely hope for eternal peace and prosperity.'[50]

And so I had my answer. A son's voice, rising at last from behind the curtain of anonymity – not to revive a legend, but to honour the man beneath it.

Notes

Foreword

1. 'From Pompeii to Detroit: Why ruins fascinate', BBC News, Fiona MacDonald, 21 October 2014.

Chapter 1: The Flags of Bataan

2. 'Marcos's Wartime Role Discredited in US Files' *The New York Times*, 23 January 1986.
3. *American Caesar, Douglas MacArthur 1880–1964*, William Manchester.
4. *The Tower of Skulls: A History of the Asia-Pacific War July 1937–May 1942*, Richard B. Frank.
5. *Samurai! The Autobiography of Japan's World War II Flying Ace*, Saburo Sakai.

Chapter 2: The Deluge and the Flood

6. *Lieutenant Ramsey's War: From Horse Soldier to Guerrilla Commander*, Edwin Price Ramsey and Stephen Revele.
7. *The Fall of the Philippines: United States Army in World War II: The War in the Pacific*, Louis Morton.
8. 'Bataan Diary of Major Achille C. Tisdelle' published in the *Journal of Military Affairs*, Louis Morton.
9. *Bataan (1943) MGM* film written by Robert Hardy Andrews, Garrett Fort, and Dudley Nichols.
10. *The Fall of the Philippines: United States Army in World War II: The War in the Pacific*, Louis Morton.
11. *Ghost Soldiers: The Epic Account of World War II's Greatest Rescue Mission*, Hampton Sides.
12. 'Bataan Death March survivor shares story' interview by Kate Blais, United States Air Force Global Strike Command Public Affairs, 5 July 2012.
13. 'Rancho Cucamonga survivor of Bataan Death March tells what it was like' by Diana Sholley, *Inland Valley Daily Bulletin*, 10 November 2013.
14. Lester Tenny interview with Atomic Heritage Foundation, 12 September 2020 and published on its website: https://ahf.nuclearmuseum.org/voices/oral-histories/lester-tenneys-interview/.

Chapter 3: Corregidor

15. 'Foundation seeks to "relocate" aggressive macaque troop out of Corregidor Island', Jonathan L. Mayuga, Manila's *Business Mirror*, 6 October 2020.
16. 'Corregidor: Gibraltar of the East', Eric Niderost, *Warfare History Network*, Spring 2013.
17. Ibid.
18. 'From Pompeii to Detroit: Why ruins fascinate', BBC News, Fiona MacDonald, 21 October 2014.
19. *Corregidor: Isle of Delusion*, Kazumaro Uno.
20. *Reminiscences*, Douglas MacArthur.
21. Speech of General MacArthur on President Quezón's Inauguration, 30 December 1941, *Official Gazette of the Philippine Republic*.

22. *Passion and Death of the USAFFE*, Leon Maria Guerrero.
23. 'The Fall of Corregidor', Hanson W. Baldwin, *American Heritage Magazine*, Volume 17, Issue 5.
24. *The Fall of the Philippines: United States Army in World War II: The War in the Pacific*, Louis Morton.

Chapter 4: Typhoon Leyte

25. MacArthur Milwaukee Forum: https://www.macarthurmilwaukeeforum.com/resources/speech-to-the-people-of-the-phillipines/.
26. *American Caesar, Douglas MacArthur 1880–1964*, William Manchester.
27. 'Strategic Aspects of the Battle Off Formosa', Vice Admiral Shigeru Fukudome, former Imperial Japanese Navy, US Naval Institute Proceedings, December 1952.
28. *The Attack on Pearl Harbour* [*sic*], Roger Parkinson.
29. *The Last Stand of the Tin Can Sailors: The Extraordinary World War II Story of the US Navy's Finest Hour*, James D. Hornfischer.
30. 'The Most Interesting Man in Dallas', Matt Goodman, *D Magazine*, February 2020.
31. *Fires on the Plain*, Shōhei Ōoka.

Chapter 5: Scorched Earth

32. 'Aquino Pledges to "Dismantle" Marcos Regime', William Branigin, *The Washington Post*, 24 January 1986.
33. *Fires on the Plain*, Shōhei Ōoka.
34. *Douglas MacArthur, American Warrior*, Arthur Herman.
35. 'Editor of *GQ* magazine quits after furore of Rommel pictures, Kamal Ahmed, *The Guardian*, 19 February 1999.
36. 'Stand off at Santo Tomás', Rupert Wilkinson, History Net, 16 February 2017.
37. *Rampage: MacArthur, Yamashita, and the Battle of Manila*, James M. Scott.
38. 'Stand off at Santo Tomás', Rupert Wilkinson, History Net, 16 February 2017.
39. 'Locked up: Inside Manila City Jail', Karishma Vyas, Al Jazeera, 17 December 2018.
40. 'The agony of a city: Manila 70 years ago', Ramon Farolan, *Philippine Daily Inquirer*, 9 February 2015.
41. 'Hell on earth, the Battle for Manila', Ramon Farolan, *Philippine Daily Inquirer*, 6 February 2017.
42. 'Battle for Manila', Ramon Farolan, *Philippine Daily Inquirer*, 1 March 2021.
43. 'Caught in the Battle of Manila', Joe Romero, Corregidor Historical Society.
44. *Rampage: MacArthur, Yamashita, and the Battle of Manila*, James M. Scott.
45. 'February 1945: The rape of Manila', Joan Orendain, *Philippine Daily Inquirer*.
46. *Rampage: MacArthur, Yamashita, and the Battle of Manila*, James M. Scott.

Chapter 6: The Tablets of the Missing

47. 'With the 503rd PRCT on Corregidor, February 1945', Don Abbot.
48. *American Caesar, Douglas MacArthur 1880–1964*, William Manchester.

Afterword

49. *American Caesar, Douglas MacArthur 1880–1964*, William Manchester.
50. 'Battle of Manila 80th Anniversary: Reclusive Son of Gen. Douglas MacArthur Makes Rare Statement', Richard Sisk, Military.com, 24 February 2025.

Dear Reader,

We hope you have enjoyed this book, but why not share your views on social media? You can also follow our pages to see more about our other products: facebook.com/penandswordbooks or follow us on X @penswordbooks

You can also view our products at www.pen-and-sword.co.uk (UK and ROW) or www.penandswordbooks.com (North America).

To keep up to date with our latest releases and online catalogues, please sign up to our newsletter at: www.pen-and-sword.co.uk/newsletter

If you would like a printed catalogue with our latest books, then please email: enquiries@pen-and-sword.co.uk or telephone: 01226 734555 (UK and ROW) or email: uspen-and-sword@casematepublishers.com or telephone: (610) 853-9131 (North America).

We respect your privacy and we will only use personal information to send you information about our products.

Thank you!